Love and War

Love and War

HOW MILITARISM SHAPES
SEXUALITY AND ROMANCE

Tom Digby

COLUMBIA UNIVERSITY PRESS
NEW YORK

Columbia University Press
Publishers Since 1893
New York   Chichester, West Sussex
cup.columbia.edu
Copyright © 2014 Columbia University Press
All rights reserved

Library of Congress Cataloging-in-Publication Data
Digby, Tom, 1945–
    Love and war : how militarism shapes sexuality and romance / Tom Digby.
        pages cm
    Includes bibliographical references and index.
    ISBN 978-0-231-16840-3 (cloth : alk. paper) : ISBN 978-0-231-16841-0
(pbk . : alk. paper) — ISBN 978-0-231-53840-4 (e-book)
    1. Sex (Psychology) 2. Man-woman relationships. 3. Sex differences
(Psychology) 4. Heterosexuality. 5. Masculinity. 6. Militarism—Social
aspects.   I. Title.

BF692.D54   2014
155.3—dc23   2014008990

Columbia University Press books are printed on permanent and durable acid-free
paper.
This book is printed on paper with recycled content.
Printed in the United States of America

c 10 9 8 7 6 5 4 3 2 1
p 10 9 8 7 6 5 4 3 2 1

Add cover/jacket credit information

References to Web sites (URLs) were accurate at the time of writing. Neither
the author nor Columbia University Press is responsible for URLs that may have
expired or changed since the manuscript was prepared.

FOR LUNA AND SANDY.

WHATEVER IS GOOD ABOUT THIS BOOK

I OWE TO THEM.

CONTENTS

ACKNOWLEDGMENTS

The conversational tone of this book reflects its origin as a series of talks I was invited to give on college and university campuses. The informality of my writing also reflects an understanding that the world urgently needs philosophers (and other scholars) to write, speak, and teach in ways that can make a difference in people's lives. That means it is essential for their work to appeal to a broad public audience.

For opportunities to present the ideas in this book to such audiences (in a multimedia format), I am incredibly grateful to Helga Varden (University of Illinois at Champaign/Urbana), Shari Stone-Mediatore (Ohio Wesleyan University), Brook Sadler (University of South Florida), Crystal Benedicks and Cheryl Hughes (Wabash College), Matt Silliman (Massachusetts College of Liberal Arts), and Jen Miller (Millersville University). Thanks also to Jen McWeeny for opportunities to present three of the chapters at meetings of the Society for Women in Philosophy (Eastern). Yet another chapter was presented at an American Philosophical Association session, sponsored by the Society for the Philosophy of Sex and Love, led by the inimitable duo Patricia Marino and Helga Varden. Versions of three chapters were presented at the Women and Society Conference, thanks to coordinators Shannon Roper and JoAnne Myers. Several chapters began as multimedia presentations at the annual International Social Philosophy Conference, sponsored by the North American Society for Social Philosophy.

During the past thirty years my feminist friends have contributed immeasurably to my growth as a person, philosopher, and feminist, especially Luna Nájera, Sandra Bartky, Jim Sterba, Valerie Broin, Phyllis Kenevan, Michael Kimmel, Susan Bordo, Alison Jaggar, Naomi Zack, Laurie Shrage, Sandra Harding, Richard Schmitt, Karsten Struhl, Tom Wartenberg, Lisa Tessman, Lynne Tirrell, Kate Wininger, Ann Ferguson, Elise Springer, Sally Scholz, Steven Botkin, Lewis Gordon, Ami Bar On, Sarah Clark Miller, Mary Ellen Waithe, Anita Superson, Joan Callahan, Nanette Funk, Dion Farquhar, Jody Ericson Santos, Ami Harbin, Kristen Waters, Becky Lartigue, Linda Lopez McAlister, Missy-Marie Montgomery, Marty Dobrow, Bobbie Harro, Barbara Love, Laurel Davis, Andrea Nicki, and my incredibly dear friend Jerry Rubenstein.

Margaret Lloyd, who is best known as a poet and artist, has been my dear friend, intellectual comrade, and department chair for seventeen years; many of our conversations manifest themselves in this book; also, she read the manuscript and gave me invaluable comments on it.

My work as a philosopher has been profoundly influenced by my students. I can only mention a few, whose names will have to represent so many others: Sarah Anderson Scafidi, Galo Grijalva, Steve Stoltz, Jon D'Angelo, Brian Duval, Chris Malia, Sonya Mickiewicz, Justin Delgado, Lisa Trimbry, Rachel DiSaia Trozzolo, June Coan, Joe Flanagan, Kate Seethaler, and Adam Taylor .

Kit Gruelle, an amazing person who works as an activist against domestic violence, read the manuscript and provided some much-appreciated supportive comments. (Kit is featured prominently in the award-winning, must-see documentary *Private Violence*.) Markus Gerke, a graduate student working with (and recommended by) Michael Kimmel, read the entire manuscript with great care, giving me a host of both substantive and editorial suggestions for improving both the book and my understanding. Larry Vinson and Robin Cooney are two longtime friends who have been astute, generous, and witty editors and commenters on the manuscript.

I am deeply indebted to Wendy Lochner, publisher for philosophy and religion at Columbia University Press, for her recognition of the importance of this project, for the astute guidance she gave it, and for her sustaining encouragement. Assistant editor Christine Dunbar was a savvy and diplomatic guide through the production process. Susan Pensak was a superlative manuscript editor whose comments led me to rethink some important points and who may have permanently cured me of commaphilia.

Marilyn Frye has influenced my approach to philosophy in many ways, one of which can be seen whenever the word *pattern* appears in this book, which reflects a more profound influence than might be appreciated by anyone unfamiliar with Frye's methodology.

Under the influence of Janice Moulton's articles on adversariality in philosophy, I have striven to use description and explanation, rather than argument, in hopes of making this book an example of non-adversarial philosophy, or as I call it, *postmilitaristic philosophy*.

The influence of the brilliant philosopher Sandra Bartky can be found throughout this book. I learned from her the usefulness of phenomenology for responding to the pressing needs of the world. Her close and profound friendship has sustained me for over twenty years.

Luna Nájera has been the most influential person in my life for eighteen years. She is the most intelligent, perspicacious, kind, generous, and fun person I've ever known and, to an extraordinary extent, she has made me the person I am today.

Love and War

1

BATTLE OF THE SEXES

WHY IS HETEROSEXUAL LOVE SO HARD?

You can't stay married in a situation where you are afraid
to go to sleep in case your wife might cut your throat.

—Mike Tyson

Consider a paradox: In most cultures, heterosexual erotic relationships are favored over same-sex erotic relationships. Heterosexual love is idealized, while same-sex love is often deemed problematic or even reprehensible, primarily on religious grounds. To the extent that any sexual orientation is problematized, it is always a *non*heterosexual orientation. But how can heterosexuality be superior to homosexuality, when the former is commonly described as a "battle of the sexes"? That expression points to a widely shared understanding that heterosexuality is inherently adversarial, so that conflict in heterosexual erotic relationships is inevitable. Isn't it paradoxical that having two persons of different sexes in a relationship tends to make it adversarial, yet that is supposed to be better than a relationship with two persons of the same sex?

I propose that, instead of problematizing same-sex love, we take a look at the problems that appear to be inherent in *different*-sex love. Let's put the culture war that is swirling around same-sex relationships aside for a while and, for the sake of straight people, let's try to diagnose what has gone so horribly wrong with heterosexuality. I'm not proposing that we try to cure straight people or that we try to pray away their straightness. My hope is that we can figure out a way to rescue straight people from the fate to which so many of them have been condemned: a lifelong and deeply tragic "battle of the sexes."

The culturally prevailing narrative about heterosexual romantic love, which we get from popular media, parents, and sometimes religion, involves two essential phases: a man and a woman fall in love and then they live happily ever after. In between, there are various plot twists and turns, but those are the two essential elements. Curiously, our allegiance to the idea that there is somehow a logical or causal connection between those two stages is rarely disrupted by doubt, despite an undercurrent of popular culture that should provide more than a little skepticism about the ostensible flow from falling in love to living happily ever after. Consider that reality TV star Kim Kardashian announced her divorce from NBA player Kris Humphries just seventy-two days after the 2011 television broadcast of what had been billed as "Kim's Fairytale Wedding." The divorce was finalized in 2013, a day after the baby shower celebrating the impending birth of the daughter she had with Kanye West.[1]

On a more ominous note, consider the Lifetime Movie Network programming for the day that I am writing this. What's playing right now is a movie called *Obsessed,* with the following synopsis: "Ellena Roberts . . . can't get (the married) Dr. David Stillman out of her head; all she can think about is their passionate affair. So Ellena is badly shaken when the police arrest her, charging her with terrorizing the man she adores—who denies the existence of their romantic relationship! Who is telling the truth? Follow this riveting courtroom drama, based on a true story, as it unfolds!"[2] Next up is *A Friendship to Die For* at 4:00 P.M.: "Rachel and Carla want money and have no problem using sex, blackmail and murder to get their hands on some cash. Will the devious duo get away with their latest scheme, or will Carla's boyfriend figure out that he's been tricked into helping them? You won't want to miss a second of this suspenseful flick where the tables are constantly turning!"[3] Too bad about those turning tables, as next it's dinner time, featuring *Engaged to Kill:* "Abby's overjoyed that her 19-year-old daughter has found herself the perfect boyfriend in Nick— or so she thought! Turns out Nick has been counting the days till he could get revenge on Abby because of some mysterious grudge. Will Abby catch on to this madman's scheme before it's too late?"[4] All in all, the message from Lifetime seems to be that love is seriously dangerous. And it should be noted that these Lifetime movies are often based on "real life" stories. In fact, in real life we are surrounded by examples of relationships that have gone awry, often with considerable emotional intensity, even rivaling a Lifetime movie.

In spite of that pattern, a connection is rarely made in popular culture between the undercurrent theme of love as danger to the surface theme of falling in love and living happily ever after. Rather, the two themes seem to be parallel strands within culture that rarely intersect, leaving intact a paradox: Heterosexuality is the preferred ideal of love, yet it is fraught with perils that are specific to heterosexuality. Indeed, those parallel cultural strands often make love seem like a scam: Supposedly, if one "truly" falls in love heterosexually, the result is automatic happiness; yet, routinely, the belief that one has fallen in love is followed by torment and misery.

As a consequence, those two parallel but contrary cultural strands—love as danger, and love as something that we fall into and then live happily ever after—function as cultural puppet strings that make us seem like very confused puppets. If we can cut those puppet strings, we can not only eliminate a lot of confusion, we can also attain greater power and freedom in our love lives. And just maybe that can increase our odds of attaining the supreme fulfillment that love can potentially offer.

To cut those cultural puppet strings we must first be able to see them. We need to identify, describe, and explain how our culture programs into us the beliefs, preferences, and desires from which our experiences of love and sexuality flow.[5] That potentially liberatory project is an example of really useful philosophy, the kind of philosophy that can make a profound difference in one's life and in the world.

✳ ✳ ✳

Let's start our philosophical project by considering a real-life story drawn from the lives of two Army sergeants. This story is emblematic of important and even dramatic changes that have been taking place in recent decades across the globe. Many women throughout the world are gaining more political power, more economic power, and more power over their own lives. Sergeant Erin Edwards was such a woman. Not only did she hold the same rank as her husband, Sergeant William Edwards, she had been an aide to a brigadier general and, like her husband, she was a veteran of the war in Iraq. Shortly after both sergeants had returned to Fort Hood from their missions in Iraq, William struck and choked Erin, dragged her outside, and slammed her onto a concrete sidewalk. She was determined to prevent anything like that from ever happening again. With the help of the brigadier general she served as an aide, a future transfer to a base in another state was arranged. She filed charges against William and obtained an order of protection. Her mother took in her two children. Her husband's commanders assured her that he would not be allowed to leave the base without the accompaniment of an officer.

Sergeant Erin Edwards had done everything possible to protect herself from her husband. Nonetheless, on July 22, 2004, Sergeant William Edwards sneaked off base and drove to Erin's house in Killeen, Texas. When she came to the door, he pointed his gun at her and pulled the trigger, killing her. He then shot and killed himself.[6]

Notice that Erin Edwards was doing work that traditionally was available only to men and that she by no means conformed to the submissive femininity of times past. She exemplified how women's lives and our cultural ideals of womanhood are changing, in the direction of women having more power over their lives. On the other hand,

William Edwards, based on what little we know about him, appears to have exemplified the ways and the extent to which manhood is not changing in coordination with the changes in womanhood.

That is not to say that manhood is not changing at all. And many of the ways it is changing are causally related to changes in women's lives. The problem is that some of the ways manhood is changing are not at all complementary to the ways womanhood is changing. Indeed, some of the ways manhood is changing are actually creating more difficulties for heterosexual relationships. To take just one example, fewer men than women are now graduating from high school, college, and graduate school.[7] As men's relative earning power declines, that can put stress on their relationships, and it shrinks the pool of ostensibly viable partners for heterosexual women.[8]

The challenges faced by heterosexual love, however, are by no means just those that have arisen in recent decades. The story of the two sergeants helps us see another, larger pattern that extends far back in time: The heterosexual antagonism that is so extreme in the tragic case of Erin and William Edwards has for centuries been a dimension of everyday life in most societies.

About two thousand years ago, when Ovid said "Love is a kind of war, and no assignment for cowards," his context makes it clear that he was talking about heterosexual love. Ovid's assertion about heterosexual love rang true to his ancient Roman audience, and his insight has continued to ring true ever since.

Confirmation of that can be found in the common expression "battle of the sexes." That phrase is by no means new; for example, D. W. Griffith's film titled *The Battle of the Sexes* was released in 1914. Similar expressions, typically interlarded with misogynistic sentiments, have circulated for millennia. In his 1952 anthology, *With Malice Toward Women,* Justin Kaplan serves up three thousand years worth of examples of what he calls "the eternally hostile tension between the sexes," acknowledging what his title suggests, namely that "men have been more vociferous than women in the war of the sexes."[9]

The persistence of the "battle of the sexes" theme has led many people to suppose that heterosexual conflict has its roots in biology. The ever provocative Camille Paglia puts it this way: "Sex is a surging power thing between the sexes. It's a sex war. . . . I feel that sex is basically combat. I feel that the sexes are at war.[10] Paglia seems to revel in this enmity between men and women, which she assumes to be embedded in biology. Fortunately for us all, she is sadly misinformed.

Paglia is mistaken about this not because biology is entirely irrelevant to heterosexual adversariality but because the causal context for antagonism between the sexes is primarily cultural rather than biological. Robert Louis Stevenson describes the cultural sources of heterosexual adversariality this way:

> The little rift between the sexes is astonishingly widened by simply teaching one set of catchwords to the girls and another to the boys. To the first, there is shown but a very small field of experience, and taught a very trenchant principle for judgment and action; to the other, the world of life is more largely displayed, and their rule of conduct is proportionally widened. They are taught to follow different virtues, to hate different vices, to place their ideal, even for each other, in different achievements. . . . So, when I see a raw youth and a green girl, fluted and fiddled in a dancing measure into that most serious contract, and setting out upon life's journey with ideas so monstrously divergent, I am not surprised that some make shipwreck, but that any come to port. What the boy does almost proudly, as a manly peccadillo, the girl will shudder at as a debasing vice; what is to her the mere common sense of tactics he will spit out of his mouth as shameful. Through such a sea of contrarieties must this green couple steer their way . . . and be ready, when the time arrives, to educate the little men and women who shall succeed to their places and perplexities.[11]

We can gain further confirmation of Stevenson's observations that source heterosexual adversariality in culture by considering cultural variations. There are some societies—such as the Mosuo of China, the Semai of Malaysia, and the Tahitians of the South Pacific—where adversariality based on sex or gender is nonexistent or rare. Further, the degree of gendered adversariality in societies that have it varies widely, both cross-culturally and across various historical periods.[12] In any case, the project of finding, describing, and explaining cultural causes of heterosexual adversariality is surely important, regardless of whether there are contributing biological factors. It is not hard to go beyond Stevenson's insights in locating those cultural causes.

✳ ✳ ✳

My search for the cultural sources of heterosexual adversariality benefited substantially when I observed two intersecting patterns: First, I noticed that heterosexual adversariality is especially common in societies that are, or have been, war-reliant, in the sense of tending to rely on group violent force to resolve problems with other societies. Second, to the extent that societies are not war-reliant, they seemed to have less heterosexual adversariality.

For people who live in a society with a militaristic culture it may be surprising to learn that not all societies are militaristic, or war-reliant.[13] Indeed, it is quite common for folks in war-reliant societies to assume (like Hobbes) that all societies are like their own with respect to militarism. Even sophisticated scholars and scientists can fall prey to this error. For example, in his widely used evolutionary psychology textbook, David Buss asserts that "human recorded history . . . reveals male coalitional warfare to be pervasive across cultures worldwide."[14] The distinguished biologist Edward O. Wilson puts aside his usual skepticism to put forth the sweeping claim that "throughout history, warfare, representing only the most organized technique of aggression, has been endemic to every form of society, from hunter-gatherer bands to industrial states."[15] There are two problems with such broad claims about the inevitability or universality of warfare among humans. First, within most societies there are many people who clearly are nonviolent or who have a disposition against violence, and within larger societies there are often even entire groups of such people who have a disposition against violence (e.g., Quakers and other pacifist religionists, antiwar groups, social justice advocates, etc.). Second, it is simply false that all human societies are war-reliant. That is a powerful, central myth in militaristic cultures, but a myth nonetheless. It is thoroughly debunked by anthropologist Douglas F. Fry: "Many nonwarring cultures do in fact exist. Not all societies make war. . . . A substantial number of cultures engage in warfare, but some do not. Thus the belief that war is a universal feature of societies everywhere, as expressed by numerous persons including some eminent thinkers, is nonetheless false."[16] Fry provides a list of seventy-four societies that do not make war, as well as extended discussions of some of them.[17] For example, the Siriono of Bolivia neither engage in war nor glorify warlike behavior. "Siriono bands interact peacefully. They do not claim exclusive territories. If hunters from one band come across signs that another band is occupying a given area, the hunters abstain from hunting in the vicinity, thus respecting the rights of the first band to any game in the area."[18] Similarly, the Paliyan of India embrace nonviolence as a way of life.

> The Paliyan usually deal with conflicts through avoidance rather than confrontation. Aggression is incompatible with the values of respect, equality, and autonomy. For the most part, the Paliyan use effective nonviolent techniques to deal with interpersonal conflict. First, individuals employ self-restraint, as reflected in this ideal: "If one strikes, the struck man keeps still. It is our main motto." Second, Paliyan avoid drinking alcohol, which is sometimes available when they encounter outsiders. Third, people remove themselves from conflict situations. Avoidance is relatively easy in this individually autonomous, nomadic society. Fourth, a third party may assist in relieving tension.[19]

The Semai of Malaysia, mentioned previously, are a particularly fascinating people on Fry's list. On average less than five feet tall, and surrounded by other groups of typical human height, the Semai have survived by consistently responding to danger by fleeing rather than fighting. Notably, their socialization of children places a primary emphasis on discouraging anger—the most militaristic of emotions.[20]

In addition to the societies on Fry's nonwarring list, it should be noted that, among modern nations, Iceland has not gone to war in seven hundred years, both Switzerland and Sweden have not been to war in almost two hundred years, and Costa Rica abolished its military after World War II.[21]

But most societies are war-reliant, and hence, culturally militaristic. Why do those war-reliant societies so consistently display patterns of men dominating women, with consequent antipathy between men and women? Why are those gender patterns more likely to prevail among war-reliant societies than among societies that do not rely on war, like the Siriono and the Paliyan, for whom gender egalitarianism prevails? Are there factors within cultural militarism that tend to engender heterosexual antagonism?

The answer to that question starts with a consideration of two of the core elements in cultural militarism, both of which are so deeply culturally programmed into members of war-reliant societies that they are rarely subjected to doubt. Each of these elements is comprised of a cluster of beliefs, values, and dispositions. The first is a faith in force to solve problems—more specifically, a faith in masculine force. This faith supports a belief in the efficacy of force, it supports a set of values that glorify people—especially men—who display forceful behavior, and it instills both individual and societal dispositions to choose force over other options for solving problems (as when torture is chosen over more effective interrogation techniques). The second element in cultural militarism is a presumption of adversariality, which often manifests itself more particularly in a presumption of zero-sumness: war-reliant societies tend toward paranoid presumptions of enmity with other societies, so that they assume they must fight to avoid gains for other societies that they assume would result in losses for their own group. This presumption of adversariality results in a kind of tunnel vision, obscuring opportunities for collaboration and cooperation with other groups.

It should be no surprise that in a society where a faith in specifically masculine force prevails, men will routinely use force to solve ostensible problems. And, in the context of heterosexuality, if those men see some of their problems as emanating from women, maybe it should also be no surprise when they resort to violent force as a way of coping with what they consider to be "woman problems."

The other dimension of cultural militarism, the presumption of adversariality, is not reserved by war-reliant societies exclusively for external enemies. Rather, there is also a tendency to find enemies within one's own society. For example, in the United States, political differences—which could in principle offer opportunities for productive collaboration—often result instead in a quite vicious, even violent, demonization of individuals who represent opposing parties or points of view. That greatly reduces the likelihood of democratic processes premised on rationality, or even reasonableness.

In war-reliant societies there is also a presumption of adversariality within heterosexual relationships that, as in politics, undermines reasonableness and promotes vitriol and violence. The presumption of heterosexual adversariality starts with the curious and false notion that sex and gender must be viewed in a binary fashion, with humans divided into precisely two groups, males and females, that are sharply delineated along both biological and psychological lines.

There is a widespread belief in many cultures that the gender binary is just the way things are, because it is persumed to be grounded in nature. Rarely is there a recognition that the gender binary is just the result of cultural programming by some, but not all, cultures. The origins of the gender binary in cultural programming becomes more apparent when we pay attention to the considerable cultural diversity regarding gender differences, and particularly when we take into account the many societies in which gendering is relatively minimal: the Vanatinai island-ers, the Semai of Malaysia, the Siriono of Bolivia, the Mbuti of central Africa, the !Kung of southern Africa, the Copper Eskimo of Canada, and the Tahitians of the South Pacific.[22]

Regarding the Tahitians, whom he visited in the nineteenth century, Henry Adams objected to their relative lack of gender differentiation: "The Polynesian woman seems to me too much like the Polynesian man; the difference is not great enough to admit of sentiment, only of physical divergence."[23] According to anthropologist David Gilmore, Tahitian men and women have "similar personalities," with "roles so similar as to seem almost indistinguishable . . . and there are no jobs or skills reserved for either sex by cultural dictate." Thus, he reports, the men feel no need either to prove their manliness or to differentiate themselves from women or children.[24]

There are also societies that differentiate women and men, but with roles that largely reverse those found in most societies. For example, among the Mosuo people of China the women are the heads of house-holds. They also are the managers of family property, resources, and labor, including assigning tasks to men. Sexual relationships are initi-ated and ended by women, not men. If a man has been "taken" by a woman, after working on his mother's farm all day, he packs a little bag and heads over to the woman's dwelling to spend the night. If he arrives to find her door closed, he knows the relationship is over and returns to his mother's farm.[25]

Even in many contemporary militaristic cultures there is a growing awareness of evidence that the gender binary has always been a myth. Traditionalists are still uncomfortable with transgender and trans-sexual people, but greater visibility means their existence cannot be denied. Further, it is increasingly difficult to find people who would insist there are roles that can be performed only by one gender, and that includes combat.

The fact is, it is increasingly difficult to maintain any clarity about gender. Consider as an example this self-description written by semipro football player and competitive strongwoman Amanda Alpert when she was a philosophy student:

> I do not wear frilly lace or pink clothes or shoes with heels. I do not wear make-up. I wear jeans and tee shirts. I am on the track team here at Springfield. I throw shot put, discus, hammer, and the twenty pound weight. I power lift. I can leg press nine hundred pounds. I am not ashamed to sweat when I exercise. I like to watch sports, my favorite is football. How many girls enjoy wrestling with their best friend? I mean serious wrestling, black and blues, but no bloodshed. As you can tell, I am neither dainty nor fragile.
>
> The media and traditions of our culture brainwash people to believe that the world should consist of delicate and petite women.... That is just not me. Neither will it ever be.[26]

There were plenty of similar examples in the London 2012 Olympics. For the first time, women's boxing was featured in the Olympics, with American middleweight Claressa Shields not only winning gold, but showing she could bloody an opponent's face as well as any man. In the gold medal tally the women of the United States actually dominated the men, twenty-nine to seventeen.[27] Of course, not all Olympic events emphasize aggression. But even in sports that do there are plenty of successful female athletes whose aggression in competition is balanced by an embrace of feminine clothing and attitudes as well, like champion weightlifter Cheryl Haworth, subject of the documentary *Strong!*, in which there is a vignette of her trying on dresses and high heels in a clothing shop. And, of course, there are the Williams sisters, Serena and Venus, known for their aggressive tennis playing, but also for their love of designer gowns and high heels.[28]

These and many other available examples show us that gender is culturally fluid, diverse, and quite often ambiguous, with a rainbow of possibilities. The idea that gender can be reduced to a binary is a cultural myth.

But it is a stubborn myth in many societies, especially those that are war-reliant or that are culturally militaristic by tradition. In such societies, the gender binary is maintained and reinforced by the culturally programmed notion that each sex is the opposite of the other; hence, the expression "the opposite sex." In that way, the two categories that comprise the gender binary become boxes, with every person confined within one and only one box. An even more apt metaphor here would be a prison, for there are strenuous cultural exertions for the purpose of policing the boundaries of those boxes.

One such cultural exertion is the inculcation in boys and men of the misogynistic idea that to be construed as a girl or woman is the worst possible fate, fear of which serves to reinforce the kind of behavior that is considered "masculine." Boys and men are continually subject to having their masculinity questioned with misogynistic taunts that they are girls, ladies, wusses, female cats, female dogs, etc. Further, an inherently adversarial relationship is presumed to exist between males and females—a "battle of the sexes," with disregard for the fact that males and females are utterly interdependent both biologically and socially. These ideas and myths about heterosexuality, including the myth of the illusory gender binary,[29] are laden with paradox and thus they fit together rather awkwardly. Nonetheless, this cluster of beliefs about gender and heterosexuality tends to be widely and deeply held, which calls for an explanation.

An initial hint is that those ideas are found in war-reliant cultures, for which they make a kind of peculiar sense: If a society is militaristic, it must make some of its members into warriors—the people who do the fighting. It would seem smart for militaristic societies to pick the biggest, strongest, meanest people to be warriors, regardless of whether they are men or women, but that's almost never what they do.[30]

Instead, they want the men and only the men to play the role of warrior, and they start preparing them for that role as boys, starting with their toys. Whenever I ask an audience or a class what best signals the boys' section of a toy store, the immediate response is "the guns." This is part of a larger pattern: all over the world, the greater the tendency of a society to fight with other societies, the more likely it is that the boys are going to play with toy weapons—toy guns, toy spears, toy knives, toy clubs, toy bows and arrows, and, of course, sticks that they use to hit each other. Of course, today toy weapons are far less likely than virtual weapons in video games, like the Call of Duty series.

Why are boys more likely than girls to be playing with toy weapons? Surely it is no coincidence that those boys are expected to have the ability and the predisposition to use actual weapons when they become men. But why do fighting societies typically select men and boys, and not women and girls, to do the fighting?

Assigning men and boys the warrior role might seem to make sense within a militaristic culture, strictly from the vantage point of the biology of reproduction: If a lot of men get killed, the population can still be replenished fairly efficiently, but not so if a lot of women get killed. So members of the comparatively more expendable sex, men, get assigned the role of combat, while the women get assigned the role of breeding and nurturing—roles with their own risks, but parts of which biologically can be done only by females.

I say that men and women are "assigned" these roles, respectively, of warrior and of breeder/nurturer, because it has always been the case that some men have been utterly incompetent and uninterested in the warrior role and that some women have been utterly incompetent and uninterested in the role of breeder and nurturer. Among the myriad examples of the latter is a recent news story with the headline "Baby Killed After Interrupting Mom's Facebook Time." A Florida woman shook her baby to death after his crying interrupted her while she was playing a Facebook game called FarmVille.[31]

A few years ago, when I first began thinking critically about the cultural programming around motherhood in militaristic cultures, and in particular about the kind of essentialism that says women are naturally maternal, I started collecting news reports about mothers who demonstrate anything but maternalism. Mind you, I was not looking for such reports, but would just quickly save the web pages to a folder on my computer whenever I happened to stumble upon the headlines. Here are some of titles of the news stories in that folder:

"German Mother Guilty of Killing Infants"
"Mom Charged with Bathtub Child Murders"
"Mom Charged with Throwing Kids in River"
"Mom Killed Her 4 Newborns, Kept Bones in Cooler"
"Mother Is Held in Slaying of 3 Children"
"Mother Kills Her 3 Children in Arkansas"
"Mother Put Girls in Car Trunk"
"Mother Tosses 3 Kids Into Bay, Father Devastated"
"My Mother Is Crazy and Terrifying"
"Woman Accused of Cutting Off Baby's Arms with Butcher Knife"
"NC Woman Shoots Five Kids in Head"
"Colorado Woman Left Estranged Husband a Note Before Shooting Their 9-Year-Old Son"

In the last case the mother killed her son by shooting him three times in the chest, once in the head, and once in the leg. When asked by her husband why she had done that, she reportedly answered, "To hurt you."[32]

I probably should say two things that are obvious: (1) these are extreme cases and (2) the fact that there are some really bad mothers is not to say anything about women or mothers in general. Rather, these cases just draw attention to the fact that being biologically female does not automatically make one a good nurturer. The culturally instilled presumption that being born female makes a person naturally maternal is a cultural trick used in war-reliant societies to camouflage the actual source of the idea that women who aren't successful mothers are defective. That belief is culturally programmed into both women and men in war-reliant societies primarily because of a need to maximize breeding, which results when a lot of their people are getting killed in battle. Secondarily, there is a need in such societies for women to be nurturing toward adult men because of the demands placed on men to have the emotional toughness of a warrior, which tends to be emotionally disabling, so they need women to "mother" them (see chapter 3, "How to Make a Warrior").

Just as war-reliant societies culturally program their members to believe that women are determined by nature to be breeders and mothers, they also program the belief that men are natural warriors. One common way to accomplish this is to promote the more sweeping belief that men are biologically determined to be both violent and emotionally tough. I have found those beliefs to be quite pervasive among both students in my classes and the audiences for my public lectures. The widespread faith in this doctrine that men are naturally violent and emotionally "hard" can be, like faith generally, extraordinarily stubborn, even though it is a doctrine that can easily be discredited.

For example, Colonel Dave Grossman—a former sniper who may be the world's leading expert on killing humans and who literally wrote the book *On Killing*[33]—insists that our brain physiology makes all of us, including males, extremely reluctant to kill other human beings.

On the other hand, men definitely fear being killed. Indeed, fear is a pervasive emotion among actual men in actual wars. Consider, for example, this description of what it was like for soldiers in the Civil War, when battle was imminent: "Sometimes this fear was so intense that men would fall to the ground paralyzed with terror, bury their face in the grass, grasp at the earth, and refuse to move."[34] The following is a historian's account of American soldiers in World War II, the so-called good war, at the Battle of the Bulge: "Down the middle of the road came the defeated American troops, fleeing the front in disarray moblike. Many had thrown away their rifles, their coats, all encumbrances. Some were in a panic, staggering, exhausted, shouting, 'Run! Run! They'll murder you! They'll kill you! They've got everything, tanks, machine-guns, air power, everything!'"[35] Such examples help us see behind the romantic facade of war, raising doubts about whether men are natural-born killers, as militaristic cultural programming would have us believe.

Indeed, one of the ways to get a group of human beings to kill is to convert them to the *belief* that they in particular are natural-born killers. That seems to be what is going on in this lecture to Marines being trained at Parris Island, as reported by military historian Gwynne Dyer: "You want to rip (the enemy's) eyeballs out, you want to tear apart his love machine, you want to destroy him, privates. . . . You want to send him home in a Glad bag to his mommy! . . . Marines are born and trained killers; you've got to prove that every day. Do you understand?"[36] The poor Marines could be forgiven if they did not understand. Were they, but not other men, killers from birth? How had they come this far without doing what they were born to do? Of course, the point of the lecture is not to bring out some killer instinct with which they were born, but rather to overcome the opposite, the reluctance to kill with which they were indeed born, according to Grossman. As Dyer puts it, the purpose of the lecture, including its graphically gory language, is to "desensitize them to the suffering of an 'enemy' at the same time they are being indoctrinated in the most explicit fashion . . . with the notion that their purpose is not just to be brave and to fight well; it is to kill people."[37] If men were such naturals at warfare and killing, such training would be superfluous, conscription would never be necessary, and it would never be necessary to shoot men for desertion.

There are two more things that must be said about this purported proclivity for violence among men. Obviously we could point to famous examples of men whose lives have been characterized by the absence of violence, like Martin Luther King Jr., whose inspiration can be seen in the exertions by folks in the Occupy Wall Street movement to keep their protests nonviolent. But in a militaristic culture those nonviolent persons, especially men, are portrayed as notable exceptions, even in the absence of any explanation of such exceptionality. For a different perspective, ask youself whether you can think of men who are gentle, kind, sweet, sensitive, and not prone to violence. Most of us can think of such men, but militaristic cultural programming instills in us a kind of forgetfulness about them. Turning our attention to those men allows us to see that biology can be resistant to militaristic cultural programming, and that helps us see that the belief that men are naturally violent comes from culture, not science.

Even more powerful indicators that men are not biologically determined to have the qualities of a warrior come from the many societies that are not at all war reliant and where men do not manifest the qualities of a warrior. For example, whenever men or women of the Semai people of Malaysia confront danger, they flee rather than fight.[38] (In militaristic societies, we tend to forget that the fight or flight response does offer two options.)

Militaristic societies rely on a gender binary, in which manhood and womanhood are so sharply differentiated from each other that each is believed to have qualities opposite to those of the other. In the following list of pairs of opposite qualities, it is easy to see which are the adjectives associated with manliness and which are associated with womanliness: dominant/submissive, aggressive/passive, hard/soft, strong/weak, confident/modest, tough/compassionate, violent/gentle, logical/emotional, taciturn/talkative, independent/dependent, analytical/intuitive, brave/timid, competitive/cooperative, insensitive/sensitive, independent/dependent, competent/ditzy.

The cultural, rather than biological, origins of the gender binary explain why societies must coerce men and women into their respective roles of warrior and nurturer, with extraordinary pressures to manifest only the qualities proper to one's gender. The penalties for the nonconformers can be heavy indeed, including bullying, hazing, harassment, and even torture and death.

There's another factor that helps explain the need for militaristic societies to culturally program their members with a coercive gender binary. Whereas the binary and its coercive framework are not altogether determined by biology, they are interrelated with male and female roles in biological reproduction. If war becomes routine for a society, there may be a need to maximize procreative efficiency in order to (1) grow the biggest possible army and (2) replace the males who get killed in battle. So it should be no surprise when a militaristic society has rules prohibiting men from having sex with men, or even by themselves. For example, when God told the ancient Hebrews not to spill their seed upon the ground in Genesis,[39] it was not because they had discovered hydroponics. The Hebrews wanted to recapture their homeland, so they needed to grow an army (not tomatoes). Thus, it was important for Hebrew men that their seed get planted where it could fulfill the imperative to be fruitful and multiply—which would not be in another man, nor on the ground.

The most notable exception to the proscription of sex between men in militaristic societies would be the ancient Spartans, who actually required boys and men to come together in sexual relationships. When men did enter into a heterosexual marriage in their late twenties or even thirties, they generally continued to live in all-male groups. For conjugal hookups, often the wife would dress in men's clothes, just to keep the marital spark alive. So how did the Spartans, one of the most militaristic cultures the world has ever known, maintain their population levels? Well, they didn't. At the time of the famous battle at Thermopylae (480 BC), the number of full citizen-warriors in Sparta was about ten thousand. By 371 BC, they were down to about one thousand, of whom four hundred were killed when the Spartans suffered a major defeat at Leuctra. After that, Sparta never regained its former status as a preeminent military and political power. There were a lot of variables that factored into Sparta's decline, so it is by no means certain that if only their attitudes about sexuality had been more supportive of procreative efficiency they could have averted decline.[40] The point is just that the case of Sparta is not inconsistent with the present explanation of the intersections of heterosexuality and militarism.

While it seems to make sense that discouraging homosexuality and masturbation could help maximize procreation, another, possibly even more efficacious, cultural strategy toward that end is the eroticization of the culturally programmed differences between men and women. The need would be for the people who can get pregnant to be turned on by people who can impregnate, and who appear to be warrior-types (say, men in uniform, tall men, strong men, emotionally reserved men) and also for those warrior-types to be turned on by women whom they perceive (however erroneously) to be inviting sexual attention by performing femininity (say, by dressing and acting in ways considered by men to be "feminine" or "sexy"). Such dynamics of attraction are likely to result in reproduction.

That's how the gender binary works: (1) everybody is supposed to be unambiguously either male or female, thereby disregarding biological ambiguities; (2) the people on each side of that gender binary are supposed to desire sex with people who are clearly on the other side; and (3) the outcome is maximum babies—male babies who can later on be sent into battle and female babies who can later on become producers of more babies.

But there's more to it. To maximize procreation, women are culturally programmed to think they will be incomplete as women if they haven't produced any offspring. And, just in case any of them are recalcitrant free spirits who resist that cultural programming, a militaristic society can make it illegal or immoral for them to control their own reproductive lives through abortion or contraception. Just for good measure, it can also tell women who use either of those ways to avoid reproduction that they'll join the gay men and masturbating boys in hell, where their flesh will burn and their teeth will gnash throughout eternity. When Heinrich Himmler created the Reich Central Office for Combating Homosexuality and Abortion in 1936, it was no coincidence that he combined those two efforts in one program, nor that he set up such a program at a time when Hitler's aspirations for expansion of Germany's military domination had become clear. Himmler was effectively—and quite explicitly—adding a procreation-maximizing feature to the Nazi war machine.[41]

Such cultural convergences of opposition to homosexuality and abortion with militarism can also be seen in contemporary United States politics. The connection between militarism and procreation maximizing is not always explicit. For example, in the 2004 U.S. presidential election, voter exit polls indicated that "social issues" like homosexuality and abortion were, as everyone expected, highly motivating factors for folks who voted for George W. Bush. What went less noticed was that the single most important factor motivating people to vote for Bush was a preference for the use of military over nonmilitary options for dealing with world problems—in other words, a greater faith in force and a stronger presumption of adversariality.[42] Note also the widespread pattern in that election of fundamentalism dovetailing with militarism, as well as with vigorous rejection of homosexuality and abortion. Rarely do fundamentalists explicitly associate their procreation-maximizing stances with their militarism, preferring to give religious or moral arguments against homosexuality, abortion, and contraception. But even more rarely does one find those moralistic stances that are effectively procreation maximizing in the absence of militarism. That continuing political convergence surely reflects cultural inertia, the grip of which gradually loosens as some political conservatives begin to notice the human tragedy that is inherent in war, yet cling to opposition to abortion and homosexuality, where they are slower to recognize the dysfunctionality of their views.

With so much procreating going on as a result of efforts within militaristic cultures to control contraception, abortion, and homosexuality, there's a need to keep the offspring alive and healthy, which is culturally deemed the responsibility of women. Thus any woman who doesn't act "maternal" enough gets demonized. If there are enough signs that a woman isn't sufficiently nurturing, willing to subordinate her interest to the interest of the children—and men— around her, she gets called shrill, cold, psychotic, a bitch, or a witch. All of which were done, not coincidentally, to Hillary Clinton during the 2008 presidential primary, by journalists who also referred to her laugh as a "cackle."[43] Such misogynistic demonization tactics related to maternalism were also used in 2011–2013 against Australian prime minister Julia Gillard, who was unmarried and had no children. Her opponents described her as "deliberately barren" and referred to her as a witch and a bitch.[44]

But if producing offspring and keeping them alive is especially important for militaristic societies, why not get the guys involved in that too? Well, the problem lies with another aspect of the warrior role that is often overlooked, even though it is even more important for a warrior than size and strength.

To be an effective warrior, what is most crucially required is this: The warrior must be able to manage the capacity to care about suffering: He must be able to selectively focus, and sometimes suspend altogether, the capacity to care about not only his own suffering and potential suffering but also the suffering of others. Thus in militaristic cultures the cultural programming of men, who are assigned the warrior role, *diminishes* their capacity for empathy, while the cultural programming of women *amplifies* their capacity for empathy. Within the militaristic cultural framework the qualities that are needed for the warrior are opposite to the qualities that are needed for a mother. The mother is supposed to care so much about her children (and her husband) that her caring for them extends to the point of self-sacrifice. No surprise, then, that any parenting that does not involve the imposition of authority is considered more appropriately done by women. Women are deemed much better at subordinating their own interest to the interests of persons they love.

Of course, the life of the warrior also involves self-sacrifice, but only in the context of combat. On the domestic scene, the warrior becomes the "man of the house," meaning not only a dominant figure but even the supreme authority within the boundaries of domestic life.

Men are culturally programmed to take on the warrior role, regardless of whether they ever go to war or not.[45] In militaristic societies, even if a man is not an actual warrior and even if a boy is not likely to become a warrior, they are culturally programmed to display the qualities of a warrior—and that has major ramifications for their erotic lives. In societies where cultural values emphasize male warriors and female nurturers, male procreation and female breeding, it is not unusual for there to be pressure on men to have heterosexual sex as part of the cultural imperative of manhood. So it is no surprise that in the United States the following headlines have appeared on the covers of men's magazines:

SUPREME SEX! MASTER THE BEDROOM'S TOUGH-EST MANEUVER!
"SEX RATED! Shred Her Sheets with These Bed-Tested Moves"

Sometimes there's an overtly military perspective:

"SEX WAR! Make Her Surrender"
"SEX TRICKS! Control Her Mind . . . Jedi-Style"
"SEX-PLOSION! How to be THE BOMB in Bed"

Recently, there may be a detectable turn to a defensive posture, as in this headline:

"Defuse Your Lady Bomb!"[46]

All in all, one gets the impression of a fantasy bedroom that is as full of action-packed adventure as combat video games like Call of Duty or Halo!

Interestingly, there is a sort of perverse complementarity when one looks at women's magazine headlines. It turns out that, corresponding to the male imperative to have as much sex as possible, there is a cultural imperative urging women to go along with the male imperative. Here are some headlines from recent issues of *Cosmopolitan* and *Glamour:*

"MEN'S SEXUAL WISH LIST—20 Requests All Guys Would
   Like to Make"
"WHAT SEX FEELS LIKE FOR A GUY—The Triggers and
   Sensations You'd Never Imagine"
"3 THINGS ALL GUYS CRAVE IN BED
"100 Sex Tips from Guys—Including the Best Ice-Cube Trick
   We've Ever Heard"

Notice the asymmetry here: men are learning how to conduct a sex war
and control women Jedi-style, while women are learning how to please
those sex warriors.

To get that picture into focus, we need to take travel back to the late
nineteenth century. By then, in both Europe and the United States,
the idea of falling in love was becoming integral to the ideal of heterosexual love (as it had not been for millennia before that). Also, the
struggle for women's equality was well underway, with pivotal events
like the Seneca Falls Convention having taken place in mid-century.
Particularly relevant to our present consideration of the asymmetry of heterosexual eroticism is a comment made by suffrage leader
Elizabeth Cady Stanton in a letter to Susan B. Anthony dated June 14,
1860: "Woman's degradation is in man's idea of his sexual rights. Our
religion, laws, customs, are all founded on the belief that woman was
made for man."[47]

Such protestations against male entitlement found reinforcement in the growing trend for heterosexual relationships to be based
relatively more on love and less on the authority of the husband.
A "love match" involved a level of mutuality, reciprocity, and individual choice that gave women in heterosexual relationships more
potential freedom and power than had been the case in previous
millennia.[48] The impact of those developments on the lives of men
was profound, and some of them responded with fear and anger.
For example, T. A. Arthur wrote the following in a popular book

called *Advice to Young Ladies,* which was published the same year as Stanton's letter:

> Singularly enough, we have in this day a class of intellectual ladies, who boldly contend for the absolute equality of the sexes. . . . They claim for woman equal civil and political privileges with man, and see nothing but tyranny in the law, or usage that has the force of law, which keeps a woman out of her country's legislative halls. Every where [*sic*] would these reformers place women in contest with men for the honors and emoluments which society bestows on the successful;—in the camp, on the bench, at the bar, in the pulpit, in the dissecting-room, or hospital, with the operator's knife in her hand,—in fact, wherever strong nerve, powerful intellect, decision, and firmness are required. . . .
>
> Let no young woman be deceived by th[is] class of reformers. . . . No good . . . has ever arisen, but much evil, from the promulgation of their pernicious doctrines. Man they are too much in the habit of representing as a selfish tyrant, and woman as his plaything or slave; and they are full of intemperate appeals to their sex to throw off the yoke that man has placed upon their necks. . . .
>
> With this idea set steadily before their minds, at the same time that they are profoundly ignorant of what really makes the difference between man and woman, they see nothing but wrong and oppression in the usages of society, and charge upon man the authorship of what is only the legitimate result of a law impressed by the hand of God upon the human mind.[49]

It's likely that most purchasers of T. A. Arthur's book were not "young ladies" themselves, but rather other gender conservative men, especially fathers who would buy the book for their daughters. However, most men in that period tried to avoid altogether the topics of love and women's equality by considering them to be matters of concern only for women. (Like today, when many men deem the problems of sexual assault, sexual harassment, and gender discrimination to be "women's issues" with which they need not be concerned.)

Not all men of that period were afraid of thinking about gender issues, though. One such courageous man was the philosopher Friedrich Nietzsche, who wrote about both love and gender equality and saw how they were intertwined.

It is important to understand that Nietzsche is not sharing his personal opinions; rather, he is describing the cultural programming that had become prevalent in Europe and the United States by the time he was writing and that continues to a great extent in the present day. According to Nietzsche, our culture programs men and women to understand love in ways that are different from, yet complementary to, each other, and those different conceptions of love stand in the way of "equal rights" in heterosexual relationships. Men and women just don't think the same way about love, he says, and each expects the other not to share the same understanding of love. "What woman understands by love is clear enough: complete surrender (not merely devotion)," without reservations or conditions. Hence, for a woman love is a kind of faith, he says.[50]

On the other hand, according to Nietzsche, a man who loves a woman wants precisely that kind of "womanly" love from her—that devotion to him, that faith in him; hence his love is altogether different from hers. Given these different, complementary conceptions of love, Nietzsche proposes the following: "A man who loves like a woman becomes thereby a slave; a woman, however, who loves like a woman becomes thereby a more perfect woman."[51] He leaves for us the rather easy task of articulating the implicit conclusion, namely, that the most perfect woman is a slave. Nietzsche grants that there are some men who experience that feminine type of love, but he says that they are not deemed to be "real men."[52] That this is still the case, we should note, is reflected in the fact that such men are commonly described as "whipped," or even more explicitly as "pussy whipped," meaning dominated by a woman.

When I have shared with audiences just that much of Nietzsche's understanding of heterosexual love, inevitably there are men present who cannot contain their delight that this esteemed philosopher has articulated their own perspective about love—male domination and female subordination, sometimes going beyond just big grins and blurting out "Right on!" or "Yeah!" Their male bonding with Nietzsche is dampened only slightly when I remind them that he is not offering a personal opinion about love, but rather is describing his culture's perspective on love.

Nietzsche's description of love aptly conveys the understanding of heterosexuality that generally prevails in militaristic cultures. Man the warrior and controller of resources dominates, and woman as mother and nurturer serves the man and his children. She is supposed to have a faith in this patriarchal figure that, like all faith, surpasses understanding. Consequently, she may stay with him even though he is emotionally or physically cruel to her. This pattern is by no means limited to Western cultures. Here is a brief glimpse into a wedding ceremony and reception presided over by Anjem Choudry, a Muslim imam who is an Al Qaeda supporter. According to Choudry, "In the West they want to say equality between men and women. . . . However, [in Islam] it is different, as surely [Allah] has given man authority over the woman . . . because he provides food, clothing, and shelter."[53] Later, Imam Choudary recites this prayer for the newly married couple (only one of whom, the groom, is present, given that the wedding reception is men only): "Allah please bless him with pious children that will continue the jihad to liberate our land. Dear Allah, please support all the mujahedeen wherever they are, in Iraq, in Chechnya, in Palestine, in Kashmir, in Fallujah, in Darfur."[54]

When I show that video clip during public lectures, the faces of those men who had previously bonded with Nietzsche over what they had thought was his personal preference for male-dominant/female-subordinate heterosexuality begin to show signs of confusion—a state that often can precipitate a philosophical breakthrough. Men who feel supported by Nietzsche in their preference for male dominance are not so comfortable about sharing that same preference with Al Qaeda.

Maybe it is reasonable to expect that, as a man, Nietzsche would have a positive view of the male-dominant model of love he has described. But it turns out Nietzsche was not writing to bond with other males. He was not giving a personal opinion; rather, he was describing his culture as a philosopher. Even more important, his take on the male dominant/female subordinate model of love turns out not to be positive at all, which becomes clear when he takes a rather sudden turn: this pattern of male domination and female subordination, Nietzsche says, leads inevitably to "antagonism" in heterosexual relationships.[55] That should not be surprising, given his earlier analogy to the relationship between masters and slaves.

All too often the antagonism that is intrinsic to this model of love goes beyond quarrels, and even becomes violent, as happened in the case of Sergeants Erin Edwards and William Edwards. Such cases help us see the bigger picture: the gendered domination-submission model of heterosexual love has its roots in the faith in masculine force and the presumption of adversariality that I earlier described as lying at the heart of cultural militarism.

Which raises the question: what does murder have to do with love? That question could only be meaningfully asked in a society where cultural militarism is such a powerful force, specifically with regard to heterosexual eroticism. For a man to kill a woman is surely the ultimate example of domination over her, with rape being a close second. Both those acts of domination occur routinely in militaristic societies, and often the perpetrator even asserts that his crime was caused by his love for the victim.

Consider a famous example: as O.J. Simpson was riding around Los Angeles in a white Ford Bronco with a gun in his lap, shortly before his arrest for the murder of his ex-wife, his friend and attorney Robert Kardashian read a statement O.J. had written on live television. It began as follows:

To Whom It May Concern:

> First, everyone understand. I have nothing to do with Nicole's murder. I loved her; always have and always will. If we had a problem, it's because I loved her so much.[56]

Hearing those words erased any doubt I may have had that Simpson had killed his ex-wife. Like most people who have studied men's violence toward women, I had already come to realize that the expression of sentiments like that are extremely common among men who have killed women they think they loved. Every day in the United States there are, on average, three men who kill women because they love them.[57] Sure, you can say that their love is not "real." That is surely the case. How could purported love that drives a man to kill his beloved be actual love? But that raises a larger question: When a militaristic society culturally programs into its members an ideal of love that calls for male domination and female subordination, which is inherently prone to antagonism, can that be real love?

At the very least, surely we can say this: the heterosexual antagonism described by Nietzsche weakens heterosexual love. That insight gets hidden among people living in militaristic cultures, where it is common to hear comments like "Fighting is an important part of love." I've even heard people say that the intensity of a couple's fighting is an indicator of how much they love each other!

But surely no one would claim that the ideal relationship is one fraught with bitterness and conflict. To the extent a relationship becomes characterized by antagonism, it is weakened and, indeed, it is moving toward the opposite of love.

So here is the picture now before us: the more a relationship conforms to the culturally programmed model of male-dominant/female-subordinate love that is typical of war-reliant societies, the more likely it is to be antagonistic—meaning fraught with tension, anxiety, instability, acrimony, and conflict, which weaken the bonds of love. Militaristic societies may typically be heterosexist, in the sense of maintaining an ideology that says heterosexual relationships offer the only opportunity for love that is morally right, but the specific model of heterosexual love they espouse is intrinsically weak and even tragic.

The heterosexualism we have is tragic not just for particular couples, but for all of us, because it lays the foundation for the strands of misogyny that run throughout our culture, including sexual harassment, sexual discrimination, sexual assault, and heterosexual homicide. And, given the current emphasis on economic factors, we should note that the annual financial cost of those strands of misogyny has got to be staggering.

And finally, let me note just one more thing: I said that the story of the two army sergeants was emblematic of changes that have been taking place in our highly gendered world. That is so in one more respect. After killing his wife, Sergeant William Edwards turned the gun on himself. It seems to have become increasingly common for men to kill themselves after killing the women they "love." This is one of a host of examples we could give that help us appreciate Beauvoir's insight that what she calls the "masculine code" is "a source of torment for both sexes." But notice that we could aptly paraphrase Beauvoir thus: the *heterosexual* code is a source of torment for both sexes.

A bleak picture, for sure, the verisimilitude of which is all too sadly confirmed by rising divorce rates and widespread domestic violence—including heterosexual homicide. If we pay attention, it is also confirmed in our everyday lives.

2

LET'S MAKE A DEAL

THE HETEROSEXUAL ECONOMY FALLS OFF A CLIFF

> I'll cook your dinner if you wash my car
> May as well keep going, hell we made it this far
> We'll both play our parts in this disaster
> I'll be the bitch and you'll be the bastard
> —Pistol Annies, "Unhappily Married"

Popular culture, from Lifetime TV to gangsta rap and heavy metal, sends us the message that heterosexual love is inherently antagonistic, and even fraught with the danger of both emotional and physical violence. The accuracy of the picture provided by popular culture is confirmed by the wealth of statistics on domestic violence, sexual assault, sexual harassment, and heterosexual homicide.[1]

Heterosexual antagonism is not hard to understand when one pays attention to how war-reliant societies tend to culturally program men and women into rigidly differentiated, even opposite, roles. The antagonism is greatly exacerbated by a further element: a notion of heterosexual love, inculcated in both sexes, that calls for men to be dominant and women to be subordinate. As a consequence, men who seem less dominant because they are emotionally responsive to female partners are disparaged by being called whipped and women who resist subordination are disparaged by being called bitches.

The antagonism that is integral to this kind of heterosexual love is further exacerbated by another factor, for which the hip-hop star Nelly offers a helpful metaphor. In his infamous "Tip Drill" video (2003), Nelly swipes his credit card between a female dancer's buttocks, as if she were a credit card terminal.[2] Nelly was unwittingly highlighting yet another factor that contributes to antagonism in the kind of heterosexual love that is common in war-reliant societies, namely, transactionality.

There are several closely interrelated elements in the cultural programming of this model of love that lead inexorably to that transactionality.

1. Love is defined as being between two persons of different sexes.
2. There are two and only two sexes.
3. Every person is unambiguously a member of one of those sexes.
4. The two sexes are so extremely different from each other that each person in a love relationship is deemed to be with someone of "the opposite sex."
5. There is a culturally assumed complementarity of these opposite sexes such that each person in a relationship is dependent upon the other.
6. Yet the persons in a relationship are not equal: the man is dominant over the woman.
7. Their oppositeness and interdependence are reinforced by making the two gender roles exclusivistic, with penalties for anyone who treads on the opposite sex's turf.

Those elements, especially the last four, are facilitated by two clusters of qualities, each of which lays out expectations that are supposed to be specific to one of the two sexes: manliness for men, womanliness for women—or masculinity and femininity, respectively.

Manliness in this cultural arrangement is largely defined by three factors. First, as protector, a man is supposed to be a potential warrior, so he has to manifest the most crucial quality of a warrior: he must be able to manage the capacity to care about the suffering of others, as well as his own suffering. Second, as a provider, a man is supposed to be a controller of resources that can be used by his female partners and their offspring. Third, a man is supposed to be a procreator, so he is expected to pursue sexual access to as many women as possible and as often as possible.

Womanliness in this model of love is defined more by a woman's role in procreation than anything else, not least because war-reliant societies are more likely than peaceful societies to experience large numbers of deaths and hence to feel a need for maximized procreation. But womanliness is further, and importantly, defined by dependence, which reinforces women's subordination to any man with whom they are in a relationship. This dependence has at least three specific elements. First, a woman is supposed to be dependent on a warrior-man for protection of herself, her children, and the larger society of which she is a part. Second, she is supposed to be dependent on the largesse of a male controller of resources. Third, she is supposed to be dependent on a man for sperm that will allow her to fulfill her culturally instilled primary mission as a breeder. In addition to those dependencies, she is supposed to be maternalistic, to emotionally nurture not just her children but also her male partner.

Regarding the seventh element in the list I have provided, gender exclusivism, women are not supposed to tread on men's turf of being the strong protector, so they are culturally defined as physically weaker, regardless of any particular woman's actual physical strength relative to men. Women are also expected to eschew the manly role of provider, so they get culturally defined as lacking competence or intelligence. While women in many cases produce more resources than men, the men take control of those resources, thereby maintaining the manly role of provider. In the other direction, gender exclusivism calls for men not to lower themselves to women's domains, such as child care, cooking, and cleaning, as participation in any of those activities is deemed to diminish their manliness.

Obviously the rigidity of those traditional roles is crumbling in today's world, but there are continuing efforts by social, political, and religious conservatives to maintain traditional ideas about gender, using both legislation and persuasion. In some cases, conservatives have even tried to dial back feminist progress, as Susan Faludi documented in her 1991 book, *Backlash: The Undeclared War Against American Women.*[3] That effort has continued unabated since Faludi's book was published. For example, consider the recent book from Suzanne Venker and her antifeminist aunt who famously took credit for the defeat of the Equal Rights Amendment, Phyllis Schlafly. Their book, *The Flipside of Feminism: What Conservative Women Know and Men Can't Say,* has been described by another famous antifeminist, Ann Coulter, as "profound" and a "must-read." Venker shared the heart of the book's message in an interview, saying, "As women have gained more freedom, more education, and more power, they have become less happy."[4] By implicitly favoring less freedom, less education, and less power for women, Venker and Schlafly are effectively proponents of the male dominant/ female subordinate model of love we have been considering. Presumably less freedom, less education, and less power contribute to greater happiness for women because those diminutions of power and stature leave more room for a real man to be in charge of a woman's life.

Sometimes conservatives get quite explicit about their preference for the kind of heterosexuality in which women are expected to be subservient to men. The conservative credentials of former Minnesota State Representative Allen Quist include serving as political mentor to Representative Michelle Bachmann, endorsement as a congressional candidate by the Gun Owners of America, espousal of the thesis that "humans and dinosaurs may have coexisted in Southeast Asia as late as the 11th century," and finally, his volunteer work going "undercover at an adult bookstore and a gay bathhouse in an effort to prove to a local newspaper reporter that they had become a 'haven for anal intercourse.'" In a newspaper interview, soybean farmer Quist cited wild animal behavior in support of his assertion that women are "genetically disposed" to be subservient to men.[5]

Similarly, Fox News contributor Erick Erickson expressed alarm about a Pew Research Center study that found mothers to be the primary source of income in 40 percent of American households: "When you look at biology, when you look at the natural world, the roles of a male and a female in society and in other animals, the male typically is the dominant role."[6] Erickson was part of an all-male panel to discuss the Pew study; all present agreed to panic about various catastrophic implications for children and society.

Like Venker, Schlafly, and Erickson, the politically powerful fundamentalist group Focus on the Family is also dedicated to conserving the traditional heterosexist ideology that prevails in so many militaristic cultures. Toward that end, they have published numerous guides for couples. Lest there be any doubt about Focus on the Family's alignment with cultural militarism, according to the section of their website devoted to marriage the whole point of heterosexual love is to fight evil: "It is a real war on a real battlefield, a real trial in a real courtroom. It's also a clan struggle, a family united against forces that are determined to deface and destroy all that is good and pure and holy."[7] Integral to that war, of course, is the "defense of traditional marriage," in other words, the kind of heterosexuality we have been describing.

Let's take a closer look at this traditional, heterosexual marriage that is so closely associated with militarism. Specifically, let's consider the transactionality that I have described as consequent to the rigidly defined gender roles required by this heterosexist ideology. Within this framework, erotic or romantic love constitutes an exchange-based economy, with men getting some things from women in exchange for some things women get from men. Here is how heterosexual marriage is supposed to work, according to conservative minister Bryan Fischer on his American Family Radio show, May 29, 2013:

From a biblical standpoint, it's very clear that men are designed to be the breadwinners for their families. That's the way God set it up. That's the way he designed it. Husbands are to use their stamina and their strength and their brain power. . . . God has given them a brain, and the purpose for using their mental ability is to provide for their families, to use their physical strength, to work hard, to work long hours, to use their physical strength to protect their wives and protect their children, and be providers for them. That is the biblical pattern. And the biblical pattern is for a wife and a mother to focus her energies, devote her energies, on making a home for her children and her husband.[8]

In short, the husband is supposed to be the provider and protector, using his brawn and the brain given to him by God (his wife seems not to have gotten one), and the wife is supposed to be a homemaker. This arrangement assures the man's dominance, because he is in charge of food, clothing, shelter, protection, and, of course, sperm. The wife serves the husband, not only through housework but also as breeder of his children and the emotional nurturer of both the children and the man himself. As a consequence of their distinct roles, each needs the other. Each has a clearly delineated role and each loses gender status by stepping outside that role or failing at it. The gender status that can be lost by men is what we call masculinity and the gender status that can be lost by women is what we call femininity.

With a nod to the reality that in most heterosexually led families today the wife is a wage earner, and so she is playing the traditional male role of provider, Bryan Fischer asserts that even if a husband just "has a wife that out-earns him, I think that's going to put some stress on his psyche." That "stress on his psyche" consists of diminished masculinity. If a wife earns more than her husband, he seems less masculine, and she seems less feminine. More broadly, if a man seems in any way like a woman, his masculinity diminishes, and if a woman seems in any way like a man, her femininity diminishes. Masculinity and femininity are ways of keeping people confined within their traditional, "biblical" gender roles, which ensure that men and women have complementary needs that can only get met transactionally. Therein lies a problem. Transactionality exacerbates the antagonism of heterosexual relationships, because it results in pressures on both "sides" in the relationship to strategize to get the most advantageous exchange, to get the best deal possible, even to the extent of exploiting the partner. In such societies, then, it is not uncommon for women to share tips with each other about getting their way with men and surviving male domination. Similarly, it is not uncommon for men to share tips with each other about getting their way with women, and in general, maintaining dominance and control. In many societies including the United States, there are magazines and websites that offer such tips, which are, effectively, about how best to exploit a partner in the context of a heterosexual relationship that is inherently transactional.

In many war-reliant societies the exploitation of women is facilitated for men by a legal system that takes transactionality to the extreme, expanding the heterosexual economy beyond individual relationships by treating women and girls literally as the property of men. In such societies, typically the woman's father owns her until he makes a deal with a prospective husband or the latter's family to exchange her for money, cattle, land, or anything else of value. So, until such a deal is made, the father and his sons make every effort to maintain her value, essential to which is her virginity and the public impression that it has not been "lost." At the slightest hint of public doubt about her virginity, or even potential public doubt about it, the pride of a father in the daughter he possesses can be so diminished—because her actual property value has been diminished— that he will kill her. Even a girl caught texting a boy can be killed—such "honor killings" have happened not just in "third world" countries (where killing a girl or woman is sometimes effectively legal) but even in the United States.[9] Even in war-reliant societies where women are no longer considered the legal property of men, there is a cultural residue reflected in the phenomenon of men killing women who have dared to leave them.

The woman as property idea was widely codified in laws in the United States until just a few decades ago. And there continue to be cultural vestiges of it in our notion of heterosexual love. When Britney Spears sings "I'm a Slave 4 U," her words and sentiments fit right into the traditional notion of heterosexuality that Nietzsche described in the following quote cited in the previous chapter: "A man who loves like a woman becomes a slave, but a woman who loves like a woman becomes a more perfect woman."[10] The implied conclusion, as we noted before, is that the most perfect woman is a slave. That metaphor is being kept alive not just by Britney Spears and her fans. A guy who appears to be responsive to, or considerate of, a girlfriend, is often called *whipped*, or even *pussy whipped*—a pejorative that works because it connotes enslavement, specifically to a woman. That lowered status is understood to be inconsistent with manliness. A girl who is similarly responsive or considerate of a boyfriend is considered to be just a good girlfriend. That is why the expression *penis whipped* has never found a foothold in the lexicon of heterosexuality.[11]

Further, even today most wedding ceremonies still commence with the traditional "giving away of the bride," in which the officiator asks, "Who gives this woman to be married to this man?" and the father says, "I do." And the overwhelming majority of women who get married maintain the tradition of wedding as property transfer by changing their last names from their father's surname to their new husband's surname, or from their previous husband's surname to their new husband's surname. Just how deeply this idea about heterosexual marriage is embedded in our culture, that a wife is the property of her husband, can be seen in a possible reversal of it: What if a husband wants to show he is property that has been given to his bride, by taking her surname (i.e., her father's surname)? Well, that goes so much against the traditional idea of only wives—and not husbands—as property that in Florida it is necessary to seek and obtain a judicial order to accomplish it.[12]

Beyond the wedding veil and Britney Spears, however, the reality is that the heterosexual notion of a wife as property is becoming increasingly quaint and even absurd. As women gradually move toward greater economic power, they are far less likely to be dependent on men. Indeed, there is now a clear trend of men becoming more economically dependent on women than they were in the past. According to the authors of a recent Pew Research Center report titled "New Economics of Marriage: The Rise of Wives": "From an economic perspective, these trends have contributed to a gender role reversal in the gains from marriage. In the past, when relatively few wives worked, marriage enhanced the economic status of women more than that of men. In recent decades, however, the economic gains associated with marriage have been greater for men than for women."[13] That is partly because more women than men are graduating from college, as well as getting graduate and professional degrees.[14] Slowly the tables are turning, with growing numbers of men now experiencing the economic interest, and even necessity, that had driven women into marriage for centuries.

It's probably unlikely that there will be a cultural shift toward viewing husbands as property of their wives, or toward a notion of heterosexual love in which the most perfect man is a slave to a woman. Nonetheless, there are widespread patterns of gradual decline for the bargaining power of men within the transactional heterosexuality that is typical of war-reliant societies.

In traditional transactional heterosexuality, women at least have had something to offer in exchange for a man's economic support: breeding and emotional nurturing. Men have been at something of a disadvantage as reciprocators in those areas. They certainly can't play the female role in breeding—except in the case of female-to-male transsexuals. As for emotional nurturing, there will be more to say about that later on, but, for now, let's just take note of an unsurprising study showing that young women struggling with depression are better off seeking support from girlfriends than from boyfriends. In an interview the study's author, Elizabeth Daley, said, "The more depressed a girl becomes, the less supportive her boyfriend is and the more supportive her girlfriend is." Commenting on the study, psychologist Nadine Kaslow explains further: "Many girls like being caretakers and caregivers. With boys, when a friend of theirs is down, they may retreat more from the relationship."[15] It should be noted that researchers sometimes essentialize their results, failing to take into account that there are some males who are, in fact, emotionally supportive of their girlfriends, and there are some females who are not supportive of female friends. Nonetheless, the research does help us see patterns (not generalizations) in the behavior of boys and girls, and men and women.

The larger pattern would seem to be this: Because of men's culturally programmed disabilities as emotional supporters, along with their diminishing ability—and women's growing ability—to contribute resources to support a relationship, men's bargaining position in contemporary transactional heterosexuality is weakening. In a growing number of cases, men are stepping outside the bounds of that traditional heterosexuality, including becoming stay-at-home dads and househusbands.

But many men are following more gender-conservative paths, looking for advantage within transactional, male-dominant heterosexuality in the form of alternatives to an ongoing relationship. One alternative where men can maintain such an advantage would be prostitutes, who generally have a weaker bargaining position than the other women in men's lives: "Prostitutes [often] join the sex industry not just for money, but to escape homelessness. Studies show that 75% of prostitutes report homelessness at some point, and as many as 95% say they want to stop selling sex, and prostitutes are eighteen times more likely to be murdered on the job."[16] While it is hard to get reliable data on just how many men exploit that vulnerability of prostitutes, a recent survey showed that 20 percent of American men had paid money for sex, and over a third of single men over thirty had paid for sex.[17]

Some of those men are contributing to the explosive growth of erotic massage parlors. The *Los Angeles Times* recently reported that there are fifteen such operations in a two mile stretch of Eagle Rock Boulevard, near Los Angeles, including an operation called Surprise Massage, which advertises "Fairytale Oriental Massage" done by "Sexy Pretty Asian Girls." Rudy Martinez, owner of a nearby sushi restaurant, says, "If you sit on our patio, you can see about 30 to 40 men coming in and out of there. They stay for 15 to 20 minutes. I've never seen one woman walk in." As with other forms of sex work, the women involved are economically disadvantaged relative to their male customers. For example, police raids have revealed undocumented immigrants working off debts at some of the parlors.[18]

In the context of transactional heterosexuality, in pursuit of an even better "bargain," many men turn to pornography. Porn images are less expensive than actual women, plus they have an added advantage: Men have no fear of being laughed at by the women in porn and, more broadly, the risk of performance anxiety is nil or at least minimal. Indeed, some kinds of porn can give men the opportunity to turn the tables, by laughing at women. In particular, the genre called *gonzo* porn by sociologist Gail Dines gives men the opportunity to gather in groups to laugh at the women in the porn and at what is done to them.[19] Gonzo porn is an extreme genre: it gives men the opportunity to see women subjected to severe degradation, often using brutality and humiliation to reinforce the subordinate status of women (examples of gonzo porn will be given in chapter 3).[20]

Like entertainment generally, gonzo porn functions as cultural programming. Dines reports that many college men she has interviewed insist that women really want to be humiliated and brutalized. She also reports that many college women report being asked by men they are with to engage in the same behavior the men have seen in gonzo porn videos—those men want more than just the fantasy of humiliating women, they want the real thing. Thus gonzo porn has become part of the cultural programming of heterosexual masculinity. And the fact that many men are enjoying gonzo porn confirms that the inherently antagonistic, male-dominant/female-subordinate model of heterosexuality described by Nietzsche over a hundred years ago is still very much alive (as we have already seen in the previous chapter).

There are many other behavioral indicators of the diminished bargaining power of men within transactional heterosexuality, which is nonetheless accompanied by an incredible sense of entitlement. For example, some men turn to predatory activity on the Internet where they think they can trade a six-pack of beer and a package of condoms for sex with a thirteen-year-old girl—a phenomenon made famous by the popular *To Catch a Predator* series on MSNBC. Men who can spend a bit more than that can buy or rent trafficked girls and women—a problem that has exploded in recent years. According to the FBI, sex trafficking has become "the third-largest criminal enterprise in the world."[21]

Another cultural development that reflects men's weakened bargaining power in transactional heterosexuality is the growing market for the RealDoll. The RealDoll, and the discourse around it, are particularly and poignantly revealing of contemporary heterosexual masculinity. Here is the opening greeting on the company's website:

> Welcome to the exciting world of RealDoll!
>
> Since 1996, we have been using Hollywood special effects technology to produce the most realistic love doll in the world. Our dolls feature completely articulated skeletons which allow for anatomically correct positioning, an exclusive blend of the best silicone rubbers for an ultra flesh-like feel, and each doll is custom made to your specifications.
>
> We offer an extensive list of options, including 10 female body types and 16 interchangable (sic) female faces. RealDolls are completely customizable, all the way down to the make up and fingernail colors. If you've ever dreamed of creating your ideal partner, then you have come to the right place.[22]

At a starting price of $5,999, the RealDoll is not quite the bargain available to men who pursue cheaper paths through the heterosexual economy, but those approaches don't offer as many optional extras, like Elf Ears, Expression Faces, and Tan Lines; even for the basic model a man gets a choice of nine faces, eleven eye colors, seventeen hair styles, and either permanent or removable vaginas.

The market demographic for such dolls brings the transactional dimension of heterosexuality in militaristic cultures into full focus. Here is what Rudy, a sales representative at the Adult Entertainment Expo in Las Vegas, has to say about that: "We do, uh, real dolls. And we're the creators and designers of that technology right there. A lot of men don't want to deal with women. That's just a lot of overhead. Here, you pay once and she never asks you for food. She doesn't want anything; she doesn't take half and when you're done with her, you put her away. Think about that. What a wonderful world."[23] Rudy is clearly in tune with the specific elements of the transactionality that define the heterosexual economy. While six thousand dollars is a substantial amount of money, the demand it places on a man to be a controller of resources and a provider of food, clothing, and shelter is a lot less than the demand he would experience in the case of an actual woman playing the subordinate role that is traditional within contemporary militaristic cultures.

Rudy's pitch for his synthetic women also takes note of two other elements in the male dominant-female subordinate heterosexual economy. The first is a matter of availability. "When you're done with her, you put her away," Rudy says. Which also means, of course, that whenever you want "her" services, you just retrieve her from wherever you had put her away. And, Rudy should have added, "she" will never ask to be taken out of the closet or box where she is stashed. Thus, there is an access differential: the doll's owner can gain access to her whenever he wants, but she cannot demand access to him at all.

From the perspective of Rudy and his customers for RealDolls, the "ideal partner" can be kept in storage until you need it, can be used whenever you desire without any reciprocity or empathy, and cannot make demands or express desires. From this perspective the "ideal partner" is totally accessible, but not alive.

Alas, those advantages men see in dolls reflect a larger pattern of gendered accessibility in the heterosexual economy. I first became aware of how this works when a chance meeting on a plane in the 1990s led to a relationship that lasted for over a year. We had been assigned adjacent seats, and when it turned out that we had both requested vegetarian meals, a conversation developed that revealed enough other commonalities that we decided to exchange contact information. She lived in Chicago, and I lived in rural New Hampshire, so I don't think either of us really expected anything further. But a telephone conversation led to a visit, which led to an ongoing long-distance relationship. While I had been teaching and writing about gender theory for several years at that point, none of that theorizing had prepared me for what turned out to be a fascinating realization. My new friend was a corporate executive, with a hectic schedule managed by an assistant and lots of international traveling. I, on the other hand, was a professor at a small liberal arts college—hardworking, for sure, but with much more flexibility in my schedule. Her situation meant that any phone calls between us had to fit into her demanding schedule. Thus a pattern developed very quickly in which I rarely tried to call her because, when I did, I would almost always learn from her assistant that she was on another call, in a meeting, or off on a trip. Instead, she would call me whenever she could find time, and usually I would be available. The only reason this was not a problem for my masculine pride was that I had learned to think critically about gender, and particularly about signs of gendered power differentials, such as asymmetrical accessibility. However, if I had been a traditional man sensitive about his masculinity, and lacking such a theoretical framework, I know that it would have bothered me a lot.

As I reflected on that experience, I began to see a larger pattern in human affairs. Differential availability seems always to reflect differential power. The more any kind of relationship between two people is defined by domination and subordination, the more the dominant person has access to the subordinate person, and the less the subordinate person has access to the dominant person. Thus the CEO of a manufacturing company feels free to spontaneously pay a visit to the factory floor, and none of the workers can voice their objections, but a visit by one of those workers to the executive suite is by appointment only, and even getting an appointment may not be possible.

Analogously, in the traditional heterosexual economy the husband or boyfriend expects the availability of sexual and other services, and even better if "his" wife or girlfriend is familiar with the aforementioned genre of articles from *Cosmopolitan* and *Glamour* magazines, like "Men's Sexual Wish List," "3 Things All Guys Crave in Bed," and "100 Sex Tips from Guys—Including the Best Ice-Cube Trick We've Ever Heard." Of course, she should also be familiar with his food preferences and should be readily available to satisfy them. Thus, the entire time I was growing up in a family structured by this heterosexual economy, my mother served bread and potatoes with every dinner and was quite adamant that she had no choice in the matter, because otherwise my father would not eat the dinner.

So far, the RealDoll that can cook dinner is not on the market, but at least, as Rudy notes, "she never asks you for food." "She" will also not ask for conversation or for emotional support, which is another big marketing point that is reflected in Rudy's comment that "a lot of men don't want to deal with women." But that points to another service, in addition to food preparation, that the RealDoll is not equipped to provide, but that—like food preparation—is expected of women in the heterosexual economy: Men in war-reliant cultures may not want to deal with women, but they do want those women to deal with them.

As Nietzsche puts it, a man in a relationship with a woman expects her to have unconditional faith in him,[24] providing emotional affirmation and support as he faces life's challenges. But as the study of depressed girlfriends mentioned earlier suggests, that faith, affirmation, and support is not reciprocal. In the heterosexual economy that is typical in militaristic cultures, a woman is expected to shoulder an unequal emotional burden: she provides emotional nurturing and sustenance to the man, but as an exemplar of warrior masculinity he lacks the ability and perhaps the proclivity to provide such emotional nurturing and sustenance to her.

Supposedly the other side of the transaction here is that he will offer protection and provisions. So the deal is, as described by Sandra Bartky, "He shows his love for her by bringing home the bacon, she by securing for him a certain quality of nurturance and concern."[25]

Bartky describes this nurturance women are expected to provide to men as "the feeding of egos and the nursing of [emotional] wounds."[26] She explains how that is done:

> It is the particular quality of a caregiver's attention that can bolster the Other's confidence. This attention can take the form of speech, of praise . . . or it can manifest itself in the articulation of a variety of verbal signals (sometimes called "conversational cheerleading") that incite him to continue speaking, hence reassuring him of the importance of what he is saying. Or such attention can be expressed nonverbally, e.g., in the forward tilt of the caregiver's body, the maintaining of eye contact, the cocking of her head to the side, the fixing of a smile upon her face.
>
> Again, the work of emotional healing can be done verbally in a myriad of ways, from simple expressions of indignation at what the boss has said about him, to the construction of elaborate rationales that aim, by reconceptualizing them, to make his failures and disappointments less terrible; or nonverbally, in the compassionate squeezing of a hand or in a hug, in the sympathetic furrowing of a brow. . . . To enter feelingly and without condescension into another's distress . . . is to affirm that person's worth.[27]

Surely anyone reading Bartky's description of emotional caregiving will appreciate its profound value for any person who is its recipient. I myself cannot read that passage without thinking I'd like to live in a world where everyone, including myself, is a proficient emotional caregiver. In my own case, there has been a gradual amelioration of those shortcomings in the years since I began studying the work of Bartky and other feminist philosophers, but I have not lost my familiarity with the society described by Bartky in this sentence: "In our society, women in most social locations stand under an imperative to provide emotional service to men, and many chafe at the failure of men to provide such service in return."[28]

Why is it that men in war-reliant societies tend not to be able to provide such emotional service to women? Further, what is it about men's lives in those societies that explains why they have a particular need for emotional nurturing, and why they seek it out primarily from women?

Consider what I described earlier as the most crucial quality for a warrior: For a man to be an effective warrior, and for a man to be continually ready as a potential warrior, what is absolutely required is this: he must be able to manage the capacity to care about suffering: He must be able to focus selectively, and sometimes suspend altogether, the capacity to care about the suffering of others, as well as his own suffering.

That fundamental requirement for the warrior will be discussed at greater length in chapter 3; for our present purposes I just need to borrow one quote from that chapter: "Just as physical fitness for battle cannot simply be turned on or off at a moment's notice, neither can emotional fitness for battle be simply turned on or off like a light switch. Neither is obtainable at a moment's notice, but rather both require training that starts in childhood. You can't just tell boys they should act like men if they happen to be in combat. Rather, in societies that are reliant on war to achieve group objectives, physical and emotional preparedness for conflict is a defining element of manhood." Alas, however, such emotional toughening up is not at all good preparation to become a lover or life partner. And it exacerbates the transactionality in heterosexual relationships by creating asymmetrical emotional abilities and needs.

So long as we continue to culturally program boys and men to have the qualities of a warrior, including emotional toughness, boys and men will at best have to struggle to become good lovers and partners. To the extent that we train boys and men to suppress the capacity to care about the suffering of others, as well as themselves, we can expect them to strive, unsuccessfully, to "tough out" their own emotional suffering and to be inept at providing emotional sustenance to others. And when they can't "tough it out" any longer, we can expect them to seek solace from the persons we culturally program to have an amplified capacity to care about the suffering of others, namely women.

As for the "bringing home the bacon" side of heterosexual transactionality, economic conditions in much of the world have changed, and the number of women who are dependent upon men to bring home bacon (or tofu) is shrinking rapidly. In countries like the United States the declining ratio of men to women attending and completing college points to a further weakening in the bargaining positions of men as a group.[29] As I have said, many men are resorting to alternatives to actual love relationships, such as prostitutes, and alternatives to actual women, including pornography and the RealDoll. It must be noted, however, that the "Conversational Cheerleader" option is not yet available for the RealDoll. So the number of men who are frustrated in their desire for the emotional sustenance of women is growing, and that can only further fuel the misogynistic resentment and rage that is manifested in the gonzo porn phenomenon.

When we add into the picture the loss of entitlement for men who are unable to play the male-dominant role in a relationship, as well as the antagonism that has always been an integral part of male-dominant/female-subordinate "love" (see chapter 1, "Battle of the Sexes"), the tragic nature of heterosexuality in war-reliant cultures comes into fuller focus. Most of those cultures have valorized heterosexuality, but for all of them there is cultural programming that systematically divides men and women, resulting in a heterosexual economy that, paradoxically, weakens heterosexual love by imbuing it with antagonism that is exacerbated by transactionality.

A way to avoid that structurally weakened heterosexual love might be to escape the heterosexual economy altogether. After all, the heterosexual economy that has prevailed for so long is the product of cultural programming, and therefore is contingent, for both individuals and societies.

The fact is, heterosexual relationships that are strong are possible outside the heterosexual economy that I have described, which weakens relationships with its cultural programming about gender and love. Heterosexual love is strengthened when it is both egalitarian and free of the gender programming that divides women and men. In this kind of heterosexuality men and women don't just want each other, they genuinely respect each other, and actually like each other, and men, rather than insisting on control of women, support them in their independent ventures. In a video clip that I use for public lectures, Coach Mike Holmgren of the Seattle Seahawks is interviewed about the fact that his wife Kathy would not be watching his team play in the 2006 Super Bowl. The reason was not because she didn't support him and his team, but rather because his birthday present to her had been an airline ticket to the Congo, where he knew she wanted to do volunteer work, in a remote village, as a nurse (she had worked there many years earlier, before they met). A quip by Coach Holmgren at a press conference may offer a peek at a broader pattern of freedom from traditional gender roles in their relationship: "I one time got her a riding mower as a birthday present, so this is a lot better, I did good on this one." After the Seahawks had won a berth in the Super Bowl, Holmgren still insisted that Kathy go on the Congo trip, saying, "This is who she is. While at times she is Mike Holmgren's wife, she's very much her own woman, and I've always loved that about her."[30] In a separate phone interview, Kathy Holmgren said, "This is Mike's wish and dream for me." According to the reporter, "He knew how much his wife still loved the people of Congo and the prospect of helping them—how much she wants to rouse a deaf world to their suffering."[31]

By contributing to the diminution of antagonism, egalitarian heterosexuality elevates the potential for stronger relationships.[32] But, as we can see in the case of the Holmgrens, egalitarianism also offers the potential for each person individually to grow stronger because of the relationship. As Shulamith Firestone says, "Love between two equals would be an enrichment [of each other]."[33]

Egalitarian heterosexuality offers a sense of connectedness that is premised not merely on desire and passion but also on the mutual respect of equals, as well as the unique joy of companionship that is defined by sharing in the fullest possible sense, uncorrupted by gendered power differentials: sharing both joint and individual aspirations and projects and, perhaps most important, sharing each other's pleasure (including sexual pleasure), happiness, and, yes, sorrow.

There's an example of such a relationship in another video clip I use for public lectures; it features two cops in San Francisco named Irene and Brian. They have been partners on the beat for twelve years in one of the city's toughest neighborhoods, the Tenderloin. When they clock out each day at 4 PM, they go together to pick up their three children from school. Brian says, "We're there for each other the whole time. I'll do the kids' showers and she'll cook, or I'll cook and she'll do the showers." And Irene says, "We communicate real good with each other, and we understand each other. We know we're not perfect—he knows my flaws, and I know his flaws, and we make it work!" Sitting next to each other on the couch, Irene says, "It doesn't seem like too much together time at all, not to me." Brian agrees, saying, "Not at all, I don't want to be anywhere else."[34]

It is important to note that what I have called weak heterosexual love is premised not only on cultural militarism but, in today's world, also on homophobia, while what we could call strong heterosexual love is utterly incompatible with homophobia, that is, with heterosexism. The reason is that strong heterosexual love is not premised on rigid roles differentially assigned to men and women, and there is no culturally programmed expectation of two people coming together in a relationship because of their culturally assigned gender differences. Hence, this strong heterosexual love draws its strength precisely from the fact that its hetero-ness is incidental. To borrow Richard Wasserstrom's famous analogy about race,[35] heterosexuality or homosexuality would matter no more than eye color if this strong heterosexual love were the prevalent kind of heterosexual love in a given society.

But of course it is not prevalent today. Instead, what is prevalent is the transactional, antagonistic heterosexual economy found in war-reliant cultures. And the ramifications of that heterosexual antagonism extend well beyond love and sex – to work, religion, parenting, politics, and every other aspect of life. In all these areas the kind of heterosexuality that is associated with cultural militarism can be seen obstructing our path to relationships of men and women that are characterized by mutuality and equality, partnership and collaboration, with each nurturing the flourishing of the other. Opening up that path would require that we liberate ourselves from the heterosexual economy and its cultural programming about love, sex, and gender so that human relationality would no longer be premised on norms of gender asymmetry, gendered transactionality, cross-gender strategizing, and exploitation of gender-specific weaknesses.

What I am proposing in this chapter is that the pattern found in most war-reliant societies of cultural militarism, sexism, homophobia, and antagonistic heterosexuality are all part of a package deal. So we need to ask ourselves: is this package a good deal? And for anyone who says it is, there is a second question: for whom is it a good deal?

3

HOW TO MAKE A WARRIOR

MISOGYNY AND EMOTIONAL TOUGHNESS IN THE CONSTRUCTION OF MASCULINITY

> In this society, if a man is called a woman, that's the biggest insult
> he could get. Is that because women are considered something less?
> —Andrej Pejić, supermodel

When people are divided into two genders, with members of each gender culturally programmed to display attitudes, dispositions, and behavior altogether different from—and generally opposite to—the other gender, it is probably inevitable that there are going to be advantages and disadvantages specific to each gender. If cultural expectations call for one of those genders to be dominant over the other, presumably the advantages for that gender outweigh the disadvantages, but that does not mean that the disadvantages are not substantial. In this chapter I want to focus on what I consider, after more than a quarter century of reflection on the subject, to be the greatest disadvantage men suffer as a gender: the cultural ideal of "man the warrior" to which almost all men in war-reliant societies are subjected, regardless of whether they function as actual warriors. As we shall see, it turns out that this cultural ideal of masculinity is also at the root of most gender-related disadvantaging of women. Thus a description of how warrior masculinity works in militaristic cultures may point to paths of escape from the zero-sum gender game that is typical in war-reliant cultures, in which there tends to be a widely accepted presumption that gains for women as a group imply losses for men as a group, and vice versa.

The expression *man the warrior* may seem anachronistic. In recent decades the expectation that men will actually become combatants in war has diminished enormously, in both Europe (since World War II) and the United States (since the Vietnam War). Today men are far more likely to engage in vicarious, rather than actual, combat—through video games and sports spectatorship. Rarely do men witness, never mind engage in, scenes like this one described by Homer in *The Iliad*:

> Idomeneus skewered Erymas straight through the mouth,
> the merciless brazen spearpoint raking through,
> up under the brain to split his glistening skull—
> teeth shattered out, both eyes brimmed to the lids
> with a gush of blood and both nostrils spurting,
> mouth gaping, blowing convulsive sprays of blood
> and death's dark clouds closed down around his corpse.[1]

Despite how few boys and men in the United States experience the gore and brutality of actual war, because of nonparticipation in the military and because of the military's shift toward the use of drones and other remote control weaponry, the sway that warrior masculinity has over the emotional lives of boys and men continues unabated, even among those who are not at all interested in becoming actual warriors and even among many who are utterly incapable of engaging in actual physical violence. This cultural inertia of the ideal of warrior masculinity is a source of great harm in the lives of both men and women.

✳ ✳ ✳

In most societies there are multiple cultural ideals of manhood. In addition to the warrior ideal, there may be ideals associated with provision of resources, procreation, self-reliance, public performance, and so on. Each of those ideals may be multidimensional, as well as interconnected with each other. In societies that have a long-standing tradition of engaging in war regularly, all the various dimensions of manliness tend to be deeply and pervasively informed by qualities associated with the role of warrior. For men who literally take on the warrior role, it means risking not only bodily injury or death, but also emotional disability, including illness caused by post-traumatic stress.[2] But beyond the ways in which actual combatants are disadvantaged, for all men there is a range of far less apparent disadvantages suffered as a consequence of gender expectations that are imbued with the qualities of a warrior.

For a man to be an effective warrior, and for a man to be continually ready as a potential warrior, what is most crucially required is this: he must be able to manage the capacity to care about suffering. That is, he must be able to focus selectively, and sometimes suspend altogether, the capacity to care about the suffering of others, but also his own suffering. In short, he must be emotionally tough.

The warrior must be able to kill another man without consideration of the suffering of the persons who loved and depended upon that man. In some cases he even has to do that as those loved ones watch. I recall reading a news account of a Marine who was engaged in door-to-door combat in Fallujah, Iraq. He confronted a man outside what appeared to be his home. The sounds of children crying and a woman screaming in fear were emanating from the house. The man was wearing loose-fitting clothes that made it impossible to see whether he was armed. The Marine shot and killed the man, unable to pause in the frenzy of battle to determine whether or not the clothes concealed a weapon, no doubt feeling that the risk of not shooting was that he himself might be killed. Similar scenarios in which people who may or may not be enemies are killed while family members watch have become increasingly common in modern warfare, most notably in Vietnam, Iraq, and Afghanistan.

That capacity to suspend caring about the suffering of one's victims plays a contributing role in military mistakes, including civilian casualties.

In such cases a diminished concern about the suffering of others can lead to a lack of the kind of caution that would be expected in noncombat situations. Adeptness at killing requires a suppression of empathy that can diminish the attentiveness required to ensure that only the intended "targets" are killed. In one such recent case, General David Petraeus, formerly commander of United States forces in Afghanistan, apologized for the killing of nine children by American soldiers in helicopters. The children had been gathering firewood in a poor rural area of Afghanistan. According to Hemad, eleven, who was the only survivor of the attack, the children were shot one after another, in repeated attacks. According to one of the villagers who found the boys the next day, "Some of the dead bodies were really badly chopped up by the rockets. "The head of a child was missing. Others were missing limbs. . . . We tried to find the body pieces and put them together."[3] The entire village was stricken with grief.

After reading the news account of the tragedy, I was compelled by the abstractness—to the point of coldness—of the ensuing formal apology by General Petraeus. It could not possibly have provided any solace to the families of the slain children. Of course, if Petraeus were to show any sign of genuine empathy with their grief—if, for example, he were to publicly shed tears over their loss or over the carnage caused by his soldiers—that behavior would be inconsistent with his warrior masculinity. Thus we can see how the warrior's capacity to suppress caring can lead not only to incautiousness in targeting people to kill, but a lack of deeply felt shame or remorse at having committed atrocities. That capacity to suppress caring is not the same in all warriors, of course, so in many cases where a warrior has committed an atrocity the feeling of horror at what he has done is so profound that it results in post-traumatic stress, sometimes so severe that he commits suicide. Within warrior cultures, though, such a case represents that individual's failure to live up to the dual, fundamental expectations of a warrior: he must be able to manage the capacity to care about the suffering of others he has harmed or killed, and he must be able to manage the capacity to care about his own suffering. In both cases, however, it is often possible for a warrior to be able to maintain only the appearance of such emotional toughness. Thus some suicides result from a man's unwillingness to seek help out of concern that being seen doing that would undermine his masculine image of toughness.

In addition to killing—whether deliberately or by mistake—the warrior must be able to maim and mutilate other men without concern for the pain and continuing disability those men will endure, and sometimes he is even expected to do those things quite deliberately to children and women.

The warrior must also be able to suppress caring about his own welfare, including fear or anxiety that he himself may be horribly and painfully injured or killed, and thereby leave behind his own loved ones to mourn. And he must suppress caring about the damage to his own psyche that may result from his actions and experiences in combat.

Even societies that are highly war-reliant need men to serve as actual warriors only from time to time, typically when a group feels threatened by another group, or when one group has something another group wants; in either case, one or both groups decide to fight it out. It's only in such specific circumstances that the men are needed to get fierce and brutal, suspending the capacity to care about the interests and suffering of the persons in the other group, as well as about their own potential suffering or death, so that they may triumph over the other group in the interests of their own.

For most militaristic societies, the circumstances calling for war arise sporadically, so men are not engaged in combat most of the time. Further, some men may be in a class that does not engage in actual combat at all, even though, as men, the qualities of warrior masculinity are instilled in them. Thus the lives of many men are devoted mostly or entirely to comparatively warm, cordial social interaction with family and friends, including other men with whom they engage in some mix of productive work and public life. During such times, the need to manage the capacity to care about suffering that is crucial in warfare is not needed and can even be dysfunctional.

It is also important to note that, even in warfare the capacity to care about particular others can actually be an important source of military strength, as is the case when powerful emotional bonds among men fighting a common enemy contribute to victory. Hence the need is not for men who are uncaring altogether, or for men who permanently suppress empathy. Rather, the need is for men who can manage the capacity to care about the suffering of others or themselves, suspending, focusing, or delimiting it when the need arises.

Even in conditions where men's fierceness is needed only occasionally, they must always be prepared for combat, and so most societies utilize various athletic activities, often specifically combat-themed, to keep men fit and ready for battle.[4] Requisite battle readiness includes not only physical fitness, but also emotional readiness. However, just as physical fitness for battle cannot simply be turned on or off at a moment's notice, neither can emotional fitness for battle be simply turned on or off like a light switch. Neither is obtainable at a moment's notice, but rather both require training that starts in childhood. You can't just tell boys they should act like men if they happen to be in combat. Rather, in societies that are reliant on war to achieve group objectives, physical and emotional preparedness for conflict is a defining element of manhood.

Therefore in militaristic societies the process of making a boy into a man requires making him physically combat-ready, but also emotionally combat-ready or, as we sometimes say, making him "tough." All war-reliant societies toughen boys up, which is a term for a kind of emotional conditioning that is absolutely essential for a potential warrior.

To get them emotionally combat-ready, boys who let their fear show, or who manifest feelings of concern for the suffering of others, are commonly admonished with imperatives like "Tough it up," "Boys don't cry," "Suck it up," "Play through the pain," "No pain, no gain," "C'mon, be a man," etc. These injunctions toward manliness direct boys not to show any fear, emotional vulnerability, or empathy for the suffering of others. The message to boys is that becoming a "real man," while dangerous to life and limb, is their ultimate goal in life.

Militaristic societies often use violence, in the form of hazing or rites of passage, to make boys into men. The sweeping pattern in militaristic societies that have rites of passage for boys (and most do) is for rites that test a boy's emotional toughness, in addition to requiring him to display physical prowess as a potential fighter.[5]

In Western societies boys are often emotionally toughened up in the context of sports. To illustrate this in public lectures, I show a short video clip from the documentary *Raising Cain*. The scene is a peewee football practice; all the boys, who appear to be about seven years old, are wearing football gear:

> INTERVIEWER (asking boy in football gear): What do you get from football that you don't get to do in normal life?
>
> BOY 1: You get to nail people (grins).
>
> INTERVIEWER: Yeah, and what's good about that?
>
> BOY 1: You get to hurt them.
>
> . . .
>
> COACH: Tad, Rockwell, you gotta start smashing people, OK? Otherwise, they're gonna smash you! OK?
>
> NARRATOR: Men often tell boys that anger is a manly emotion, but feelings of vulnerability and fear are not.
>
> . . .
>
> INTERVIEWER: What is it that makes a man a man?
>
> BOY 3: Not cryin' over nothin'.
>
> BOY 4: A man is somebody who is not a wuss, and doesn't cry all the time.
>
> BOY 1: Tough, never cry (pauses, before revising that)—doesn't cry a lot.[6]

Crying is natural, and caring about human suffering is natural, which is why boys have to be *taught* not to do it. The imperative that they not cry imposes an emotional sacrifice on boys and men, for it runs counter to primal human urges and needs. When folks claim that masculinity has its determinants in nature, I want to ask this question: if it were unnatural for boys and men to cry, then why would so much cultural capital be expended on getting them not to do it? An even more powerful response comes with another video I use in public lectures. It is a clip from an

NBC News report in which Richard Engel interviews Sergeant Louis Loftus, a young soldier fighting in Afghanistan. Engel asks him about a fellow soldier who had been killed the previous week. Loftus responds:

> Right now I'm kind of numb to it. Like, to be honest, I just don't really feel much. I pray for his family, I pray for his soul that he, you know—yeah. [Has begun crying, tears flowing down his cheeks, trying to choke off the sobs.] You see, I try not to think about it because when you think about it, then I get like this, and it's not—you're not—yeah. [Still struggling not to cry.] So, yeah, you know, everyone deals it their own way. I try to hide it, I try not to think about it because I got to stay 100 percent. You know, I got to—I got to keep a good example in front of the other soldiers. [Still sobbing.] I'm sorry.[7]

Throughout that last passage, Sergeant Loftus is struggling mightily, even heroically, not to cry, but he quite clearly just can't fight it off—it is utterly impossible for him not to cry. For anyone who would claim males are biologically determined to be emotionally tough, I would propose consideration of the following question: in that glimpse into the life of a young soldier, which part was determined by nature—the crying or the struggle not to cry?

Suppose someone says that, while emotional toughness may not itself be biologically determined for males, nonetheless toughening males up does respond to some biologically determined need that males have. As it turns out, Richard Engel did a second NBC News report on Sergeant Loftus several months later, after he had left the army and returned home. According to Engel, "An Army psychologist told Loftus he's too emotionally distraught to even be evaluated for post-traumatic stress disorder."[8] The broader pattern here is that we toughen up boys and send them off to war, and, despite all that emotional toughness that has been conditioned into them, about 40 percent come back with PTSD and other mental disorders, and in the last few years military suicide rates have been setting new records every year.[9]

Consider this: to love and be loved, to care for others and have them care for you could hardly be more crucial to human happiness and flourishing. So how have we managed to get so many persons to take on a role that, in its very essence, requires such impoverishment of their emotional lives, such detriment to their psychological health, so that, for example, later on as men they'll be twice as likely as women to commit suicide? Given that the warrior role requires a heavy emotional sacrifice, regardless of whether one actually engages in combat, how is it possible to get men not only to take it on, but to do it with the deep internalization and enthusiasm the warrior role also requires?[10] There is surely a clue in the fact that it is precisely men who are almost universally given this role. The belief is instilled in boys that if they don't take on the warrior role they simply cannot become real men, along with all the privilege and power that potentially accrue to that status.[11] And we hide from them all the disadvantages of becoming a real man.

What is the alternative to being a "real man"? The cultural presumption here is that gender is intrinsically binary. This is not a sexual, physiological binary that is ostensibly determined by different roles in reproduction. Rather, it is an unequivocally cultural binary that is fraught with peril—especially for boys and men, who daily confront the danger of being tossed over to the other side of the gender binary by being called girls, ladies, pussies, wimps, sissies, wusses, bitches, fags, queers, fruits, and so on, or by being directly accused of being gay. Clearly homophobia is a factor with some of these terms, but the cultural work being accomplished in such cases includes policing of the gender binary—if you are deemed gay, that means you are not masculine, and under the rules of the binary the only alternative is that you are feminine, in other words, that you are not a real man.

It is interesting to note recent research suggesting that as homophobia slowly declines among young men its power to alter the behavior of boys and men is diminishing.[12] In contrast, the power of misogyny to maintain the gender binary continues unabated. While part of the cultural work of misogyny is to confine girls and women within the limitations of femininity, it is also used to enforce the expectations of masculinity, and particularly those expectations that epitomize the ideal of warrior masculinity.

We saw some of that with the peewee football player who didn't want to be a wuss. Consider another example, the "Hurt Feelings Report" that was (unofficially) fabricated by one or more soldiers and then distributed around U.S. military bases at locations where the troops could go for help with PTSD:

Hurt Feelings Report

Date:_____
Time of hurtfulness: _____am / pm

A. Which ear were words of hurtfulness spoken into: Left or Right or Both
B. Is there permanent feeling damage Yes No
C. Did you need a tissue for the tears Yes No

Reasons for filing this report: Please circle Yes or No

1. I am thin skinned   Yes
2. I am a pussy   Yes
3. I have woman like hormones   Yes
4. I am a Queer   Yes
5. I am a little bitch   Yes
6. I am a cry baby   Yes
7. I want my mommy   Yes
8. All of the above   Yes (circle this one since all most likely apply)

Name of "Real man" who hurt your sensitive little feelings:_____

If you feel that you need someone to hug go home to mommy and let her hug you and change your diaper. If you feel as though need to speak to someone to soothe you please call this number: 1-800-CRY-BABY or 1-888-SIS-GIRL

Girly man who filed report:_____
Signature of girly man:_____

Real man (person who is being brought up on charges) :_____
Signature of Real man: _____

Superintendent's Signature: _____

Most of the power of the "Hurt Feelings Report" to control men's behavior, and specifically to constrain them within the boundaries of masculinity, derives from its exploitation of the misogyny that is intrinsic to the cultural ideal of warrior manliness. When I show this document to an audience, there are always young men who laugh. They impulsively join in with the cultural project of ridiculing any man who does not live up to the cultural ideal of warrior manliness. This is a useful indicator of the cultural breadth of the misogyny embedded in the ideal of warrior manhood, such that it is not located only within the military as an institution, but rather is in much broader cultural circulation, particularly in academic culture, business culture, and sports culture—including peewee football. Indeed, some high school football coaches have adapted the "Hurt Feelings Report" for use in the project of toughening up their players.[13]

The "Hurt Feelings Report" exemplifies this larger pattern in militaristic cultures: any tendency to show anxiety, emotional vulnerability, fear, or a need for help is taken not just as a sign of weakness or lack of bravery but also as a sign of not being a man at all, and the only alternative according to the culturally programmed gender binary is to be a woman. For a man to be perceived as womanly is the worst possible fate that could befall him—it is a kind of gender death, which is often perceived by men to be even worse than physical death.

Clearly the threat of being deemed a woman or girl is taken incredibly seriously by any boy or man who has been subjected to this militaristic cultural programming. To say that a man is womanly is not like mistaking his eye color. Rather, it is the most profound insult that can be hurled at men, precisely because they buy into the profound stigmatization of women that is inherent in misogyny. To be deemed a girl or woman is not only a sign of failure as a man, it is a sign of having fallen to a status that is implicitly understood to be profoundly inferior. To be female is to have a status that is deeply despised—and feared—by boys and men. That is why misogyny is such an effective means of culturally policing their lives. Misogyny is at the emotional core of the gender binary as it is experienced by boys and men in militaristic societies.

The intensity and range of misogyny in militaristic cultures can be illustrated by a wide array of available examples. For example, consider the Sambia bloodletting practices, which occur after the boys have been removed from their mothers and confined to an all-male group. The boys are flogged by the older men until blood runs down their backs. Sharp blades of grass are thrust up into their noses to cause copious nose bleeding. A third practice is no longer used: the forcing of a sharpened cane down the throat to cause bloody vomiting. These violent acts serve the purposes of initiation; they are part of a cluster of rituals that purport to make boys into men. The idea behind the bloodletting is partly to prepare boys for the bloody violence they will experience as warriors. But there is also another purpose: blood is symbolic of ongoing womanly—and therefore pernicious—influences coming from their mothers. Those influences are viewed as inhibiting masculinization. The bloodletting represents the purging of those womanly influences.[14] In societies that are reliant on war, any indication that a man is dependent upon any woman—upon any member of that inferior, stigmatized class—is inconsistent with warrior masculinity. Hence, in the "Hurt Feelings Report," the ridicule of "I want my mommy" is premised on misogyny every bit as much as "I am a little bitch" or "I have woman like hormones." Dependence on a woman, even on one's own mother, is almost as unmanly as being deemed a woman oneself.

Much of the misogynistic policing of masculinity takes place when men are gathered in groups. Typically in such cases, a man is acutely aware of the gaze of other men, is acutely sensitive to the taunts of other men, and feels intense pressure to join in with the "male bonding." In some cases the bonding of a group of men is rooted in mutual caring and shared fear, as when soldiers mourn the death of a fallen comrade during a period of respite in the midst of battle. But more often the bonding is not grounded in shared caring, but rather shared hate, and often that hate is directed at women.

Many male college students who play team sports have recounted to me their experiences of such shared misogyny. Here is one example:

> I play hockey, which is considered to be a manly, violent sport. . . . The hockey locker room is also a good depiction of how women are regarded in our society. All the guys try to prove how manly they are by bragging about how many chicks they have hooked up with. *In my experience, I have noticed that the more men disrespect women the more respect they get from men.* They want women to act weak and rely on men to get what they need. To a man, the perfect woman is one that performs in beauty pageants. These women are constantly smiling and never bother men with their problems [emphasis added].[15]

The student's central point is exceedingly perspicacious: the more men disrespect women the more respect they get from men. That respect that men get from other men by disrespecting women is not moral respect, it is not respect for their character; rather, it is respect for their manliness, for their exemplification of the masculine ideal that is found in militaristic cultures. These are not men who are good, they are men who are good at being men.[16] Notice that the elevated masculinity in the present case is not a reward for aggression toward the enemy (whether enemy soldiers or a rival hockey team), nor is it a reward for bravery or the ability to withstand pain. No, the reward of elevated masculinity is being given by male peers because a man has shown a generalized disrespect for women.

There may seem to be a contradiction here between masculinity that is grounded in misogynistic disrespect for women and another concept often associated with masculinity, particularly in militaristic cultures, namely chivalry. But, paradoxically, misogyny does not imply an absence of chivalry. Chivalry is individualistic, whereas misogyny is directed toward a group. Chivalry is directed toward an individual woman, and signifies her dependence upon a particular chivalrous man to defend her, to open doors, or to pull chairs back from the table at a restaurant. So chivalry is not at all premised on actual respect for a woman; rather, it is premised on an assumption that a woman is weak and dependent on a strong man. That helps us see how chivalry is not only consistent with misogyny, it reinforces it. As the hockey player noted, misogynistic men "want women to act weak and rely on men to get what they need."

When that masculine desire for the dependence of individual women is merged with the ideal of womanhood that is epitomized by the beauty pageant contestant, the result is a woman who is "constantly smiling" and who never bothers a man with her "problems," yet who simultaneously displays weakness and dependence on that same man. In effect, becoming the ideal woman means not burdening a man with your actual humanity; it means, effectively, becoming a non-person. In that way, misogynistic desire strips a woman of her humanity, of the reality of her life and personhood, leaving behind an empty, smiling, acquiescent shell—a Stepford Wife, or one of the RealDolls discussed in chapter 2.

Taking away personhood, not at all coincidentally, is one of the methods used by warriors to suppress their caring about the suffering of persons they are fighting. That is the purpose of using pejoratives for enemy soldiers, like *gook, raghead, hadji, nip,* and *kraut.* It is easier to kill or maim someone who is not deemed a full person. Likewise, to the extent men don't treat women as full persons, to the extent they dehumanize women, it becomes easier for men not to care about women's suffering, about "their problems."

Recently I learned about a particular context in which young men gather in groups for a particularly extreme activity that strips women of their humanity, and—despite my three decades of studying, teaching, and writing about gender—I have to say I was stunned. This is a case that goes well beyond men gathering in groups at strip clubs. It is an activity in which extreme misogyny is blended with the emotional toughening up of boys and men to manage the capacity to care about the suffering of others. I owe my awareness of this phenomenon to sociologist Gail Dines, who gave a multimedia presentation on pornography at a scholarly conference I attended a few years ago. Some of the ideas, such as the commodification of sexuality, were familiar ones, but what I was not at all prepared for was an introduction to what Dines calls *gonzo porn*, her term for what seems to me to be the most extremely misogynistic pornography imaginable. The whole point of gonzo porn is to degrade women in extreme ways, taking the preexisting misogyny of its viewers and amplifying it to the maximum extent possible.

In most cases where men use pornography, the point is to have a solitary experience of sexual pleasure. But the "enjoyment" of gonzo porn seems comparatively more likely to occur in groups of men. When I returned to my campus after experiencing Dines's presentation, after I related some of what I had learned to students in a class, one male student reported that groups of men in his dorm would get together for gonzo porn sessions, with lots of raucous laughter. From the uncomfortable looks on other men's faces, it appeared that some of them had participated in such events.

In the phenomenon of gonzo porn parties, the synergy of misogyny and emotional toughness in the construction of masculinity is manifest in multiple ways. First, just as ethnic slurs are used in war to make it easier for soldiers to kill people, and racial slurs are used to ease the conscience of the racist, in gonzo porn, misogynistic slurs such as *bitch, cunt, whore, slut,* and *cumdumpster* are used to help men suppress their compassion for the women who are being abused.[17] But that is just the start. For gonzo porn to work its misogynistic magic on groups of men, they must join together in laughing uproariously at the sight of other men brutalizing and humiliating women. (I need to offer a trigger warning for readers, as the next several paragraphs contain graphic descriptions of extreme misogyny, degradation, and violence.)

Of all the genres of gonzo porn, one stands out for its misogynistic entertainment value. As Dines reports in her book, *Pornland: How Porn Has Hijacked Our Sexuality,* "Probably the most degrading of acts in contemporary porn is ass-to-mouth (ATM), where a woman is expected to put a penis in her mouth that has just been in her anus (or in another woman's anus)." Fans discuss their favorite ATM scenes in forums dedicated to the subject. After reviewing some of those forum threads, Dines concludes that "the pleasure for many of these fans seems to be in watching the real looks of disbelief, disgust, and distaste flash on the women's faces when they realize just what they are going to have to put in their mouths. It is a pleasure gained from watching somebody totally dehumanized and humiliated."[18] According to Dines, one of the most extreme gonzo porn producers, and a pioneer of the genre, is Max Hardcore. In a 2005 interview, he brags about the creativity of his porn:

> Positions like pile driver, where I would gape the girls asses wide open, and provide a clear view for the camera, was unknown before I came along. I also created the technique of cumming in a girl's ass, having her squeeze it out into a glass, and then chuck the load down. . . .
>
> Over time, I developed many other unique maneuvers, most notably, vigorous throat fucking, creating gallons of throat slime over a girl's upside down face, and even causing them to puke. A little later, I started pissing down their throats several times during a scene, often causing them to vomit uncontrollably while still reaming their throats.[19]

Max Hardcore's pornography brings together in one package the misogyny and emotional toughness that are central to the construction of militaristic masculinity. He goes beyond misogynistic discourse, to misogynistic performance, violently acting out his hatred on actual women. For a man to do what Hardcore does to women requires emotional toughness, the ability to manage the capacity to care about the suffering of others.

And for men to watch his violently misogynistic videos requires that they, too, have that emotional toughness that is so crucial for the warrior. When men watch gonzo porn in groups, they put their misogyny and emotional toughness on display for other men to see. The male witnesses serve as gender police for each other, with each man knowing that if he does not toe the line of manliness he risks the punishment of ridicule or worse. So long as no one in the group deviates from the pattern of masculine misogyny and emotional toughness, male bonding occurs, on the basis of a collective passing of this test of manhood, in which each man performs misogyny for the others.

It is illuminating to place gonzo porn in the broader context of cultural militarism, and particularly the two elements that are central to it: adversarialism and the faith in masculine force. The adversarialism that is at the heart of militarism is manifest in the violence and dehumanization that characterize gonzo porn. Violence and dehumanization are what is done to enemies, whether the context is a "shooting war" or whether it is the "battle of the sexes"—of which gonzo porn is a manifestation. As we have seen in chapter 1, there is a widespread pattern in war-reliant cultures of antagonism between men and women. Gonzo porn not only serves as an obvious example of this heterosexual antagonism, it also helps us see how that antagonism is implicit in warrior masculinity, where the required emotional toughness is reinforced and policed by misogynistic teasing of men. When a man shows signs of caring about the suffering of others (compassion) or himself (fear), he gets called a *pussy*, *bitch*, *wuss*, or some other word that gets its pejorativeness from the fact that it refers to a female, which is misogynistically assumed to be an extremely bad thing.

The second central element in cultural militarism is a faith in masculine force, as in Max Hardcore's "pile driving" and "reaming their throats." The faith in masculine force actually has two components: a faith in its utility and a faith in its goodness. Faith in the utility of force tends to blind militaristic societies to ways of solving problems that do not involve masculine force. Faith in the goodness of masculine force is manifest in the widespread admiration—from both women and men—for superheroes and badasses. As I write this, the movie *Thor* has smashed its way to the top of the box office.[20] According to Ben Thompson, in his just published book *Badass: The Birth of a Legend:* "Thor was the head-smashing Norse god of Lightning, Thunder, storms, being awesome, and killing Giants in the face with a meatnormous magical hammer. The son of the god Odin and the goddess Earth, Thor was the defender of the heavenly land of Asgard, the toughest warrior among the gods, an original Avenger, best friends with Captain America and Iron Man, and the guy who everybody called on whenever they needed some pompous douche's ass kicked out through his forehead [sic, sic, sic, and sic]."[21] In real life, faith in the goodness of masculine force is reflected in our admiration for military and police heroes, especially when their successful use of violent force against enemies or criminals places their own lives at risk.[22]

The faith in masculine force obviously makes it more likely that war-reliant societies will choose violence over other options for dealing with other societies who are deemed to be enemies. And in most militaristic societies women are deemed to be enemies of men, especially in the context of eroticism. One form of violence that can be engendered by the faith in masculine force is the torture of presumed enemies. Isn't that precisely what is happening in Max Hardcore's videos? But would anyone assert the goodness of Max Hardcore? Well, yes. Here is a comment posted at the end of the previously quoted interview with him: "You really have to respect a guy like Max. He makes no apologies for his career, and just forges ahead despite a lot of criticism and legal scrutiny. He's rich, too . . . so that's got to be a plus!" All those fans who have made Hardcore wealthy would presumably agree with that statement. In their eyes, Hardcore's use of masculine force against women is something to be admired. I've never met a Max Hardcore fan (so far as I know), and I don't know of any demographic studies of his fans, but it is with considerable confidence that I can describe his fans as being misogynistic, prizing emotional toughness, tending toward adversarialism, and valorizing violent masculine force. They see those traits in Max Hardcore, that is precisely why they admire him, and there are enough of these presumably all-male admirers to have made Max Hardcore rich. I don't know how rich, and I don't know what percentage of men are his admirers, but it's worth pointing out that the four traits that make Max Hardcore admirable to his fans are four traits that are at the heart of warrior masculinity. In the United States that is a notion of masculinity from which virtually no boy or man can be entirely free.

✳ ✳ ✳

Both men and women are disadvantaged by the warrior ideal of masculinity. Men are more likely to be disadvantaged individually, while women are disadvantaged both individually and as a group.

Men are disadvantaged individually by the culturally programmed supposition that their lives, as quasi-warriors, are physically and emotionally expendable. The expectations of masculine "toughness" can impoverish their emotional lives, even to the point of emotional disability, so that men are far more likely than women to commit suicide. In recent years there has been an epidemic of suicides in the military, with substantially more troops dying by their own hands than enemy hands in 2012.[23] Iraq war veteran Daniel Somers's case is instructive. In his suicide letter Somers described his struggle to be emotionally tough: "During my first deployment, I was made to participate in things, the enormity of which is hard to describe. War crimes, crimes against humanity. Though I did not participate willingly, and made what I thought was my best effort to stop these events, there are some things that a person simply can not come back from." Ten years later he was still struggling with the emotional disability that resulted from his effort to manage his capacity to care about the suffering he had caused for others: "My mind is a wasteland, filled with visions of incredible horror, unceasing depression, and crippling anxiety, even with all of the medications the doctors dare give."[24]

As perhaps the ultimate indicator of fear, anxiety, and weakness, suicide is anything but masculine. But masculinity can make it a lot more likely to happen. Bushmaster, the company that makes the assault rifle that was used to kill twenty children at Sandy Hook Elementary

School in Connecticut in 2012, understood the connection between masculinity and guns when they ran a series of ads featuring a picture of their rifle and the slogan "Consider your man card reissued."[25] The association of masculinity and guns is surely a causal factor involved in the fact that thirty-one thousand people are killed with guns each year in the United States. It is overwhelmingly men doing the killing with guns, and it is overwhelmingly men getting killed. In fact, in two-thirds of the cases it is men who kill themselves.[26] That's more likely to happen in Wyoming than any other state in the country. Shawn Wagner, the owner of a gun store there, says it has to do with the cowboy myths that are especially prevalent in Wyoming. Wagner, whose own brother tried to shoot himself, says, "The Marlboro cowboy didn't go and get mental health—you know, appointments, and talk it out with his shrink, you know. And that's kind of the mentality of Wyoming—is man up; you're a man."[27]

Wagner's comment helps us see that suicide is only the tip of the iceberg regarding the psychological problems caused in individual men by warrior masculinity. Many boys and men who don't kill themselves are nonetheless trapped in what Kevin Powell calls an "emotional prison" with walls made of fear.[28] There is a paradox here. The emotional toughness at the heart of warrior masculinity is comprised of fear: fear of being seen as weak, fear of being seen as compassionate, fear of being seen as sensitive or empathetic, fear of being seen as like a woman, and, above all, fear of being seen as fearful. Yes, at the core of masculine emotional strength is fear—and particularly fear that very real things about a man's life will be seen by others.

Implicit in a man's fear of his reality being seen by others is that he must constantly be on guard against himself as a potential leaker of his fears to others. So he fears himself in addition to fearing others. In effect, he is his own potential enemy, for at any moment he could reveal his fears to other people, making himself vulnerable to them, thereby becoming complicit in their potential adversariality. Other people are viewed as potentially capable of seeing his hidden fear, and hence they are viewed as potential enemies. That is the case even for his own heterosexual lover, who is already culturally programmed as an enemy in the battle of the sexes (as we have seen here and in the past two chapters). Surrounded by potential enemies, intimate or not, and in continual fear of being complicit with them by revealing his fear, a man's emotional isolation becomes his citadel. But again, the paradox: his citadel is constructed out of fear. Confined within that emotional citadel, he faces the further paradox: the only way to ensure his safety, the only way to liberate himself from fear, is to kill himself.

Now it is clear why men are disadvantaged individually by warrior masculinity, more so than as a group. The pursuit of the ideal of warrior masculinity radically individualizes a man. If he opens up to others about his relative masculinity, if he exposes the citadel walls made of fear, he thereby undermines his manhood. Most men are unable to keep themselves entirely confined within that citadel of manliness, but for a man who can, for a man who experiences those walls of fear as absolute, there is a radical isolation in which the ultimate victory is also the ultimate defeat: suicide. Having become his own enemy completely, he has demonstrated the warrior's ability to kill, as well as the warrior's willingness to be killed. His greatest strength and his greatest weakness have converged.

In militaristic cultures the ideal of masculinity is not something that is supposed to be pursued by women. However, its pursuit by men affects women's lives every bit as much as it affects the lives of men. Men's pursuit of warrior masculinity draws them into behavior toward women that disadvantages women not only as individuals, but as a group. Men's maltreatment of women emanates from the fusion of the misogyny and emotional "toughness" that form the emotional core of warrior masculinity, along with the adversariality that we have seen to be intrinsic to heterosexuality in militaristic cultures. Hence it is not only individual women who become the victims of "manly men," it is women in general.

Here is an undoubtedly incomplete catalog of the ways women in general are affected by the widespread behavioral and attitudinal cultural patterns that are common among men in militaristic cultures; all these examples derive from the fusion of the hatred of women with the warrior's capacity to manage caring for the suffering of others:

1. Acceptance of the normality of rape and acceptance of the ways women's lives are structured by the fear of rape (e.g., higher rent, greater expense for cars and car repairs to avoid danger that could result from a mechanical failure, less freedom to be alone in public, fear of the night).

2. Acceptance of the normality of sexual harassment, as well as the normality of men who engage in it.

3. Acceptance of discrimination against women in employment (hiring, promotions, salary) and a general lack of concern for how women's lives are harmed by economic discrimination.

4. Resentment of women's advancement, especially in cases where it is perceived to be at the expense of a man or men generally (e.g., Title IX).

5. The emotionally calloused treatment of women in heterosexual relationships, including the inability to listen to women.

6. A lack of respect for women generally, which in politics can be manifested in two ways: (1) not taking female political candidates as seriously as male candidates and (2) treating women who are obviously less qualified as serious candidates primarily because of their erotic appeal (e.g., Sarah Palin).

7. The widespread assumption that it is primarily women who should do housework, child care, sexual servicing, and cooking—except, of course, in the case of barbecues.

All these patterns together point our attention to an extremely important meta-pattern in militaristic cultures: the tendency to assume that all the items in that list are not men's issues, but rather women's issues or, even more narrowly, feminist issues. So any man who takes them seriously suffers a major loss of masculinity points. And, yes, any woman who takes them seriously runs the risk of being called a feminist, thereby losing femininity points.

4

KEEPING THE BATTLE OF THE SEXES ALIVE

FAITH AND FANTASY

Everybody fusses, everybody fights
With all of the baggage you and me carry
We'll spend forever unhappily married
—Pistol Annies, "Unhappily Married"

Why is it that so many of the mistakes people make in their love lives are so incredibly familiar to us all? There are patterns of mistakes that are so common that it is hard not to think of them as just part of the human condition (a dubious phrase, for sure). For example, why are so many women attracted to jerks? When I raise that question in a public lecture, it always gets a lot of smiles of recognition and often a bit of nervous laughter. Everyone is familiar with this widespread pattern in human behavior, and they are also aware that there is something inherently absurd about it.

Sometimes I pair that question with this one: "When a group of straight women are talking about guys, how long does it take on average for someone to say something like 'guys are such assholes' (or dogs, pigs, dicks, jerks, etc.)?" Again, there is immediate recognition of the pattern, and laughter over the absurdity of it. The absurdity becomes even more obvious when I emphasize that the question was about straight women, whose erotic preferences are understood to favor men. And, by the way, the answers women give about how long it takes before such a comment is uttered range from thirty seconds to three minutes. There are lots of other similar examples available, of course, all pointing to ongoing and long-standing patterns of absurdities in human behavior that suggest we humans may be considerably less reasonable than Aristotle surmised when he said we are "rational animals." In this chapter I want to explore a factor in human irrationality that is a particularly powerful force for conserving some of our stubborn cultural absurdities, namely faith. My concern is not faith in the context where it is most commonly discussed, namely religion, but rather in the context of our love lives. I'll be paying particular attention to the faith we tend to have in ideas about love and gender that often are little more than culturally programmed fantasies—regardless of how prevalent and persistent they are.

Faith typically means believing something that you don't have adequate reason to believe. As the title character, played by Denzel Washington, says in the film *The Book of Eli*, "It means knowing something even if you don't know something." I interpret Eli as meaning that faith feels like knowledge, even though it lacks the prerequisites normally expected of knowledge, like evidence. It is not easy to separate that epistemically tinged sense of faith from another way the word is used, which means a kind of allegiance, commitment, or confidence, or a blend of those things. So used, the word *faith* is typically followed by the preposition *in,* as when we speak of faith in a doctrine, divinity, church, or person. It is probably the religious notion that most people tend to have in mind when they hear the word *faith,* but it is also routine to use that word in an altogether secular way to refer to confidence in a person, especially confidence in a person's abilities.

Having faith in a person, idea, or thing is not inherently positive or negative—the effect of faith on people's lives is sometimes helpful, sometimes harmful. Ascertaining when it is helpful or not can be difficult, but it is not always impossible. For example, up to a point having faith in your own ability can be helpful in achieving your life goals, although having faith in your ability to fly can be decidedly unhelpful in achieving those goals.

One common source of faith is what I have been calling cultural programming, meaning the manifold ways in which a culture effectively programs habits of belief, desire, preference, and behavior into its members. Sources of cultural programming include parenting, education, religion, peer pressure, movies, books, television, online videos, music, and social media. I've borrowed the word *programming* from the computer world, of course. Although cultural programming works in a much less precise way than computer programming, it does result in lots of automatic behavior. To the extent that, unlike a computer, we can become conscious of how we have been culturally programmed, we have a chance of interrupting that automatic behavior and moving toward comparatively more autonomous behavior.

Faith is the glue that keeps us stuck in those habits of belief, desire, preference, and behavior that have been culturally programmed into us. Faith can keep us stuck in those ruts by shielding our cultural programming from critical scrutiny, thereby leaving us with the sense that our beliefs, desires, and preferences emanate from "within" us, perhaps from a self or a soul. That feeling of emanation from within makes us feel that our actions and preferences are our own and that, because we have something called *free will*, we could freely choose to think, feel, and act differently. So we believe that we are in control of our lives. That belief gets in the way of any attempt to free ourselves from our cultural programming, or even to see it, thereby reinforcing faith as the glue that keeps us stuck in those ruts of thinking, feeling, and acting. Thus, faith in the existence of free will stands in the way of attaining actual freedom from the ways we have been culturally programmed.

The kind of faith we have been considering lies at the very heart of heterosexual love. So if we want to interrupt the absurdly tragic repetitions in our love lives, we must interrogate our faith in the fantasies of love and gender that form ruts, dooming us as individuals and as a society to making the same mistakes over and over again.

To apprehend the faith that underpins notions of romantic love, it is helpful to start, however paradoxically, with the role that faith plays in war. In societies that are war-reliant (and not all of them are—see chapter 1), there is a faith in the utility of masculine force, typically involving violence or the threat of violence by men. To the extent that a society is reliant on war, and to the extent that it assigns the task of fighting wars to men, it has faith in those men to engage in violence that serves the needs and aspirations of the entire society. As we have discussed in previous chapters, it is men, and not women, who are assigned the role of warrior primarily because significant numbers of warriors tend to get killed in war, and men's contribution to procreation makes them comparatively more disposable.[1] All of those factors in war-reliant societies are part of a pervasive pattern that we could call cultural militarism, which, in addition to faith in masculine force, often includes one or more of the following faith-based beliefs: (1) there are always enemies who threaten our society, (2) hence adversariality with other societies is inevitable, (3) hence war is often necessary or desirable, and (4) war is mainly a job for men.

These faith-based elements in cultural militarism ramify throughout our culture, intersecting with and informing every other part of social life, including what we call romantic or erotic love. Because most war-reliant societies experience significant pressures to procreate efficiently, they tend to have a strong cultural preference for heterosexual love over other kinds of love and sex. But the preference is not just for any heterosexual relationship. War-reliant societies culturally program into their members certain ideas about heterosexual love that are informed by the larger patterns within cultural militarism regarding adversariality and faith in masculine force.

Faith in those culturally programmed ideas about love plays a crucial, pervasive role in how we understand and experience heterosexual love in all of the forms it takes, including romance, marriage, eroticism, and what we now generically call *relationships*. All those terms can also be used for same-sex love, of course. But with a few intriguing exceptions, like ancient Greece,[2] war-reliant societies have tended to have cultural preferences for love that is more likely to lead to efficient procreation. In any case, my research suggests that all war-reliant societies culturally program their members into distinctly differentiated gender roles (and not all societies have such roles—see chapter 1). To the extent such gender programming is efficacious, the effect of faith on a given person's love life depends largely on which of two genders has been programmed into that person, especially in the case of persons who have been successfully programmed to identify as heterosexual.

✳ ✳ ✳

Consider the description of heterosexual love by Nietzsche we discussed previously. It is important to understand that Nietzsche is not giving his personal opinions in this passage, nor is he moralizing, that is, telling us how we ought to behave. Rather, he is describing the cultural programming that was prevalent in Europe and the United States at the time he was writing, in the late nineteenth century. Eventually he offers a devastating pragmatic critique of the cultural patterns he describes in this aphorism, saying that they inevitably lead to antagonism between women and men. As we shall see, his insights turn out to be helpful even now, well over a century later.

According to Nietzsche, women and men are culturally programmed to understand love in ways that are different from, yet complementary to, each other.

Man and woman have different conceptions of love; and it is one of the conditions of love in both sexes that neither sex presupposes the same feeling and the same concept of "love" in the other. What woman means by love is clear enough: total devotion (not mere surrender), with soul and body, without any consideration or reserve, rather with shame and horror at the thought of a devotion that might be subject to special clauses or conditions. In this absence of conditions her love is a *faith*. . . .

Man, when he loves a woman, wants precisely this love from her and is thus himself as far as can be from the presupposition of feminine love. Supposing, however, that there should also be men to whom the desire for total devotion is not alien; well, then they simply are—not men. A man who loves like a woman becomes a slave; while a woman who loves like a woman becomes *a more perfect woman*.[3]

Nietzsche leaves for us the task of articulating the implicit conclusion: The most perfect woman is a slave. For a hint of the continuing relevance of Nietzsche's insights, we need look no further than that would-be perfect woman Britney Spears and her (previously mentioned) 2001 hit song "I'm a Slave 4 U," in which the title line is sung repeatedly. Lest anyone be tempted to put Britney's philosophical chops in the same league with Friedrich Nietzsche, let me note that the song was written by Pharrell Williams and Chad Hugo. More important, however, is how to understand this culturally programmed idea of woman as slave, including its effects in heterosexual relationships.

Central to the idea of woman as slave in heterosexuality, according to Nietzsche, is the faith she has in the man she loves. It is not hard to see how a woman whose faith in a man is characterized by complete surrender and devotion might wind up as his slave, effectively. And to the extent she has been culturally programmed to construe this as love, it may be hard for her to grasp what is happening to her, that is, what her faith in this man is doing to her. Calling this experience of submission by the name *love* has a camouflaging effect and, indeed, makes it seem like something truly wonderful is happening. The work of cultural programming that produces this camouflage is powerfully assisted by biology. During the period of infatuation, or "falling in love," there is a potent cocktail of chemicals released into the bloodstream (including phenethylamine, or PEA) that makes you feel really good and tends to make your partner look really good. Neither the camouflaging provided by cultural programming about love nor the biochemical changes that accompany infatuation are factors of which a person is explicitly conscious. So it makes perfect sense to call it *falling* in love—it feels like something that happens to us, rather than like something we consciously do. Thus, infatuation, or falling in love, could hardly be called a rational process. If there is any doubt about that, just notice how often people who are falling in love do really stupid things!

Which brings us to the case of Hedda Nussbaum. When police arrived at the Greenwich Village apartment she shared with Joel Steinberg on November 2, 1987, they saw on the refrigerator the typical kinds of photos of a couple falling in love, taken at Coney Island and other fun locations, from as far back as 1975, when Hedda and Joel met. Back then, she was employed by Random House as an editor and author of children's books, and Joel was a lawyer. According to Hedda, "The romance developed pretty quickly." They dated for two months, but Hedda became concerned. "When I would say I had something else to do, he would always convince me to change my mind. And I felt . . . that I was too easily persuaded, and broke it off with him because I felt that he brought that out in me." Somewhat later, they ran into each other again, and went out for what turned out to be a romantic dinner. "I was in love," Hedda says. "And he was in love, apparently." Her parents provided affirmation of the relationship: "They loved him. They thought he was terrific."

But eleven years later, when Hedda opened the door, the police saw a crushed nose, a split upper lip, cigarette burns, bruises, missing teeth, a damaged eye, and, a bit later, broken bones that had not healed properly. The occasion for the police visit was not about anything that had been done to Hedda, however. They had responded to a 911 call about a six-year-old girl, Lisa, who was unconscious. That turned out to be because of a blow to the head. Lisa—who had been illegally "adopted" by Joel—later died without regaining consciousness.

I have not said in this narrative who was responsible for the injuries to Hedda and Lisa. Nonetheless, most readers have probably surmised that the perpetrator in both cases was Joel, because that would fit with a larger picture about domestic violence with which we are all famil- iar. They would be correct. Most readers would also presume that the injuries already described fit into a larger pattern of violence by Joel. Indeed, Joel once beat Hedda so severely that doctors had to remove her spleen. One of his favorite ways to maintain "discipline" was to submerge Hedda in an ice cold bath until her teeth were chattering so much she could not talk. He did that one of the six times she tried to leave him, saying it would "clear her head."

After all that torture at the hands of Joel, as well as his murder of Lisa, Hedda nonetheless said, "I was still in love with Joel." Her deep faith in him was redolent of religiosity: "To me he was like this godlike person." But alas (and the analogy here with the story of Job is ines- capable), "Over the years, (the abuse) just kept escalating." At his trial, after she limped to the witness stand as a result of a knee injury he had caused, Hedda was asked why she had not escaped from his control. She said, "I worshiped him."[4]

"Worship" is more than a metaphor here. Regardless of whether it is a man, a god, a godlike man, or an idol who is the object, worship requires faith. Praising a "higher power" is intrinsically not a rational process; rather, it is grounded in emotion-laden beliefs about a being who is purportedly in control, and in whom one has faith that he will exercise that control benignly. Hedda's situation helps us see that such worshipful faith is likely to be misguided, even illusory.

Hedda Nussbaum's case is obviously an extreme one. Nonethe- less, it is entirely consistent with a quite familiar pattern, which is why anyone could easily have guessed that a boyfriend or husband or "ex" had caused the injuries to Hedda and Lisa. The familiarity of the pattern derives primarily from our awareness of the regularity of news reports of domestic violence. But its familiarity also reflects a tendency among some men (and even some women) to accept domes- tic violence as normal, or even good. Consider, for example, a Face- book poster circulated by men's groups that features a photograph of a woman's face with a black eye, along with the inscription "1/3 OF WOMEN ARE PHYSICALLY ABUSED—2/3 OF MEN AREN'T DOING THEIR JOB." The familiarity of the pattern of men abusing wives and girlfriends also fits into a larger pattern about which explicit awareness is less likely, namely the cultural programming of male-dominant heterosexual love that Nietzsche described and that is typically found in militaristic societies like ours—a pattern of cultural programming with a range of negative consequences extending well beyond domestic violence.

✳ ✳ ✳

In war-reliant cultures the faith in masculine force is so pervasive, and so far-reaching, that it leads to sweeping patterns of domination by men, not only in domestic life, but in the realms of politics, economics, religion, and popular culture. We're talking here about patterns, not generalizations, so the point is not that all men are dominant everywhere all the time, nor that women and only women are universally dominated by men. The exceptions to the patterns include cases of women dominating men, of course. But it is also important to note the widespread pattern in militaristic societies of men being dominated by other men, typically by men who excel at the use of force.

So the overall pattern is that men who manifest a high capacity for the use of masculine force are understood to "be in charge." In these societies "being in charge" and "taking charge" are strongly associated with manliness—a "real man" is a "take charge kind of guy." Thus it is generally understood that in a heterosexual relationship (1) it is the man who controls the woman and (2) the woman should have faith in that particular man and his control of her—she surrenders to him, she is devoted to him. These words, used by Nietzsche, but also found widely in the literature of romance, remind me of a hymn we sang in the Southern Baptist church my family attended when I was growing up. It is called "I Surrender All":

All to Jesus I surrender;
All to Him I freely give;
I will ever love and trust Him,
In His presence daily live.

Refrain:

I surrender all,
I surrender all;
All to Thee, my blessed Savior,
I surrender all.

All to Jesus I surrender;
Humbly at His feet I bow,
Worldly pleasures all forsaken;
Take me, Jesus, take me now.

All to Jesus I surrender;
Make me, Savior, wholly Thine;
Let me feel the Holy Spirit,
Truly know that Thou art mine.

All to Jesus I surrender;
Lord, I give myself to Thee;
Fill me with Thy love and power;
Let Thy blessing fall on me.

All to Jesus I surrender;
Now I feel the sacred flame.
Oh, the joy of full salvation!
Glory, glory, to His Name![5]

Just in case it is not obvious why Nietzsche's description of heterosexual love reminded me of this hymn, notice the emphasis not only
on surrender but also on being taken. Similarly, Nietzsche describes a
heterosexual woman's love as a kind of surrender, and he adds that she
"wants to be taken and accepted as a possession. . . . Consequently, she
wants someone who takes [her]."[6]

So: I surrender all, to him I freely give, I will ever love and trust him, take me, make me thine, etc. I don't think the parallels of these two cases of surrender grounded in faith are at all coincidental, and, indeed, they help us understand what Hedda Nussbaum meant when she said she worshiped Joel Steinberg, whom she viewed as a godlike person.

Further, in both cases, the word *devotion* is used as a synonym for this surrender grounded in faith. Well, isn't the ultimate devotion that of a willing slave? And it's not just Britney Spears and Hedda Nussbaum who confirm the contemporary relevance of Nietzsche's slave metaphor for describing heterosexual love. Even today, among college students, the expression *whipped* is used for a man who shows even the smallest sign of not being in control of his girlfriend or, worse, that she might be in control of him—i.e., that she might be "wearing the pants" in the relationship. Further, traditional weddings continue to start with the officiator asking who gives the bride to the groom, and the overwhelming majority of brides in the United States change their surname from their father's surname to their new husband's surname, which traditionally signified a change in ownership. That view of women as property owned by men has been reflected in laws, which traditionally have deemed a woman, just like a slave, to be some man's property, whether it be her father, husband, or brother.

As feminist movements have, since the mid-nineteenth century, gradually weakened the grip of those laws in many militaristic societies, they have been replaced in heterosexuality by faith—specifically the faith of the woman, both in a particular man and in a particular idea of heterosexual love. As Nietzsche observes, the faith of a woman in a heterosexual relationship is inseparable from romantic passion.

A woman's passion in its unconditional renunciation of rights of her own presupposes precisely that on the other side there is no equal pathos, no equal will to renunciation.

Woman wants to be taken and accepted as a possession. . . . Consequently, she wants someone who *takes*, who does not give himself or give himself away; on the contrary, he is supposed to become richer in "himself"—through the accretion of strength, happiness, and faith given him by the woman who gives herself. Woman gives herself away, man acquires [her].[7]

The culturally programmed expectation of women in this notion of heterosexual love is that they willingly, even passionately, embrace being treated, effectively, as a man's property. The notions of property and faith intersect here: Nietzsche says that her "faith [is] given him by the woman, who gives herself." Her unconditional faith in this man and his control, in this "higher power," is effectively a way of gifting him with herself. "Woman wants to be taken, adopted as a possession," so as to make the man "richer."

Today, more than a century after Nietzsche wrote about love, people feel uncomfortable talking about women as "property." I definitely can't imagine any woman today saying that she wants to be some guy's property. But except for the use of that particular word, Nietzsche's perspicacity about our culturally programmed notions of heterosexual love has not much diminished over the past hundred years. There continues to be a cultural expectation that heterosexual women will aspire to find and fall in love with "A Take-Charge Kind of Guy." In an interview with precisely that title, the following exchange takes place between romance novelist Christina Dodd and her interviewer, Michelle Buonfiglio:

MB: We hear a lot, in romance, about alpha males, and alpha males are just the hottest thing there is, believe me. But it's hard to define why they are so hot. Tell us, what is an alpha male?

CD: These are the guys who are the big brawny guys. . . . They are the richest guys. They always have an immense amount of power, and it is about power, I think. Women like men with power.[8]

Dodd's 2011 book is called *Taken by the Prince*. The prince, Saber Lawrence, is a warrior in a revolution against a despot in Moricadia who is keeping him from his rightful place on the throne. According to the book's description, "Saber kidnaps Victoria to ensure her silence and vanquish her reserve." According to the *Publisher's Weekly* review, the book "delivers sensual sizzle, though some readers will flinch at scenes of aggressive seduction that verge on the nonconsensual."[9] It was in 1882 that Nietzsche published the passage about heterosexual love I have quoted. The publication date for Christina Dodd's *Taken by the Prince* is April 5, 2011. I should also note that Dodd's novels have been translated into twelve languages, and one of them, *My Favorite Bride,* spent fifteen weeks on the *New York Times* bestseller list. It would be too sweeping to claim that cultural programming about heterosexual love has not changed at all in the last 129 years, but perhaps it would not be too extravagant to observe how remarkably little the cultural programming directed at women has changed (despite the huge changes in women's actual lives).

What about the cultural programming of men? Nietzsche says that what men want from love is perfectly complementary to what women want: "Man, when he loves a woman, wants precisely this [feminine] love from her." He wants her complete and utter devotion, and not merely surrender, to him. He wants her unconditional faith in himself. For a contemporary popular culture reference to pair with the aforementioned Britney Spears song, let me cite an ironic authority on the subject, George Michael. In, "Faith," a song he wrote and that he sings in an album with the same title, he avers that he is unable to accept love "without devotion." Assuming the persona of a "strong man," he sings "I've got to have faith."[10] Does George Michael speak for men generally? Does a *strong man* who is heterosexual expect faith and devotion in the love of a woman? Some men who seem to *think* they are strong, like Joel Steinberg, want a woman's unconditional devotion and faith so much that they will use their strength to physically and emotionally torture, even kill, to try to get that kind of love from a woman—

although whether it is love that they get may be doubtful. Those men suppose such strenuous efforts to be driven by love; remember, this submission of a woman is what a heterosexual man wants "when he loves a woman," says Nietzsche.

In today's world it is increasingly hard to find a man who would say out loud that his love for a woman means that he desires her overt submission to his authority. But consider some more subtle ways that Nietzsche's insights about heterosexual love continue to apply in men's attitudes. For example, most young men today expect a potential partner to have a career, and most of them appreciate the economic advantages of a two-career partnership. Nonetheless, I recently heard a man express precisely those attitudes, but he added that he does not want to take "second place" to a woman's career. I want to call attention to two things about his comment. First, men who express such sentiments tend not to notice that the very notion of a second place implies there is a first place. In this context a man's wish not to be in second place seems to mean that he wants to be in first place. But few men in Western cultures today would say explicitly that they want to be in first place, dominant over their female partner in second place. Even less, though, would a man want to emasculate himself by trading those places, with a girlfriend or wife in first place dominant over himself in second place.

Second, if a man says that he doesn't want to take second place to a woman's *career*, he is probably not even thinking about this as an issue about whether one person or the other will be in first place in the relationship. He thinks he is talking about her career, not her as a person. Such a distinction between a woman and her career might have made sense in the past, say the 1960s and before, just because white middle-class women were generally not allowed to have careers at all. For men it was opposite to that: a man's identity and sense of self-worth were inseparable from his job.

Now our culture is getting close to a consensus understanding that for women, too, identity and self-worth are inseparable from a job or career. Alas, women are getting to that understanding about women faster than men are. And that is a problem for heterosexual relationships, for it means that, as a widespread pattern, men are not understanding how important a woman's work and career are to her own personal flourishing. But women who do understand it are increasingly reluctant to put their own personal flourishing, including a career that is an important part of it, in "second place" to any man's personal flourishing.

I suppose it is obvious why women are quicker than men to appreciate and value the changes in their lives that are moving them ever so gradually toward greater equality. Many men, however, tend to see these changes as a threat. They see the privilege and entitlement that have traditionally been associated with manhood slipping away.

I have gotten some sense of that concern when I have given public lectures to college students. When I have shared with them Nietzsche's description of heterosexual love, including the parts about the perfect woman being a slave, women wanting to unconditionally surrender to a man and wanting a man who will take her as a possession, and women wanting a man who "is supposed precisely to be made richer in 'himself'—through the increase in strength, happiness, and faith given him by the woman who gives herself," inevitably there are men present who cannot contain their delight that this esteemed philosopher has articulated their own ideas about love. There are big grins, and one or two will even blurt out "Yeah!"

From the perspective of those men, while the changes that are coming about in women's lives may be welcomed for taking some of the economic pressure off men, the implications of these changes for men's erotic lives are feared. That sheds light on a developing phenomenon that initially puzzled me. Up until recently it was the women in my classes who would be more likely than the men to buy into the myth of falling in love and living happily ever after. The women were also more likely to believe in "soul mates," understood as the idea that for each person there is someone out there who would be the perfect mate, so that the challenge for attaining romantic bliss is to find that person. In the last few years I've noticed a gradual reversal, so that now more men buy into these myths than women. Some recent research has confirmed this pattern.[11] Men, it seems, are becoming more romantic, as women are becoming less romantic, and men are now more likely than women to believe in falling in love and living happily ever after. A young man today is not just likely to want a woman to have faith in him, he is likely to want her to have faith in love itself.

Relationship therapist Terri Orbuch shares this telling anecdote: "A girlfriend of mine told me her boyfriend asked her last week which she preferred—opals or pearls. She said, 'Ink cartridges.' Her boyfriend was crestfallen when she explained that she'd prefer that he gift wrap a six-month supply of those expensive little ink cartridges for her printer/scanner than slip her a romantic necklace the night before Christmas."[12] Orbuch saw this anecdote as reflective of a larger pattern. Men, she says, are now typically more romantic than women. By that she means that men are more likely to have beliefs about love that reflect traditional romanticism. So men were more likely than women to mark "True" in the following recent survey:

True / False—I believe in love at first sight.

True / False—I fall in love easily, and when I do, I fall hard.

True / False—I believe there is a perfect soul mate out there somewhere for me.

True / False—If I don't have passionate feelings for someone right away, chances are s/he's not "the one."

True / False—No matter what challenges life presents, love can conquer all.

True / False—When you're truly in love, passion never fades; it can last forever.[13]

The term I use for this developing pattern of more men buying into traditional myths about love is *masculine romanticism*. One element in this gradual shift is a reversal of the long-standing assumption that most men tend to resist long-term commitment. Men on college campuses are now more likely than women to say that they want a committed relationship.[14] And according to a 2013 survey, African American men are now substantially more likely than African American women to say they are looking for a committed, long-term relationship.[15] That particular study did not look at other races, nor did either report address beliefs about falling in love, soul mates, and living happily ever after. Nonetheless, when put alongside Orbuch's research those two reports of men's increased interest in long-term relationships may provide some insight into the shifting attitudes among men that I am calling masculine romanticism.

To understand what is driving this twenty-first century trend toward masculine romanticism, and why that expression may no longer be an oxymoron, we need to look at other gendered changes that are taking place in the twenty-first century, contextualizing them with Nietzsche's insights about gender differences regarding love from the nineteenth century.

As women are moving forward in their lives, elevating their economic status and their self-esteem, although the *Taken by the Prince* version of romance may continue to have an attraction for some of them on the level of fantasy, in real life sometimes they would rather have ink cartridges. Many women are gradually pulling free of the traditional romantic cultural programming described by Nietzsche, in which men are takers and women are givers and, more broadly, in which men are viewed as dominant over women.

The grip of that cultural programming on women's lives is loosening as they become less financially dependent on men. For example, consider the actual life history of romance novelist Christina Dodd, shared by her in a 2005 interview (also with Michelle Buonofiglio):

MB: Who is the most heroic person you know?

CD: My mother. My father died unexpectedly while she was pregnant with me, my sisters were 8 and 10, and since this was the 50s, she was the typical unemployed housewife. Yet she managed to deal with some really grinding poverty, get a job, put food on the table, and raise her three daughters. She's the reason I wanted to write—she read to me all the time when I was a kid. She's the reason I was so persistent (10 years!) in trying to get published—by example, she taught me to keep fighting no matter what the odds and sooner or later, you will succeed. And she's the basis for my heroines— the impoverished yet determined woman who, in spite of adversity, fights to take control of her life and always wins.[16]

In an era of strong women who fight to take control of their lives, as Dodd's mother did, it should not be surprising that women are becoming less patient with men's efforts to maintain the control that traditional romantic love gave them.

It should also not be surprising that as women gradually remove themselves from the traditional romantic formula, men are clinging to it ever more tightly. Men are becoming more fully cognizant of, and allegiant to, the ostensible benefits of a kind of love in which a woman is unconditionally devoted to a man. As that kind of love starts to slip away from men's grasp, its perceived value to them becomes greater. There is an analogy that is useful here from the work of the philosopher Martin Heidegger. He says that, when using a hammer to drive in nails, a carpenter's focus is on the work that is being done, not the hammer. But, if the handle of the hammer breaks, the carpenter's attention is suddenly turned to the hammer itself and how crucial it has been to the larger project. The lost usability of the hammer reveals its full value to the carpenter.

Likewise, as more and more women gradually—very gradually, we should emphasize—lose interest in romantic love, and in the romantic attention of men, seeing both as having diminished value in comparison with pragmatic factors that actually make a difference in the attainment of more fulfilling lives, men begin to see the immensity of the entitlement they are gradually losing. As the culturally programmed traditional model of heterosexual love increasingly appears to be broken, as it begins to slip away, men are beginning to see the value it offered them, and they don't want to lose it. So they are becoming "more romantic" and increasingly trying to persuade women to share their romanticism.

Alas, they may have gotten on the love train a bit late. The relationship specialist Orbuch describes the following gendered scenario:

> If you are a man, you may be frustrated by your girlfriend or wife's practical approach to lovemaking and romance. Does she roll over, put on her bathrobe, and start checking her e-calendar moments after you've made love? . . .
>
> If you are a woman, you may feel put off by his amorous advances when you're trying to study at night. Or his complaints that you don't seem to care about him anymore. . . . It's fine to be practical about your love relationship, but at least some of the time, let him feel like the two of you are in a movie. Take the time to create a romantic mood or scene for him.[17]

Let him feel like the two of you are in a movie? Putting aside whether that is good advice, it does bring into sharp focus that the traditional ideas about romantic love have always been a fantasy. Anna Breslaw describes the fantasy specifically as it tends to be found in movies: "The rules of movies were as deeply ingrained in me as the laws of physics or the pledge of allegiance, and they went something like this: The best relationships aren't easy. Without conflict, you can't have a happy ending. If a guy doesn't hurt you so badly that he has to perform some grand and cinematic gesture (typically with pop song accompaniment) to win you back, then who cares?"[18] Breslaw says that she recently found a list of boyfriend desiderata she had written at the age of twelve and that she had learned from movies. Two of the five desired traits are particularly interesting: "bigger than me" and "not too nice." Commenting on the latter, she says, "The 'not too nice' part followed me to college and film school and morphed into Mr. Darcy Syndrome, the endless pursuit of a jerk in the hopes of being able to peel back the layers to discover his secret, gooey, nice-guy center. But inside I'd just find more layers of jerk, smaller and smaller, like Russian nesting dolls."[19]

Obviously, Breslaw can today look on this cinematically programmed fantasy with detachment. Today there are many women who understand that the traditional male dominant/female subordinate model of romantic love is a fantasy. They may see it as an arena for play, which they prefer to enjoy only when they want a break from the more important things in their lives, such as careers.

Men, in contrast, may be trending toward taking romantic love *seriously* and seeing their happiness as dependent upon it. Of course, what that really means, though, is that they are more likely to feel dependent on achieving an entirely unrealistic fantasy that entitles them to the possession of a woman. Thus, paradoxically, heterosexual men becoming "more romantic" does not bode at all well for their love lives or for heterosexual love generally.

To unravel that paradox, consider that the traditional model of romantic love as described by Nietzsche is really all about entitlement for men and subordination for women. The striking complementarity of the feminine and masculine conceptions of love in this cultural construct tends to camouflage the complete lack of equality noted by Nietzsche at the start of the passage we have considered. This is a model of heterosexual love in which men own women, and where that's considered perfectly all right, because women supposedly want to be owned by men.

In the past, because women were economically dependent upon men, and because their membership in society was premised on being owned by some man, whether father, brother, or husband, their very survival often meant being a man's property. In such a context the cultural programming of women to buy into the traditional romantic love fantasy might make some sense, given that there was just no way for most women to escape material and social conditions that made them little more than chattel.

Today, however, that romantic fantasy can remain alive for women only because of cultural inertia—no doubt fueled significantly by commercial interests for which femininity and romantic fantasies have been incredibly profitable. Nonetheless, growing numbers of women now conceive of romantic fantasy as *nothing but* fantasy, having its nostalgic place only in the fictive worlds of novels and movies, and perhaps in the occasional role-playing scenario in the context of an actual relationship.

Countering that trend in contemporary heterosexual love is the growing depth of men's faith in traditional myths about romantic love that I have called masculine romanticism. Will men's growing commitment to romantic fantasy save heterosexual love? We'll answer that question in the next chapter.

5

CAN MEN RESCUE HETEROSEXUAL LOVE?

MORE FAITH AND FANTASY

"Don't you see Elisa? I love you the way a drowning man loves air. And it would destroy me to have you just a little.

—Hector in Rae Carson, *The Crown of Embers*

A traditional, culturally programmed fantasy about romantic love is the idea that if one can just find and fall in love with the right person, one will live happily ever after. In the previous chapter we took note of a slowly developing trend among women in the direction of losing faith in those fantasies, seeing them merely as fantasies, rather than as indicators of realistic aspirations for their actual lives. This trend is not surprising, given that it fits perfectly with developments in the material and social conditions of women's lives in many parts of the world: the survival of a woman has become far less likely than in the past to require a male partner to provision and protect her, and she can now procreate without a male partner to supply sperm. These factors mean that for women to pursue traditional heterosexual romantic fantasies in which a woman is dependent on, and subordinate to, a male partner, is no longer in their material interest. Hence, those romantic fantasies are kept alive only by cultural inertia, which is powerfully reinforced by commercial interests in the entertainment media and the beauty-industrial complex. For the companies involved in those businesses, traditional romance and associated notions of femininity are immensely profitable. Their advertising and media campaigns ensure that traditional romantic fantasy qua fantasy will continue to bring pleasure to many women.

As we saw in the last chapter, there may be yet another developing factor keeping heterosexual romantic fantasies alive. Seemingly in correlation with the diminishing faith in fantasies about romantic love among straight women is what appears among straight men to be a growing faith in traditional fantasies about romantic love. We've already taken note of some of the signs of this masculine romanticism: men seem more likely than women to believe in the myth of falling in love and living happily ever after, more likely to believe in soul mates, and, among African Americans at least, men are much more likely than women to be interested in long-term, committed relationships.

Why at this particular time would the faith of men in notions like "true love" and "living happily ever after" be on the rise? For an explanation of that phenomenon, let's first recall from our earlier discussions the advantage accorded to men by the traditional model of heterosexual love, given that its asymmetry tilts in their favor, offering them a woman's faith, devotion, and surrender—even to the extent of virtual slavery, according to at least two authorities, Friedrich Nietzsche and Britney Spears. Nonetheless, despite the advantages men get from traditional romantic love, generally they have had less interest than women in talking and writing about love, and have even deemed interest in romantic subjects to be primarily a womanly thing, and hence unmanly. Just before quoting the Nietzsche passage about gender and love that has figured prominently throughout this book, in which he explains how the male dominant/female subordinate model of heterosexuality inevitably leads to antagonism, Simone de Beauvoir tacitly concurs with a line she quotes from Byron: "Man's love is of man's life a thing apart; 'Tis woman's whole existence." But, as we discussed in the previous chapter, among many women such a preoccupation with romantic love is becoming less prevalent, a trend that is easy to understand in the light of women's changing material circumstances. What could account for the opposite trend among men? Why would there be an uptick in men's faith in romantic love?

Consider that not only are women today more likely to have careers that make them financially independent, men are gradually beginning to be less likely than women to focus on careers. There are many signs of this, one being that men are now less likely than women to go to college, and, when they get there, they are less likely to appreciate the value of education, which seems to be reflected in a lesser degree of academic commitment.[1] When I ask the students in my classes who studies more, men or women, they actually laugh. For them, there is an obvious pattern of the women being more likely to be serious about their studies than are the men, who are more likely to be devoting large amounts of time to playing video games and watching sports. That pattern fits with another one: Men are less likely than women to go to graduate or professional school. These are just patterns, not generalizations about all men or all women, but they are significant patterns.

These patterns of decline in men's educational commitment and career prospects help explain the results of the study discussed in the previous chapter, which found that 43 percent of single black men say they are looking for a long-term relationship, compared to only 25 percent of single black women. That surprised a lot of people, not least because of a previous spate of media reports about the difficulties black women supposedly have in finding a suitable black male mate. In response to skeptics, Robert Blendon, who was codirector of the study, cited the substantially greater percentage of black women, compared to black men, attending college and attaining postgraduate degrees. Blendon acknowledges this pattern can be found among whites, too, but he contends that it is more pronounced among blacks.[2] It is true that 63 percent of bachelor degrees earned by African Americans in 2009–2010 went to women, while 55 percent of bachelor degrees earned by whites went to women.[3] The differences can be explained, of course, by the history of race in America.

The range of educational and economic opportunities for black men has always been dramatically constricted, compared to white men, and that has always had a substantial impact on black heterosexual relationships.[4] But now white men are less likely than white women to avail themselves of the kind of educational opportunities that formerly were an element of white male privilege. This substantial gender disparity in educational attainment for both whites and blacks is important. The growing concern of straight women about the economic prospects of straight men of both races is a significant factor for the purpose of understanding changing patterns in heterosexual love and sexuality.

One consequence of men's comparatively lesser emphasis on education that can enhance career prospects is that men's desirability as heterosexual partners is lowered. That is not just because of the obvious economic considerations. It is also because a man with lesser career prospects is perceived as less masculine. The context here is a widespread pattern in militaristic societies for men to be the controllers of resources that are necessary for the survival of women and children, which in turn has meant that in those societies a man's control or potential control of resources is likely to be the most important factor in a woman's mate preference,[5] so it is not surprising that men in those societies understand that maximizing their control of resources enhances their prospects for finding and keeping a female partner. Thus it is not uncommon for men to lie about the size of two things we refer to with *p* words, one of which is *paycheck*.[6]

Indeed, the pattern among war-reliant cultures is for a man's control of resources, which are provided to wives and children—and sometimes the broader society, to be one of the three most salient elements in masculinity. Thus, to the extent that boys and men appear to have comparatively less motivation for pursuits that can contribute to greater control of resources, like education and careers, their masculinity declines. That also means that their appeal to heterosexual women diminishes, given the heterosexual cultural programming in most militaristic societies that instills strong desires and preferences for erotic relationships with members of the opposite sex, with the oppositeness being marked by qualities we associate with masculinity and femininity.

That decline in the factors that contribute to masculinity, and hence that make men seem desirable to heterosexual women, has implications for a second aspect of masculinity in militaristic cultures: factors related to procreation. In many societies this is not necessarily about actually producing lots of offspring; often it is more about appearing to have lots of sex, which is tacitly understood to have a causal relationship with the production of offspring. As with the provider role, there is a decline in the salience of this procreative factor for masculinity, because of some interrelated reasons. First, in both developed and developing countries around the world, the emphasis on maximum procreation is rapidly diminishing. Even in many militaristic societies, including the United States, the impact of war casualties on procreative pressures is far less than it was in earlier centuries. Second, as they place growing emphasis on careers, women are choosing to procreate at a far lower level than in the past, or not at all, which results in diminished opportunities for men to procreate. The impact of that on men's opportunities for sex is complicated, not least by the increased availability and effectiveness of contraceptives that make nonprocreative sex the norm. All other factors being equal, safer sex means more sex, but, with sex being increasingly nonprocreative, the specific need of women for male sexual partners is diminished. The widespread availability of vibrators, dildos, and other sex aids for women, and their greatly improved quality, has also contributed to that diminished need of women for male partners.

Hence, it should be no surprise to find on the other side of the heterosexual binary that so many men are also turning to alternatives to actual heterosexual sex, like pornography, sex dolls, and other sex aids—men's use of all these has grown exponentially in recent decades (see chapters 2 and 3). Of course, for men, pornography and sex dolls are mostly about masturbation, and in militaristic cultures that valorize procreative efficiency frequent masturbation does not raise one's masculinity quotient—it is more likely to lower it. Indeed, after sex columnist Dan Savage reported in a recent podcast on the growing use of vibrators by men for masturbation, he noted that when a woman says she has a vibrator she is viewed as empowered, but when a man says he has a vibrator he is viewed as pathetic.[7]

* * *

With both the provider and procreative roles gradually shrinking in their relevance to manliness, let's turn to the third role that contributes to masculinity, which has sometimes been called the protector role, but is really about having the qualities of a warrior, like aggressiveness, dominance, and emotional toughness. Masculinity in a militaristic society means, in large part, to be dominant and to be ready and willing to use violent force to exert that dominance. In battle men try to dominate male enemies. And in heterosexual relationships they try to dominate female lovers.

However, many contemporary militaristic societies, including the United States and European countries, are relying less and less on masculine force in war, for a variety of both technological and cultural reasons. Concomitantly, most men in these societies do not perform military service at all. Still, many men continue to try to dominate other men in other contexts, including sports, video games, business, politics, and religion. But for men to dominate other men with violent force generally no longer has the utility, or presumed utility, that it did in past centuries when men were expected to be actual warriors.

Thus all three of the most important dimensions of masculinity in war-reliant cultures are gradually evaporating, however slowly. Nonetheless, we continue to be culturally obsessed with masculinity, especially warrior masculinity, and with boys growing up to be "real men." Masculinity is, however, increasingly virtual, grounded in video games or sports spectatorship, or just "acting tough" when one is subject to the gaze of other people. So perhaps it should not be surprising that in their approach to heterosexuality men are also increasingly turning in a virtual direction, for example, to pornography and sex dolls.

Yet another such turn toward virtual masculinity is what I have called *masculine romanticism* (see the previous chapter)—what seems to be a growing pattern among some men to embrace, and have faith in, traditional myths and fantasies about romantic love. What makes that romanticism masculine is not just that it's men who are embracing it, but also the part of traditional romantic love that involves a woman unconditionally devoting herself to a man, and the man taking possession of her. That has always been at the heart, so to speak, of romantic love, yet only now is it becoming interesting to frame such a model of romantic love as masculine, because only now are men gradually displacing women as the people who take romantic love seriously.

Alas, the success of any effort by straight men to actualize their fantasies about "true love" and "living happily after" requires that they get women to buy into them as well. And that, as we have discussed, increasingly goes against the material, psychological, and emotional needs of women, which is why their faith in such fantasies is declining. That does not bode well for would-be masculine romantics, as it means their love ambitions are likely to be thwarted. When the trend toward unfulfilled masculine romanticism is combined with the continued emphasis on socializing boys into a warrior model of manhood, in which the only emotion deemed manly is anger, the result is a recipe for a dangerous masculinity cocktail.

That danger is exacerbated by another factor: in war-reliant societies manliness is open-ended, so a man can never feel completely secure about it. As an ideal that is inherently impossible to fully and finally realize, manliness is never a settled matter. Hence the demands of manliness are experienced by boys and men as making them continually vulnerable to feelings of inadequacy, aggravated by ubiquitous insults coming from other males. That produces insecurity, anxiety, and fear, which generally cannot be expressed by tears because crying is unmasculine. If a boy seeks emotional nurturance from men, the best response he is likely to get is something like the advice Coach Eric Taylor gives to a member of his high school football team in the television series *Friday Night Lights:* "Suck it up—that's what being a man is."[8]

That's a real problem in militaristic cultures, where masculinity is the most crucial dimension of a boy's or man's identity, and the impossible demands of masculinity mean that repeated failures to be unequivocally a "real man" are inevitable. Because of that inescapable sense of failure, right at the heart of one's identity, boys and men regularly experience a profound need to turn to somebody who can offer comfort and reassurance. It is understandable why a man would be reluctant to seek that from another male, and not just because of fear of an insult that would make his insecurity even worse. In war-reliant cultures an emotional disability is socialized into boys that results in men being more challenged than women at offering emotional comfort. Boys are socialized to be emotionally "tough," for that is the most crucial capability of the warrior, as it enables the warrior to suppress the capacity to care about the suffering of others, as well as himself—that's why crying is inconsistent with warrior masculinity. In militaristic cultures, then, men who are good at empathy and emotional nurturance are likely to be the exception, not the rule.

So if a man wants emotional nurturance, or even to cry, better that he shed his tears in front of his mother or sister or aunt or grandmother, where he may get a hug of reassurance and encouragement to open up and talk about the ways in which he feels vulnerable. Most boys grow up understanding that it is better to cry in front of a woman than to cry in front of a man. Also, girls and women in militaristic cultures tend to be socialized to have an amplified capacity to care about the suffering of others.

Now we are in a better position to understand the rise in masculine romanticism. For an adult heterosexual male in need of emotional nurturance, but perhaps without available female relatives with that skill, the traditional model of romantic love, along with its associated fantasy about living happily ever after might seem to be a great idea. After all, it does feature a female lover who will unconditionally devote herself to him, which is enticing beyond the sex and cookies, for "unconditionally" surely must mean her devotion will not waver even if he cries or otherwise needs emotional nurturance. That traditional model of heterosexual love offers him the masculinity boost that comes from having a male-dominant, female-subordinate relationship, plus he's got a presumed source of emotional sustenance to help him deal with his inevitable failures at being maximally masculine in other departments, like being fearful or anxious, being unable to violently dominate other men in war or elsewhere, or being unable to get a good enough job to be a good provider.

Of course, all those advantages for men have always been there, at least theoretically, in the traditional model of heterosexual love as described by Nietzsche in the passage we have discussed throughout this book, that is, male dominant and female subordinate love. What is happening only now is a growing realization of men that the fantasies about true love and living happily ever after, which have long been associated with heterosexual romance, offer a specific advantage for contemporary men, who are immensely challenged by the dramatic changes occurring in the lives of women. Here is the advantage: if a straight man can persuade a woman to buy into the fantasies of true love and living happily ever after, that might serve to draw her into a traditional heterosexual relationship or to dissuade her from escaping one. That is an advantage, particularly when it is becoming more and more difficult for women not to notice that traditional romantic love does not actually serve their interests.

A man who adopts the masculine romanticism strategy faces numerous obstacles. The most obvious one is the challenge of finding a woman who wants to be not only his sex slave but also his surrogate mother. But suppose the miracle happens and his OK Cupid profile or Craigslist ad produces a long queue of candidates at his door, all with a reactionary attachment to traditional romanticism and subordinate femininity (perhaps his profile or ad should target fans of Christina Dodd's novels?),[9] from whom he chooses the absolute best and most old-fashioned of them all, and he and she have so fallen in love that he's now ready for the happily ever after part.

Congratulations to our lucky guy for such a wonderful demonstration of faith in fantasies about romantic love. Alas, Simone de Beauvoir has some unfortunate news for him regarding that anticipated happily-ever-after phase. But bad news can always wait—how about a little romantic diversion first? Let's travel south of the border to Mexico City. Lucy Williamson, host of a recent BBC radio documentary called "Family Matters, Episode 2—Mexico"[10] is our guide: "Dusk on a warm spring evening in Mexico City can be irresistibly romantic, and if the old Spanish style buildings rising behind the palm trees don't get you in the mood, try coming here to Garibaldi Square where Mariachi groups in black and silver sombreros sing age-old songs of how boy meets girl, falls in love, gets married. Here with a little tequila inside you it's easy to embrace the time-honored ideas about love and family. It's what the young couples cuddling to the music say they want." Alas, says Williamson, those ideas are "beginning to look as dated as the musicians' eighteenth-century costumes." Outside Mexico City's Central Divorce Court, she meets nineteen-year-old Deanna, who is one of about a hundred young women waiting to file for divorce, sitting on the benches outside the court—although there are not enough seats for them all, so divorce court has become SRO. Asked what she had expected marriage to be like, Deanna responds: "I expected it to be like it was before we were married when we were boyfriend and girlfriend, when there was a lot of attraction, a lot of chemistry between us, but it wasn't like that. He started spending much more time with his friends than with me, and we began to fight. I thought marriage would be for life. But I feel fine about it. Why stay with somebody if the relationship is not working?" Good question. But why are so many relationships not working?

Here is where Beauvoir is helpful. First of all, she quotes the passage from Nietzsche that we have discussed in previous chapters, which is in a section he titled "How Each Sex Has Its Prejudice About Love."[11] Then she takes its perspicacity a couple of steps further, showing how it explains the following: "Men have found it possible to be passionate lovers at certain times in their lives, but there is not one of them who could be called 'a great lover.'" The reason is precisely that their desire is to possess a woman, rather than to devote themselves to loving her. As Beauvoir says, "The beloved woman is only one value among others."[12] That is, the man has his career, his hobbies, and of course his other possessions—and, besides, if a beloved woman were to be at the center of his life, if he were to be utterly devoted to her, well, as Nietzsche says, he would not be a "real man." Deanna's case is particularly instructive here. She says her new husband started spending a lot more time with his friends than with her. We can easily imagine that if he were to resist his male friends' pressures to hang out with them so that he could spend more time with his wife, they would signify his diminished masculinity by calling him "whipped."

To be a truly great lover, I think Beauvoir is suggesting, would require a man to have a devotion to his beloved so strong that it would be inconsistent with the male-dominant/female-subordinate model of love described by Nietzsche. That is why Nietzsche says a man who has that degree of devotion is not a real man— in the traditional model of love such devotion is characteristic of precisely what a man is not: a woman. Beauvoir helps us see that when a man places his faith in the traditional model of heterosexual love by trying to exert dominance over "his" woman, he becomes disabled as a loving partner. His effort to compensate by adding into the mix a faith in the fantasies of true love and living happily ever after only offers the prospect of prolonging the tragedy.

"Before we were married," Deanna says, "when we were boyfriend and girlfriend, there was a lot of attraction, a lot of chemistry between us." Here, again, Beauvoir is helpful, offering further insight into why that chemistry tends eventually to evaporate in heterosexual relationships based on the traditional male-dominant/female-subordinate model.

According to Beauvoir, in a society that is premised on male dominance (a pattern that prevails among war-reliant cultures), a woman is "habituated in seeing in him a superb being whom she cannot possibly equal," and so she will "dream of transcending her being toward one of these superior beings, of amalgamating herself with the sovereign subject." This situation is intensified by her economic dependence, which is characteristic of such societies.[13] Hence, Beauvoir continues, "she chooses to desire her enslavement so ardently that it will seem to her the expression of her liberty." To borrow the title of Christina Dodd's book discussed earlier, she wants to be "taken by the prince." When Beauvoir adds, "Love becomes for her a religion," we are further reminded of the centrality in romantic love of faith—in both the culturally programmed model of love and in her male lover.

A central doctrine in that religion of love is that masculinity is superior to femininity, and that it is only through femininity that a woman can attain some share in the superior status of masculinity. So for the adolescent girl who has resigned herself to not having the superior status accorded to males, Beauvoir says, she "seeks to share in their masculinity by having one of them in love with her." The female romantic quest is for a lover "to represent the essence of manhood."[14] It is important to note, given that masculinity in militaristic cultures is inherently hierarchical, with men constantly judging each other's masculinity quotient, that it is primarily men, not women, who define the essence of manhood.

The aspiration of a girl or woman to share in a man's masculinity by having him in love with her represents an inherently impossible demand. For a woman who wants this traditional kind of love, which requires her to serve a man, the man had better be worth it. And so she puts him on a pedestal, a masculinity pedestal, and strives to keep him on that pedestal. According to Beauvoir,

> The woman in love tries to see with his eyes; she reads the books he reads, prefers the pictures and music he prefers; she is interested . . . in the ideas that come from him; she adopts his friendships, his enmities, his opinions; when she questions herself, it is his reply she tries to hear. . . . She lets her own world collapse in contingence, for she really lives in his.

> The supreme happiness of the woman in love is to be recognized by the loved man as a part of himself; when he says "we," she is associated and identified with him, she shares his prestige . . . she never tires of repeating—even to excess—this delectable "we."[15]

That is a really big investment for a woman to make. And it is an ill-fated investment. "This glorious felicity rarely lasts," Beauvoir says, for "no man really is God."[16] Hence, she adds: "Familiarity is often sufficient to destroy his prestige."[17]

The problem is twofold. First, as previously noted, manhood is a cultural ideal that cannot be finally and unequivocally realized by any man. It is "The Big Impossible," as the traditional Fox tribe of Iowa put it.[18] A man's masculinity in militaristic cultures is always subject to questioning by other men, as well as by women (who draw on the masculinity standards that have been defined by men). Thus no man can live up fully and consistently to the expectations of a woman whose faith in him is premised on her investment in both the cultural ideal of masculinity and the traditional, romantic model of heterosexual love. And, second, to the extent that she has subordinated herself to a male lover, and to the extent she has devoted her life to him, she is so invested in him that her expectations of his manliness are even higher than those of other men, including the men from whom he is likely to seek manly affirmation—friends, brothers, coworkers, etc. Her devotion makes her status dependent upon his status, and thus her self-esteem becomes parasitic on his masculinity—which is parasitic on other men's affirmations.

Because it is always subject to question and doubt, masculinity is inherently unstable, and masculine perfection is forever out of reach. A man's masculinity quotient fluctuates throughout his life, throughout the day, sometimes even from minute to minute. At any instant he may display a hint of fear, or be revealed as sexually inadequate, or suffer a setback at work—maybe even losing his job so that he can no longer be a provider. Or he may suffer an illness or injury so that he can no longer play the protector role. Or he may experience sexual impotency, or discover a diminished sperm count, so that he can no longer play the procreator role. Sooner or later, one way or another, every man's status as a "real man" will be revealed, for an instant or forever, as a facade.

When a man's inevitable fall off the masculinity pedestal occurs, the woman who has devoted herself to him may struggle to put him back on it. She may use taunts of the sort men use with each other, suggesting his effeminacy (calling him an "old lady" or a "little bitch"), thereby relying on the misogyny that is inherent in such taunts (see chapter 3). But taunts and teasing cannot have the desired result; they create a double bind for the man. Suppose he does start acting more masculine; in that case he owes his masculinity to the pressure from her, so his manhood has become dependent on a woman. That not only in itself undermines his manliness, it pulls back the curtain on both the artificiality of the manly ideal and his quixotic pursuit of it—which makes him seem less manly, and even ridiculous. Or suppose he rebels against his culture and resists its demand that he put on a more convincing masculine act. In that case each new taunt reinforces the previous ones, with the accumulation of taunts bringing his masculinity quotient further and further down.

It's a lose-lose situation. The more effort a woman puts into making a man act more masculine, the more his masculinity is undermined, and therefore all of her efforts redound negatively to her own status, as a woman who has made a life choice to invest herself not just in this male person, but in his masculinity—on the basis of a faith in the whole fantasy structure of the traditional model of heterosexual love.

The salience of the element of choice becomes more apparent when Beauvoir contrasts a woman's relationship with her father to a heterosexual erotic partnership. Her father, too, will inevitably fall from the masculinity pedestal, momentarily or forever. In both cases, father and husband, her status or even her very survival may make her dependent on the man. But she has not chosen her father, and while in the traditional family model she may be subordinate to him, that is not because of her choice. In contrast, when she chooses to enter into a heterosexual erotic relationship with a particular man, and to unconditionally devote herself to him, and to be possessed by him, her status becomes dependent on his masculinity precisely because she has chosen him.

When Deanna says that the "chemistry" has been lost between her husband and herself after six months of marriage, we now have a possible explanation, involving the inevitable fluctuation, or even steady decline, in the man's masculinity. While that is not the only conceivable explanation, one would expect it to be increasingly relevant in a world where masculinity is becoming more and more confusing. In many countries around the world there is a widespread decline in societal needs for men to be singled out for service as providers, procreators, or warriors, and when those roles are subtracted from masculinity, as it has traditionally been defined in war-reliant cultures, there is not much left. Further, in many societies there are way too many young men who are either unwilling or unable to take on the challenges of productive work lives, and who are instead pursuing masculinity by taking on the warrior role, as with gangs fighting each other in absurd battles over turf, or in individual fights to prove their brutality and toughness to each other and to themselves, or by taking guns to schools or shopping malls or churches to kill as many people as possible.

Mexican psychologist Vidal Schmill, who is interviewed in the "Family Matters" documentary, says, "Mexican men haven't caught up with modern realities."[19] He explains that the role of women in society has changed dramatically, with women far more likely to work, and to work specifically in what had been exclusively male jobs. Mexican women are increasingly likely to be taken seriously, even in bullfighting and wrestling. Men, he says, have not been changing in response to the changes for women. But I would ask this: Why would heterosexually inclined men, in Mexico or anywhere else, change if the only way for them to be erotically or romantically attractive to women is to demonstrate machismo? What I am getting at is that men cling to what vestiges of masculinity remain, what little is left that distinguishes manliness from womanliness. With the provider role no longer being uniquely masculine, and with a greatly diminished need for a manly role in actual procreation,[20] the remainder of masculinity primarily consists of its warrior elements. And so increasingly that is the only avenue open to men to prove their masculinity, and, in the absence of some substantial cultural shift, their prospects for heterosexual sex and love continue to rely on that proof.

I'm guessing that the hundred women lined up with Deanna outside the divorce court now have doubts about the kind of traditional romantic love that calls for them to unconditionally devote themselves to a man with no job who spends every day hanging out with his friends. Maybe their experience with marriage is giving them second thoughts about investing themselves in a man and his masculine status.

In Mexico and elsewhere, it appears that women, as I have suggested, may be losing their faith in the culturally programmed model of heterosexual love faster than men are. To see more evidence of that, let's turn our attention to American college campuses, where men are finding themselves in a quandary.

Throughout their lives, young men in war-reliant societies are culturally programmed to see sexual activity as central to establishing their manhood. And the urgency of fulfilling that imperative is powerfully reinforced by a hormonal torrent coursing through their bloodstream. Getting laid is number one on their to-do list. That should not be hard to accomplish, according to all the signals they are getting. Everywhere they turn, there are images of beautiful, seductive women—the line between pornography and popular culture, especially in advertising, has virtually disappeared. But never mind images—they are surrounded by actual women, too.

So here's the situation: Straight college men urgently want sex, they are surrounded by images giving them the message that women want sex just as urgently, and maybe also they perceive the attire of the women in their classes as confirming that message—what could be the problem? Well, news flash: it turns out that most women don't actually want to have sex with most men! All those signals men are getting, as they themselves are interpreting them, turn out to be false signals.

Those false, or falsely interpreted, signals become an even greater problem when we consider that straight men are increasingly challenged by the project of making themselves as appealing to the women as the women are to them. For example, one of the factors in earlier times that made men attractive to straight women is becoming much less important. The joke on campuses used to be that women were there to earn "MRS degrees," i.e., that they were in college only to snag a husband. And husband candidates were evaluated on the basis of their prospects as providers for a woman and her children. Now, as we have considered previously, college women plan to have their own careers, and while most hope to partner up with a second wage earner, the provider role is no longer exclusively male. Increasingly, demonstrating potential as a provider is seen as attractive for a partner of *either* sex—so the display of great potential as a provider is no longer such an important part of masculinity.

That may help explain why boys and men may be less motivated to get the education that could help them become better providers—the pursuit of masculinity is a declining source of pressure to get an education and a good job. We discussed indicators of that diminished motivation early on in this chapter: the majority of college applicants and college graduates are now female, women are more likely than men to take their studies seriously, and men are more likely than women to drop out of both college and high school.[21] None of this comparatively lesser academic commitment should be surprising, given that the provider role has virtually disappeared as one of the three crucial components of masculinity. Getting a good education and getting a good job are less important as pillars of what it means to "become a man."

That change was exacerbated by the 2008 recession, which raised the overall unemployment rate to about 9 percent, making jobs substantially less available to men. And, early on, the recession hit men even harder than women. Before the recession there was virtually no gap in the unemployment rate for men and women, but by June 2010 the gap was about 2 percent.[22] That's one reason fewer men have jobs now than in the 1950s. About 96 percent of American men in the age range twenty-five to fifty-four worked in 1954, and during the 1950s and 1960s the number of men working never fell below 91 percent.[23] Now the number of men in that age range who are working is only 80 percent.[24]

So the diminished significance of the provider role in defining masculinity has resulted partly because of structural economic factors that have substantially increased the difficulty of being a successful provider. But, as we have noted, its decline as a factor in masculinity is also because we are no longer culturally programmed to view the provider role as exclusively male, and this declining significance of the provider role in masculine identity diminishes the ambition of men to be good providers and to pursue education that can help them as providers.

It is also the case that far fewer college men are trying to prove their manhood through an even more salient path in war-reliant cultures, by signing up for combat service as a warrior. That's not to say, though, that they are not being culturally programmed in the warrior direction. The boys' section of a toy store is where one finds the toy guns, toy swords, toy uniforms, and other toy military gear. Eventually most boys stop playing with toy guns, except maybe paintball guns, and either they play with real guns or they get their inner warrior on through video games. That has an interesting implication for their heterosexual sex prospects, however. Although women in my classes report that they are still turned on by men in military uniforms, they laugh when I ask if they are turned on by a guy who is really good at playing combat video games like Call of Duty or Battlefield. Turns out virtual warriors are not nearly as sexy as real warriors.

So, on the contemporary campus heterosexuality scene, guys are far less likely than in the past to attract women on the basis of success in either the provider or the warrior role, in large measure because guys are less likely actually to be engaged by, and in, those roles. Sure, they have a culturally programmed faith in those elements of traditional masculinity in the abstract, in the image of the masculine warrior or in the fantasy of being wealthy, but their faith is not strong enough to lead to the actual exertion that is requisite for either role.

The changes in men's lives with regard to the third of the three main dimensions of masculinity in militaristic cultures, sometimes called the procreator role (but which is really about having lots of sex) are even more complicated. In today's world there is a greatly diminished need in most societies for actual procreation. Further, with the advent of readily available contraception, and a growing moral consensus in its favor, sex and procreation have been largely separated, so that for a man to have lots of sex no longer necessarily serves the need specific to a militaristic society for maximum procreation.

But, unlike the warrior and provider roles, the procreator role has a powerful biological foundation that is often called "the sex drive." That biological force is greatly amplified culturally in societies that traditionally have been war-reliant, as a consequence of the associated procreative pressures. Even in societies that no longer have those pro-creative pressures, there is a cultural inertia of competitiveness among men regarding sexual activity, even though it no longer makes sense. Most young men continue to have faith in the culturally programmed notion of sexual promiscuity as a kind of masculine competition.

Thus on college campuses sexually "scoring" continues to be supremely important as a way to display masculinity. A "high scorer" does not necessarily gain points with heterosexual women, but that is not the point. The competition among young men is primarily for an audience that itself consists of young men.

One of the challenges men face in that competition is the fact that the sexual activity that advances a guy's standing in this competition must be heterosexual. And while a man's great ambition to be a wealthy pro-vider or an effective warrior may attract the admiration of both women and men, a man's ambition to have a lot of sex does not excite similar admiration. A straight guy who overtly appears to intensely crave sex all the time, and who appears to exert copious amounts of time and energy to get sex, is not sexy—rather, he is more likely to be seen as a bit creepy. So, when all this is put together, the result is a growing number of young men who are either not pursuing the traditional paths to manhood and masculinity or are pursuing them only virtually. In either case, this presents us with a crisis in the heart of heterosexuality. We still culturally program women to strongly prefer heterosexuality, and we continue to place a high premium on masculinity and femininity as the primary markers of viable heterosexual partners. But with a growing number of men withdrawing from the roles that contribute to masculinity, or playing those roles only virtually, in the words of conservative columnist David Brooks, "These men will find it hard to attract spouses."[25] Looking at it from the other side of the heterosexual divide, the number of viable male candidates for women to be heterosexual with is shrinking.

Because we are talking about patterns that are continuing to develop, the forecast would seem to call for growing numbers of frustrated straight men and straight women. But the problem is far, far worse than that, especially if we focus on those straight men. After David Brooks mentions that men without jobs will find it hard to attract female partners, while he is talking only about the employment problem, he follows that with a highly suggestive assertion that hints vaguely at broader dangers: "Many will pick up habits that have a corrosive cultural influence on those around them."[26] Examples of what that sentence might mean, regardless of what Brooks himself intended, are readily available. I mentioned earlier that when men's thwarted romantic and sexual ambitions are combined with anger, which is the one emotion that militaristic cultures deem masculine, that is a recipe for a "dangerous masculinity cocktail."

Let's look at some examples of that cocktail, particularly from the realms of virtual masculinity, and, just to be clear, virtual *heterosexual* masculinity. It is also important to keep in mind that this mixture of thwarted romantic ambition and anger is more likely to be found in some straight boys and men than in others. Presumably the level of both anger and actual peril would rise in correlation with the degree that a boy or man has been culturally infused with the qualities of warrior masculinity, particularly the capacity to suppress empathy, the urge to dominate, and a proclivity for violence.

First, consider the fourth installment of the hugely popular video game series, Grand Theft Auto. On its very first day on the market, GTA IV: The Ladies of Liberty City: Very Bad Things, set a record by selling 2.5 million units in North America.[27] Some of the scenes from a video montage of the game are described by Matt Ezzell:

> The Ladies of Liberty City opened with graphic images of women stripping, pole-dancing, and giving the protagonist [Niko] a lapdance. The next scene showed Niko shooting a woman in the middle of the street. It went on to show Niko picking up prostitutes. . . .
>
> He approaches one woman who says, "I'll suck your cock real nice." "Get in," he replies, before driving her to a baseball field. Once parked, he says, "You get what you pay for, right?" The woman sits on his lap. As they bounce up and down, the woman squeals, "Fuck the shit out of it! Yeah, you nasty fucker!" They finish, and Niko says, "Life is strange, don't you think?" The woman gets out of the car and walks away. As she does, Niko pulls out a gun and shoots her several times. You can hear her scream as Niko says, "Stay down or I will finish you off!" She does not get up.[28]

Here we have an example of men's traditional disdain for a woman who is not virtuous—with virtue understood to mean either not sexually active at all or sexual exclusively with a man who possesses her. In militaristic cultures, for men to torture and kill unvirtuous women is generally considered either acceptable or not nearly as objectionable as doing those things to virtuous women. In the case of Grand Theft Auto IV, the victim is a prostitute, which would put her among the most unvirtuous of women.

So the basic attitudes in this video game scenario are quite traditional and fit within the notions of heterosexuality and gender that typify war-reliant cultures. However, in such cultures it is unusual for men to go out of their way to put themselves into situations where they torture or kill an unvirtuous woman. It is also unusual for men who do something like that to acknowledge enjoying it as opposed to claiming it is done because of religious or familial duty. So what makes Grand Theft Auto IV interesting is that large numbers of boys and young men in contemporary militaristic societies (1) typically pay money for the game, (2) vent their misogynistic rage by vicariously exploiting a woman sexually and then killing her, and (3) acknowledge that they enjoy that. There is a lot of controversy over whether what happens in that realm of virtual masculinity spills over into the real world, where actual men interact with actual women. Without jumping into that thicket, let me just say that it is impossible for me to imagine a person who enjoys virtual misogyny but who does not also harbor a substantial amount of anger toward actual women.

For a second, even clearer, example of what can happen in the realm of virtual masculinity when anger gets mixed with thwarted sexual ambition, let's turn our attention to a new kind of pornography that has become popular among college men. The role of pornography in the lives of boys and men has been changing in recent years, in correlation with the other changes in gender, love, and sex that we have explored. Prior to these recent developments (and still for many men today), the primary purpose of pornography was to serve as an aid to masturbation. It was a way for men to have imaginary sex with the models in photographs or videos, with female models for straight men and male models for gay men.

But as pornographic videos targeted at straight men have become more and more "hardcore," where hardcore typically means featuring abuse, degradation, or overt exploitation of women, there has been a trend on college campuses in particular toward men—primarily white men[29]—enjoying pornography in groups. That is the case with the "gonzo porn" that was discussed in chapter 3, and it is also the case with what could be called *bangbus* porn, after the name of one of the websites sites that serve it up. So far as I have been able to ascertain, the point of watching gonzo porn or bangbus porn in groups is not for straight men to masturbate together. Nor is the point primarily for a group of straight men to have an opportunity to share an erotic experience with each other. Rather, the primary point with both these new genres of pornography is less about having a sexual experience and more about something else, as aptly described by Michael Kimmel in his book, *Guyland:* "The sexual fantasies of many young men become more revenge fantasies than erotic ones—revenge for the fact that most of them don't feel they get as much sex as they think they are supposed to get—or as they think everyone else is getting. The ubiquity of pornography in Guyland is . . . also about guys' anger at women for withholding what they, guys, believe is their due: sex" (175). Of course, for most women to withhold sex from most men is not new, but the factors we have explored throughout this chapter help us understand why that withholding might be on the rise, relative to centuries past.

As far as "just sex" is concerned, however, a counterdevelopment is the hookup culture that has purportedly become prevalent on college campuses, which substantially increases the apparent availability of sex. I say "purportedly" and "apparent" because (1) the data on hookup culture is sometimes unreliable, unclear, or otherwise problematic, and (2) the expression "hooking up" can refer to a wide range of behaviors, from just hanging out as a couple, to "playing around," to coitus. When a man reports he and a woman hooked up, he is hoping that his male friends will think he had sex, even if the reality was far less than that. On the other hand, when a woman who actually had sex with a guy reports to her female friends that she hooked up with him, she may be hoping that they think she means something less than sex.

For both women and men, a general de-linking of sex and love is integral to the phenomenon of hooking up. In the past a woman who acquiesced to a man's urging to have sex typically would have been hoping that her "gift" would be reciprocated with an ongoing relationship, or at least a phone call the next day. But, in the context of the hookup culture, women who don't withhold sex are likely to withhold the prospect of a relationship or love. That obviously fits with the pattern we have discussed throughout this chapter, and here again we can see an absence of symmetry or coordination between the sexes, with men remaining stuck in the notions of male sex-entitlement and love-entitlement that are integral to the traditional culturally programmed ideas about heterosexual love and sex, as well as becoming more invested in fantasies about true love and living happily ever after. Those presumed male entitlements that derive from traditional male-dominant and female-subordinate eroticism collide head-on with the love-withholding, and sometimes sex-withholding, of women who are finding fewer and fewer men who are worthy partners, and who are finding that the culture or phenomenon of hooking up actually facilitates that withholding, especially of love.

The response of many men to that collision is reflected in *bangbus* porn, which Michael Kimmel describes as follows:

> On sites such as slutbus.com, bangbus.com, and bangboat.com, a couple of young guys who appear to be in their early twenties go cruising in a minivan (or boat) with a video camera looking for young women. They offer the women a ride, and once she gets in the van, they offer her money, typically $100, to take off her clothes. Gradually, the guys up the ante until she agrees to have sex for money. The rest of the video shows her having sex with several guys in the van. When it's over, and the woman gets out, one of the men leans out with a wad of bills. But just as she reaches for the money, the driver revs the engine and the van peels off, leaving her running after it, angry and frustrated that she's been both "had" and "taken." The guys in the van have a good laugh at how "stupid those bitches are." (176)

The women in these videos look like they could be college students, and sometimes are even portrayed going to classes, which no doubt contributes to the feelings of revenge the standard bangbus plot offers to college men. One guy interviewed by Kimmel said, "Those girls think they are so hot and all stuck up, and for a couple of hundred, they'll do it doggy-style." A student at the University of Massachusetts said he shares a website membership with his friends so they can watch together. He says, "We're all like 'oh, bang that bitch!' and 'fuck that little ho.' And they're like college girls! It's like so cool."

A student at the University of Georgia explains why he likes a similar genre of pornography: "I love where these stuck-up college bitches are like drunk and finally just give head to like 20 guys and get fucked by the whole football team and all. It's like they're always walking around campus in their little shorts and you can see their shaved pussies sometimes, but they think they are like, way too hot for me. But then these films, man, they're like these same bitches, and they finally get what's coming to them" (182–83). Presumably men who have that sort of response after watching these videos were already strongly inclined toward the traditional model of male-dominant and female-subordinate heterosexual eroticism, as well as the misogyny that is inherent in that model—otherwise they would not enjoy the videos so much. But when they are introduced to these new erotic fantasies in the context of male-bonding groups, through the medium of what purport to be "real life" documentaries, it is hard to see how their misogynistic sexual preferences could fail to be reinforced by the experience.

Of the men Kimmel interviewed about bangbus porn, about half knew about the sites and had been to them. Based on his interviews, Kimmel concludes: "We . . . learn that the guys think that after using these women for sex, it's funny to humiliate them by not paying them. All women are basically whores and will have sex if the price is right. But since they are whores anyway, why pay them? Better to just peel out and leave them angry too" (177). So in the scene from Grand Theft Auto IV discussed previously, young men get the notion that prostitutes deserve to be tortured and shot, and they get an opportunity, virtually, to experience doing that as satisfying, even enjoyable. Bangbus porn confirms, in their minds, that "all women are basically whores."

When they look around the classroom and see women who are dressed in ways that they view as deliberately provocative, what are they thinking? To the extent that they have been subjected to these new forms of cultural programming about women, bangbus porn and gonzo porn, whatever misogyny had already been instilled in them as part of traditional notions of masculinity and male-dominant/female-subordinate heterosexuality is ratcheted up to new levels of rage and resentment.

It should also be noted that those men don't just party with other men. In fact, most parties on most campuses are given by men, who make every effort to maximize the number of women at any party not devoted to misogynistic porn. It is also men who typically supply the alcohol at parties. According to sociologist Kimmel, "the most treacherous time for a college woman is when she is at a party, drinking, with people she thinks she knows" (223). Sexual assault at parties has become so common that there is now a term for it commonly used by journalists, scholars, and the U.S. Department of Justice: "party rape." A report by the DOJ describes party rape as a rape that "occurs at an off-campus house or on- or off-campus fraternity and involves . . . plying a woman with alcohol or targeting an intoxicated woman" (223). This is one of the reasons why college women are at greater risk of sexual assault than both women in the general population and women in general who are of a similar age.[30] Party rape reflects a range of factors that contribute to misogyny on campus, and gonzo porn and bangbus porn are among those factors.

Now I would guess that any man who is a fan of bangbus or gonzo pornography is not likely to provide that information to a woman he wants to have sex with, and is even less likely to provide it to a woman with whom he thinks he is falling in love. Most men know that they must at least maintain the appearance of being respectful and courteous toward women. So it may be difficult for women to know which men are into hyper-misogynistic porn and which are not. There are, however, conversational strategies women can use to get men to share their ideas about gender, love, and sex. So if a man is a fan of these genres of porn, there is at least some hope that his misogynistic sentiments, or at least hints of them, can be revealed.

For straight women, just to be aware of bangbus porn and gonzo porn may make it more likely that they will put the effort into trying to uncover misogyny among prospective male partners. Alas, that further shrinks the pool of viable partners for straight women. And no doubt the pool would be shrunk even more if straight women were to observe groups of men guffawing and raging together as they watch the women in pornography and video games get degraded, abused, and subjected to either virtual or actual violence.

What are straight women to do, in the face of a declining ratio of men to women opting to go to college, and with those men who do enter college turning ever more to virtual masculinity, virtual eroticism, and misogynistic entertainment? How can straight women respond to the fact that the pool of worthy male partners is shrinking? Some may turn to hooking up in an effort to fulfill the heterosexual imperative. Some may look for ways to enhance their competitiveness with other women for the diminishing supply of worthy men, and if that doesn't attract one of those men, at least it may impress other women. Hooking up allows fulfillment of the desire for heterosexual erotic experiences without commitment to the kind of traditional romantic relationship that women increasingly perceive not to be in their interest, and without investing themselves and their self-esteem in a man who is not worth it. All in all, these patterns signal that the flame of women's faith in fantasies about heterosexual romantic love may be flickering a bit.

Other women are giving up heterosexuality—to one extent or another, or even altogether. They are finding other ways to attain sexual pleasure, fulfilling human relationships, and life satisfaction. Some are choosing solitude, some are discovering that they don't have to be confined to a heterosexual orientation, and some are exploring alternative ways of sexually and socially relating to other people. The changing material conditions of contemporary life and the gradual relaxation of culturally programmed ideals are opening up new possibilities for women to see that a fulfilling life does not require traditional heterosexuality.[31] Even if what appears to be a growing level of misogyny among men is actually just its greater visibility, it is easy to understand why growing numbers of women might be losing interest in erotic relationships with men.

For a more optimistic vision of the future of heterosexuality, there is this consideration: To paraphrase Simone de Beauvoir, men are made, not born. It is not being genetically male, or having a complete set of male gonads that makes a man an unworthy partner for a woman. I'm not saying that biology is altogether irrelevant, but biology does not make a man misogynistic. Rather, war-reliant societies, for reasons that I have explained in other chapters, culturally program boys and men to be misogynistic. If we want erotic relationships between women and men to work, we can do that only by doing away with that cultural programming. That's a monumental task, and it can only be accomplished gradually. In the meantime, what is needed is also a big challenge: helping boys and men to become liberated from the misogynistic cultural programming to which they have been subjected.

It is only by taking on those challenges that we can ever get to a place where we don't need faith to support fantasies about love, and where we don't need fantasies to trick ourselves into getting into, and staying in, relationships. We need the kind of philosophy that can uncover our cultural programming about gender and love and sexuality so that we can see the myths promulgated by that programming. Only then can we imagine a future in which love is premised not on faith in culturally programmed fantasies, but rather on mutually shared joy, fulfillment, devotion, and pleasure.

6

GENDER TERRORISM, GENDER SACRIFICE
GETTING BEYOND ZERO-SUM HETEROSEXUALITY

> I didn't just screw Ho Chi Minh. I cut his pecker off.
> —Lyndon Johnson, after bombing North Vietnam, 1966

The cultural programming that produces a gender binary, dividing human beings into two "opposite sexes," results in antagonism between men and women. But the damage does not end there. There are also harms that are specific to each gender. There are harms men experience solely because they are men, such as the expectation that they be willing to sacrifice their lives, limbs, and minds in pursuit of masculinity defined by the warrior ideal. And there are harms women experience solely because they are women, such as discrimination, harassment, violence and subordination of their own needs to the needs of the men and children in their lives.

In this chapter, we'll look at how amelioration of the harms that are specific to men is interwoven with amelioration of the harms that are specific to women, and vice versa, which will allow us to see that gender liberation is not the zero-sum game it is often assumed to be, where gains for women imply losses for men, and gains for men imply losses for women. Instead, for either men or women to "win," they both must win. If that is so, then for individual men and women to flourish in their personal lives would require escape from the notion that relations between men and women comprise a zero-sum gender game.

Most of the critical and imaginative thinking about gender over the past several decades has come from feminist theorists, and their insights are crucial to this project of getting men and women out of the zero-sum gender game. However, there is an antifeminist named Warren Farrell whose heartfelt concern about male victimization is also helpful. Now it should be noted that there are some men today who seem rather quick to assume the mantle of victimhood in relation to individual women or in relation to certain categories of women that seem threatening to them. Farrell himself does not always seem free of such aggrieved posturing; nonetheless he directs our attention to some real harms some men experience just because they are men that mostly go unnoticed.

Many of the harms to men discussed by Farrell are rooted in what I have described as the warrior ideal of masculinity. The image of the warrior evokes not only combat and killing but also getting killed. Not surprisingly, to the extent that a society associates masculinity with war, there tends to be a more general embrace of behavioral patterns in which men risk life and limb, as well as a widespread understanding that men's lives are more expendable than women's lives. Women's lives in militaristic societies are viewed as expendable—in the sense of risking life and limb—mostly in the context of pregnancy and childbirth. The expendability of women's lives is in the service of procreation, so ideals of womanhood tend to revolve around defining women as breeders,[1] not fighters. In a nutshell, as Farrell says, "Women expected to risk life in childbirth; men expected to risk life in war." He proposes the goal of "fewer women killed in childbirth; fewer men killed in war."[2] I find it curious that antifeminist Farrell doesn't realize that virtually all feminists would sign on to that goal (including myself in an article published ten years prior to Farrell's statement of that goal).[3]

Farrell claims that singling out men for service in combat is a form of sexist discrimination against men and further claims that feminists bear some responsibility for that sexism because they did not protest the military policy that excluded women from combat prior to 2013.

Farrell is mistaken about the latter point—feminists quite vigorously protested the exclusion of women from combat roles, because that policy had the effect of obstructing the career advancement of female soldiers. Regardless, there is a much better explanation than anti-male sexism for the widespread pattern in militaristic societies of assigning the role of warrior only to men. If a lot of men get killed, that has far less effect on replenishing the population than if a lot of women get killed. So members of the biologically more expendable sex, males, are assigned the task of combat where they might die, while the females are assigned the roles of breeding (for which they are uniquely qualified) and nurturing children (a role that a male could also do, but less well to the extent that he has internalized the values of warrior masculinity).

Given this biological underpinning of the differential gender role assignments in militaristic societies, it makes no sense for Farrell to blame feminists or women for the danger, suffering, and death faced by men who serve as warriors. Actually, the most effective way to ease the burden of combat on men would not be to spread the burden of combat to women, but rather to diminish a society's reliance on war, something most feminists have strongly advocated.

Farrell quite vividly and passionately describes the cultural project of getting men and boys to pursue the inherently sacrificial ideal of warrior masculinity. In particular, he has a harshly critical perspective on the use of violent sports to instill in boys and men the qualities of the warrior, saying, "We are more than blind to violence against men: We reward it. We call it football, rugby, ice hockey, boxing, boot camp, rodeos, car racing."[4] Ratcheting up the sarcasm, he suggests that "male child abuse might be fun to watch, but taxpayers should not be required to pay for it."[5] Strong words indeed, which he backs up with this elaboration:

> Men's exposure to violence is . . . supported . . . by socialization, schol-
> arship incentive, and the education system (telling men who are best
> at bashing their heads against 11 other men that they have "scholarship
> potential"), via approval and "love" of beautiful women (cheerleaders

cheering for men to "do it again"—to again risk concussions, spinal chord [*sic*] injuries, etc.), via parental approval and love (the parents who attend the Thanksgiving games at which their sons are battering each other), via taxpayer money (high school wrestling and football, ROTC, and the military), and via our entertainment dollar (boxing, football, ice hockey, rodeos, car racing, westerns, war movies . . .). After we subject only our sons to this violence (before the age of consent), we blame them for growing into the more violent sex. . . .

This is deeply ingrained. Virtually every society that has survived has done so via its ability to prepare its men to be disposable—to call it "glory" to be disposable in war.[6]

Getting men to accept their own disposability by risking the sacrifice of life and limb in exchange for glory is indeed part of a larger cultural pattern. Regarding the role of football in particular, we have seen in recent years a growing chorus of voices (consisting of former football players, parents, and journalists) sounding alarms about head injuries. What may have been the first alarm was sounded in 2002 by a pathologist, Dr. Bennet Omalu, who autopsied Mike Webster, a center who helped the Pittsburgh Steelers win four Super Bowls in the 1970s. By the time of his fatal heart attack, the venerated football hero had gone bankrupt, his marriage had fallen apart, and he was spending nights in a bus terminal. Omalu found that Webster had suffered from chronic traumatic encephalopathy (CTE), a brain disease that had resulted from repetitive impacts, which likely caused Webster's behavioral problems. After Omalu alerted the National Football League, instead of doing something about the problem, NFL managers formed a committee to publish a series of skewed, deceptive, but purportedly scientific articles denying the dangers of football head injuries. What's more, they claimed that returning to play after a concussion was not a problem, even for high school football players.[7]

A series of articles in the *New York Times* in 2007 reported on how the NFL had been misleading players about the dangers and proper treatment of concussions and CTE, and how such injuries had resulted in serious impairment and early death for many players. No doubt concerned about liability, the NFL responded by commissioning a study by the University of Michigan. Alas, that study found that NFL players are nineteen times more likely to get dementia than is normal for men in the thirty to forty-nine age range.[8] With the rapidly escalating threat of legal action, NFL officials and owners have become cagey when talking about the problem of head injuries. And with mounting evidence that the game of football sacrifices players and their families for the entertainment of fans, the public relations nightmare threatens fan disenchantment, which could have major potential implications for this multibillion dollar empire.

Paradoxically, another challenge faced by the NFL in dealing with brain injuries comes from demands by fans for the very kind of violent, bellicose, football action that makes injuries more likely. The NFL epitomizes the militaristic values that pervade the broader culture. This is often quite explicit, as in the Hank Williams Jr. song "Are You Ready for Some Football" that introduced the NFL's Monday Night Football show from 1989–2008. The song relies heavily on language like "ready to strike," "special forces," "battle," and "invasion" to convey the cultural militarism integral to the game.[9] In a militaristic culture it is not unusual for people to revel in seeing men's violence against each other, whether it be in wrestling matches, on the football field, in the hockey rink, on the NASCAR track, or in cages and arenas where men fight each other either one-on-one or in a group melee. In the case of professional sports, any effort to diminish that violence runs the risk of diminishing fan enthusiasm and therefore profits.

There are important parallels between the way the "manly" NFL has been "tough" in its treatment of injuries to football players and the ways politicians with "manly" images have been tough in their treatment of injured war veterans. Since Ronald Reagan, the Republican Party has projected an image of being the manly party, not least through an aggressive foreign policy and a lot of militaristic bluster. So one might expect the GOP to be a staunch advocate for military veterans. Yet, quite the opposite has been the case. The 2008 Republican presidential candidate John McCain, who has often been touted as a "war hero" and who regularly advocates military intervention in various conflicts in the Middle East, was given a rating of 20 out of 100 by the Disabled American Veterans for his handling of veteran's issues as a senator. In contrast, the DAV gave his Democratic opponent Barack Obama a rating of 80. Similarly, the Iraq and Afghanistan Veterans of America advocacy organization gave McCain a grade of D, and Obama a grade of B+ in 2008.[10] Both the IAVA and the DAV are nonpartisan, rating legislators strictly on their voting records. Their ratings reflect a larger pattern of differences between the two political parties with regard to caring about the suffering of troops and their families. Despite the GOP's pro-military image, the DAV gave its top rating of 100 to 207 Democrats, but only 13 Republicans in 2006.

Despite the failure of Republican politicians to support veterans through actual policies, the GOP has been able to maintain a pro-military facade. That may be a muddled consequence of their preference for pro-militaristic policies. On the surface, one might expect that the GOP's predilection for using war and the threat of war as a primary tool of foreign policy would be accompanied by policies providing health care and educational benefits to returning warriors. The fact that the opposite is the case can be explained by two factors. First, adequate care for disabled veterans raises the overall financial cost of war, which could make it harder to garner political support for war. Second, a key element in warrior masculinity is emotional toughness, including the ability to manage the capacity to care about human suffering. Even a "masculine" politician who supports aggressively militaristic policies must have an ability to suppress caring about the suffering and deaths of the troops who will be carrying out those policies at the level of combat. And that ability to suppress caring makes it possible for a pro-war politician to sacrifice veterans' health care, especially in the case of veterans whose injuries make them no longer able to fight in the politician's wars.

Among pro-war politicians there are also patterns of failure to protect men from potential injury or death by providing adequate planning and support. For example, political leaders rushed into the Iraq War without planning for sufficient numbers of troops, without adequate armor for soldiers' bodies and vehicles, and even without adequate quantities of ammunition for their weapons. Similarly, it has been only after many years of external pressures that NFL executives have begun to emphasize at least modest regulation of hyperviolent behavior on the football field.

In both cases, the politics of war and the business of violent sports, there are patterns of policy decisions that clearly reflect a lack of compassion for the men who are injured or killed. Those decisions reflect a crucial requirement for the effective warrior, which comprises the core of warrior masculinity: the ability to manage the capacity to care about the suffering of others and the suffering of oneself. More broadly, in both cases, war and violent sports, deeming men and their health to be expendable reflects an embrace of the inherently sacrificial nature of the warrior masculinity that is at the heart of cultural militarism. Warrior masculinity is sacrificial masculinity.

✳ ✳ ✳

Let's broaden our perspective on that ideal of sacrificial masculinity. Several years ago, I wrote the following about the gendered harms to men in an article called "Male Trouble": "I am going to focus [in this section] ... on what I consider, after more than a quarter century of reflection on the subject, to be the greatest disadvantage men suffer as a gender, especially because it is the root of most other male disadvantages, namely, cultural ideals of manhood that are deeply informed by the role of warrior. For men who literally take on that role, this means risking not only bodily injury or death, but also emotional disability."[11] While that risk of emotional disability is most obviously exemplified by PTSD (post-traumatic stress disorder), it is much broader than that. In the article I go on to consider how emotional disability results not just from the experience of war but also from qualities that militaristic societies inculcate even in very young boys so that they will be prepared to serve as warriors as they become older. That is the only way for militaristic societies to assure a ready supply of warriors—it is necessary for most of their men to have the emotional prerequisites of a warrior, regardless of whether they ever actually serve as warriors, and that requires that their socialization into the warrior role must begin in childhood.

Adult males, such as fathers, brothers, uncles, coaches, military officers, politicians, and teachers, are largely responsible for both maintaining the warrior ideal in our culture and inculcating it into boys. But women contribute to those projects, too. Warren Farrell writes about the role of cheerleaders, for example:

> When a cheerleader says, "first and ten, do it again!" she isn't saying "first get in touch with your feelings again." Nor is his coach. Nor are his parents cheering in the stands. All of us are unwittingly supporting him to "risk a concussion again." His motto is, "When the going gets tough, the tough get going" (they don't cry to the school therapist). If, instead of getting a touchdown, he gets in touch with his feelings, and quits his position on the team to avoid the concussion, the cheerleader doesn't say, "Next week I'm going to cheer for you—I noticed how open and vulnerable you were when you were playing football." Yes, next week she does cheer. But she cheers for his replaceable part.[12]

So there definitely are women and girls engaged in the project of encouraging boys and men to internalize warrior masculinity, even if they have a somewhat lower status in the gender hierarchy. However, Farrell's attempt to blame feminism for the ways society harms boys and men is utterly misguided. For example, Farrell fails to notice that those cheerleaders urging men to risk concussions are not doing so as feminists. Indeed, feminists are more likely to be found writing critically about both cheerleading and football, as Mariah Burton Nelson does in her book, *The Stronger Women Get, the More Men Love Football*.[13]

Indeed, it is feminist theorists (both male and female) who are providing the critical insights into masculinity and femininity that can lead to the liberation of men from being sacrificed on the altar of masculinity, as well as the liberation of women from sexism and misogyny. As I suggested at the outset of this chapter, those gender-specific harms are inextricably interlinked, so when feminist theorists write about harms to women there tend to be implications for harms to men, and vice versa. As Pierre Bourdieu puts it, masculinity and femininity are constructed diacritically, so that whatever can be said about one necessarily implies something about the other.[14] When Warren Farrell and other "men's rights activists" assume that feminism is the enemy of men and boys, they are profoundly confused.

✳ ✳ ✳

Toward an explanation of how that interlinking works, let's take a look at the connection between the warrior ideal of sacrificial masculinity and one of the greatest harms faced by women in militaristic societies, the threat of rape. Consider this 2007 news report from the Iraq War: "Three female soldiers had died of dehydration in Iraq, which can get up to 126 degrees in the summer, because they refused to drink liquids late in the day. They were afraid of being raped by male soldiers if they walked to the latrines after dark. . . . The latrines were far away and unlit . . . and male soldiers were jumping women who went to them at night, dragging them into the Port-a-Johns, and raping or abusing them."[15]

Women veterans of the Iraq War reported that "the danger of rape by other soldiers [was] so widely recognized in Iraq that their officers routinely told them not to go to the latrines or showers without another woman for protection." Military policewoman Mickiela Montoya says she carried a knife with her all the time. "The knife wasn't for the Iraqis," she says. "It was for the guys on my own side." One factor in this situation is that women have become more integrated into the military than ever before. But 1 out of 3 women in the military have been sexually assaulted, twice the rate of sexual assault among civilian women.[16] It has been calculated that a woman in the military was 180 times as likely to have been sexually assaulted than to have died during deployment to Iraq or Afghanistan during the past 11 years of combat.[17]

The dehydration deaths in Iraq illustrate that the effects of the threat of rape in women's lives extend much more broadly than the crime itself. For this broader range of effects I have used the term *rape terrorism*. In the article "Male Trouble" I noted that

> The threat of rape, which is perhaps the ultimate expression of misogyny, terrorizes virtually every woman in the United States. Few men, and not all women, are aware of the pervasive effect of the threat of rape in women's lives. Tim Beneke made the effort to talk to women about this, and came away transformed. He learned that the threat of rape alters the meaning of the night, makes women dependent on men for security, inhibits their ability to enjoy solitude in nature, requires them to spend more on rent to live in safe places and more on cars to insure safe transportation, constrains their public expressions and the freedom of their eyes, and inflects with fear their experience of male company— even the company of friends.[18] [I myself have] found consistently that in a class with twenty or more female students, it is possible for every woman in the class to name a strategy she uses on a daily basis to avoid sexual assault, without a single repeat. At the end, many women say that they routinely take all of the measures that have been named. Not only does this open the eyes of the men, women themselves are surprised, for typically they have not given conscious attention to the omnipresence of the threat of rape for the same reason a fish doesn't notice the water.[19]

That pattern of women altering their behavior as a result of being targeted by the threat of rape may not be what we normally have in mind when we think of terrorism. But if we consider the range of instances to which we routinely apply the word *terrorism*, and if we aim for a definition of it that would be neither too broad nor too narrow in relation to those instances, we get a definition like this: terrorism is the use of violence or the threat of violence to control or alter the behavior of members of a targeted group (or sometimes an individual person). So defined, the word *terrorism* is actually exemplified by the everyday threat of rape, based on the range of effects on women's lives that I have previously described. And it is worth noting that rape terrorism represents a far more sweeping harm to human beings than is the case with the typical threats we call terrorism.

In the years since I first wrote about the concept of rape terrorism, I have come to realize that the term is too narrow. For example, the threats of domestic violence and sexual harassment also function as terrorism against women, both individually and as a group. The need for a broader term for terrorism directed against women became particularly clear to me when I read Joan Walsh's article, "Men Who Hate Women on the Web."[20] It is about a prominent software programmer, public speaker, and blogger, Kathy Sierra, who was subjected to a campaign of incredibly vile abuse on various blogs, including violently misogynist altered photographs of her, culminating in graphic death threats and the posting of her address, her social security number, and other personal data. Sierra suspended her blog; in her final post she apologized to her fans for not attending a forthcoming conference where she was scheduled to speak and then said this:

> I have cancelled all speaking engagements.
> I am afraid to leave my yard.
> I will never feel the same.
> I will never be the same.[21]

The content of the terroristic harassment of Kathy Sierra manifested a clear intention to terrorize all women who work in this male-dominated field. What those men did was not just anti–Kathy Sierra, it was anti–women. It reflected a generalized hatred of women. Thus the appropriate term for what those men did is *misogynistic terrorism,* an expression that can encompass the complete range of terrorism against women: rape, domestic violence, sexual harassment, sexual discrimination, online threats, and so on.

I would expect most people reading about what was done to Kathy Sierra by her attackers to respond with anger, not just because of the harm they perpetrated in her life, but because their hate was implicitly aimed at all women. Anger is a natural response to misogynistic terrorism. However, the utility of anger is limited when it is directed only at the individual men who terrorized Kathy Sierra or only at the individual men who have assaulted female soldiers in Iraq and Afghanistan or only at the individual men who have assaulted, harassed, and discriminated against women in other contexts. Part of the problem with that narrowly focused anger is that the perpetrators of misogynistic terrorism are replaceable. In a society that culturally programs men to be misogynistic, there is always a ready supply of men to engage in misogynistic behavior. Focusing on an individual perpetrator does little about the unlimited supply of perpetrators who are all too ready to engage in misogynistic terrorism.

There is a further problem when it is a man who is angry toward individual male perpetrators who have victimized individual females. That's what I call *chivalrous anger.* Chivalrous anger conforms to the conventions of cultural militarism perfectly, fulfilling the cultural programming of men to be protective of women. Chivalry is even a core element in that programming, calling on men to rescue the "damsel in distress" and to serve as avengers for female victims. Thus chivalrous anger responds to cultural programming that deems men to be more powerful than women and that considers women to be dependent upon men. In short, chivalrous anger reflects and conveys the cultural message that men should be dominant over women.

That's not to say that anger cannot be an important motivator for getting something done about the overall problem of misogynistic terrorism. But to focus on revenge or punishment of individuals can distract from a broader, crucial, specifically philosophical project: identifying, describing, explaining, and critiquing the cultural programming that systematically produces the perpetrators of misogynistic terrorism. That philosophical project can open a window on potential changes in child rearing, where the cultural programming of boys to become misogynists gets its start.

This use of philosophy will also help us see, more broadly, how the problem of misogynistic terrorism is interwoven with sacrificial masculinity, and how neither problem can be solved independently of the other. This particular interweaving of gendered harms will serve as one example of why zero-sum thinking is not useful in dealing with harms that are specific to women or to men, and how instead it obstructs efforts to deal with those harms.

✳ ✳ ✳

Consider that in a militaristic society such as ours the process of making a boy into a man requires making the boy not only physically combat-ready, but emotionally combat-ready or, as we say, toughening him up. Toward that end, boys who let their fear show, or who manifest feelings of concern for the suffering of others, are commonly admonished with imperatives like "Boys don't cry," "Suck it up," "Tough it up," "Play through the pain," "No pain, no gain," "C'mon, be a man," "Don't be a girl," "Don't be a pussy," "Don't be a little bitch," etc. They are learning to be "tough," which in this context means being able to manage the capacity to care about the suffering of oneself and of others, or at least seeming to do so. And simultaneously they are learning that nothing is worse than being a girl or a woman, for that is the precise opposite of being a man.

That gender binary is reinforced and policed every day in the life of a child through the use of emotional terrorism by both other children and adults. In a narrative by Linda Rubin about a case of emotional terrorism, a five-year-old boy learns a compelling, life-changing lesson about the importance of staying on the correct side of the gender binary. On the day before Kirk started first grade, his mother took him to buy a new lunch box. Kirk selected what he considered to be the most exceptionally cool lunchbox out of an array of brightly hued possibilities featuring fun-looking cartoon characters. His mother was totally unprepared for what happened the next day. Kirk was crying when he got home from school. He ran out to the garage and tossed the new lunch box into a trash receptacle, screaming, "Get it away from me! I hate it!"

Unbeknownst to Kirk and his mother, the character featured on the lunchbox was female. The result was ridicule by Kirk's peers at school. But that was not the end of the little boy's torment.

From that first day of school, Kirk was emotionally terrorized every single day. Other boys would stand nearby and cough as they barked out the word *fag*. Kirk was frequently and openly called names intended to hurt: *gay, queer, homo*. He was told he was a "girl." By the time Kirk entered middle school, other boys would push and trip him as he walked down the hallways. In the locker room his genitals were grabbed. By now he hated school and was afraid to go.

This anecdote serves to direct our attention to a broader pattern of everyday *gender terrorism*, in which boys and men are subjected to humiliation, violence, and the threat of violence as ways of controlling their behavior so that they will conform to the code of what I have been calling *sacrificial masculinity*.

Consider also the case of Derrion Albert, a sixteen-year-old honor student who was on his way home from school in Chicago, wearing his school uniform and carrying his books, when he encountered a fight between two rival gangs. Both the attire and the books were clear signs of the young man's failure to measure up to the gangbangers' thuggish ideal of masculinity. However, they were also signs of potential success in relation to other notions of masculinity that prevail in the dominant culture. As a living symbol of the masculine norms of the dominant culture, in which education is presumed to lead to a man's success, both financially and romantically, Derrion's very presence constituted a symbolic threat to the subaltern masculinity of the gangbangers. And in militaristic cultures around the globe, a threat to the masculinity of a boy or a man is often responded to with violence. So the rival gang members joined together in collaboratively beating Derrion to death with railroad ties.[22] News accounts of the murder tended to focus narrowly on the brutality of the crime without addressing the murder of Derrion Albert in terms of the larger pattern in gang culture of terrorizing boys into staying within the confines of a sacrificial, self-destructive ideal of manhood.

The kind of gender terrorism involved in the cases of Kirk and Derrion does not just come from other boys. It also comes from parents, coaches, clergy, teachers, and other adult agents of cultural programming who are devoted to conserving and continuing the sacrificial warrior ideal of manhood as an integral part of the broader pattern of cultural militarism. Given the central place of violence in cultural militarism, it should be no surprise that these adults are willing to use hitting, whipping, spanking, humiliation, and other forms of physical and emotional violence to coerce boys into conforming to the demands of a misogynist, warrior masculinity.

We sometimes describe this process of making boys into men as toughening them up. Making a boy tough means to inculcate in him the most fundamental quality of the warrior, which I have described as the ability to manage the capacity to care about his own suffering and the suffering of others. If we're going to have a militaristic society, we need to do that to boys so that they will be prepared to serve as warriors as they mature. And in order to urge them on in that sacrifice of their own intrinsic interest, we need to tell them that this is how one avoids being a "girly man," wimp, lady, pussy, bitch, fag, etc., all of which represent a horrible fate, namely femaleness. Such a fate is horrible not just because it signifies a boy's failure to be like a "real man," but also because it means he would effectively become an enemy to all boys and men, for in the "battle of the sexes" a member of the "opposite sex" is an enemy. Here we can see some of the incredible power of insults to masculinity, for they imply not just loss of masculine status, but a betrayal of all manly men.

✳ ✳ ✳

After such fear and antagonism directed at femaleness has been instilled in a boy or man, and after he has succeeded in developing that capacity to suspend caring about the suffering of another person, how does that affect his behavior toward women? To focus the question a bit more, to the extent that a man has cultivated that capacity to suppress empathy with others and has cultivated that antagonism toward womanhood, doesn't that convergence of supremely masculine qualities make him more likely (compared to men without those qualities) to engage in misogynistic behavior, including rape, domestic abuse, sexual harassment, sex trafficking, patronizing child prostitutes, buying gonzo porn, etc.?

With regards to rape in particular, rapists often express misogynistic feelings, including resentment and anger toward women in general. For example, John Albert Taylor, who was executed in 1996 for the rape and murder of an eleven-year-old girl, and who had also been charged with the rape of a woman, said, "When I raped or molested, it was a way for me to get back at the female race."[23] Commenting on Taylor's statement, Jane Caputi, author of *The Age of Sex Crime,* describes rapists as "acting out masculinity in totally dominating the feminine."[24] Such domination lies at the heart of culturally programmed heterosexuality in militaristic societies, as we have seen throughout this book. Thus, rape is not an aberration in militaristic societies—rather, this supremely misogynistic phenomenon lies at the heart of the "battle of the sexes."

To fully understand rape, it is necessary to consider another factor alongside its inherent misogyny. Rapists describe being able to enter a state of mind—a zone if you will—where they are unaffected by the terror, screams, and crying of their victim.[25] Indeed, one of the greatest risk factors for a man to become a rapist is the ability to have "emotional detachment, leaving the offender relatively impervious to cues of victim distress and thus unempathic."[26] In other words, the rapist must be able to manage the capacity to care about the suffering of others. Another element in warrior masculinity also makes it more likely that a man will rape: a willingness to use force to satisfy one's desires and attain one's goals.[27]

In sum, there are five factors that enable a man to rape: (1) misogynistic attitudes, including not just antagonism toward women, but also a belief that men should be dominant over women; (2) a desire for revenge against women who show signs of not submitting to male dominance or who show disrespect for a man or for men in general; (3) the reinforcement of misogyny by the constant threat and fear of being deemed a girl or woman or "fag," which implies betrayal of the masculine project of domination over women and therefore betrayal of men generally; (4) the ability to suppress the capacity to care about the suffering of his victims; (5) a willingness to use violent force to satisfy desires and attain goals.

It should be emphasized that those are not qualities, attitudes, abilities, and dispositions that one can simply choose to have; rather, they must be instilled by cultural programming. And in militaristic societies those qualities are systematically and routinely inculcated in most boys, with varying degrees of success.

The larger picture is now coming into focus: The cultural programming that inculcates warrior masculinity into boys has the same elements as the cultural programming that would enable those boys to become rapists, and more broadly to become misogynistic terrorists. Hence, this sweeping pattern: militaristic cultures are misogynistic cultures, so in militaristic cultures rape is routine.

No surprise, then, that rape is inevitably part of war. Mostly the victims of military rape are enemy women. However, after the Normandy invasion by Allied troops in World War II, there were widespread rapes of French women by the GIs. Among the many angry letters received by the mayor of Le Havre complaining about rape and other crimes, one described "a regime of terror imposed by bandits in uniform."[28] And as the numbers of women in the United States military have increased, the number of men choosing to rape fellow soldiers has also increased, as previously noted. That pattern is compellingly demonstrated by the documentary *The Invisible War*. The *New York Times* describes the subject of the film as "the epidemic of rape within the United States military" and further characterizes military culture as "steeped in a belligerent, hypermasculine mystique."[29] That is an apt characterization of military culture, although the word *mystique* is misleading, suggesting that belligerent hypermasculinity is inexplicable. It is not at all inexplicable, as this book has demonstrated.

The belligerent hypermasculinity that is integral to military life is grounded in misogyny, a faith in the use of force to satisfy desire, and the ability to suppress empathy. Which makes one wonder: how could there not be more rape in the military than among civilians?

✳ ✳ ✳

Warrior masculinity is a primary source of male pride in militaristic cultures. However, it is not hard to see that there are components of warrior masculinity that are not generally advantageous to individual men. Misogyny problematizes one's relations with the half of the population that is female, which is not advantageous to men, especially those who are heterosexual. Reliance on force to satisfy desire calls into question a man's own undesirability, which is not to his advantage. Finally, the suppression of empathy is not advantageous with regard to the most important sources of human happiness and flourishing: to love and to care for others and to have others love and care for you. My point is not to deny that there is ever any personal advantaging attributable to warrior masculinity, for it surely can bring glory and respect. Nonetheless, regardless of any such particular instances of advantage, the requirements of warrior masculinity make it inherently sacrificial.

Those relative deprivations of human fulfillment by the demands of masculinity help to explain the statistic that young white men are responsible for 80 to 90 percent of all suicide deaths in the United States.[30] They also help to explain why boys and men are responsible for all mass shootings (so far). It is in the teen and early adult years that males are most likely to be anxious about their masculinity and therefore feel impelled to exert themselves in "proving" their manliness. That helps explain why most of the mass shootings, including Columbine, Virginia Tech, Aurora, and Newtown, are carried out by boys and young men—who notably tend to wear military garb and kill with military weaponry. Further, the expendability factor that is integral to warrior masculinity helps us understand why these shooters, after killing as many people as possible, usually turn the gun on themselves.

The centrality of sacrificial hypermasculinity in military culture also helps explain why suicide has become a growing problem in the armed forces, specifically. The already sacrificial nature of masculinity is exacerbated by the stress of the multiple combat tours that have become routine for a country at war for thirteen years, increasing the military suicide rate dramatically. In the calendar year 2012, more members of the military were killed by their own hand than were killed by enemy fighters.[31]

✳ ✳ ✳

Consider a pair of questions: First, what percentage of violent crimes are committed by men? In my experience, people always assume the number to be high, but it is even higher than folks guess: 85 percent. Second, who are more likely to be the victims of violent crime, women or men? When I ask this question of a group, the first people who answer typically say women, although most folks are unsure about how to respond. When they learn that 85 percent of the victims of violent crime are men, the initial surprise slowly dissipates as what seems to have been tacit understanding comes into focus.[32]

I suspect that one factor for the uncertainty about whether women or men are more likely to be victims of violent crime may be this: when women are the targets of violence, the fact that they are women is often a crucial factor. That is one reason why the expression *war on women* is so meaningful and widespread. When a woman is raped, it would not have happened if she were not a woman. Men who rape women have regular social interaction with both men and women, but only consider women as potential victims.

On the other hand, when a man is raped, the situation is more complicated. In prison a male rape victim is not singled out from a group of both women and men, and sometimes the perpetrator rapes a man only because a woman is not available. In other cases of prison rape a man is assaulted as a way of demonstrating the dominance of the perpetrator or as a means of revenge or punishment. Outside of prison, though, the gender of a male rape victim is typically a factor in his being targeted. In the case of a priest assaulting an altar boy, the perpetrator may have a particular desire for sex with boys. In the case of hazing that includes sexual assault, gender is a factor, although there is another element that makes hazing similar to many prison rapes. A primary aspect of hazing is the humiliation of the boy or young man. That larger purpose can be seen in the many non-assaultive hazing techniques that have been employed to humiliate a victim, such as requiring him to clean a toilet with his toothbrush, demanding the use of subservient language in addressing "superiors," embarrassing him through public nudity, or forcing him to get so drunk that he behaves stupidly.

Far more powerfully humiliating than any of those practices, however, is to symbolically turn a boy into a girl by sexually penetrating him, a practice that has become increasingly common in recent decades, particularly among student athletes. In a recent case near

Chicago, fourteen-year-old boys on the soccer team were attacked by older teammates, under the approving eye of a coach. According to a lawsuit, the older players tore off the boys' underpants, grabbed their testicles, and penetrated them anally with fingers and sticks.[33] Around the same time (September 2012), four soccer players at La Puente High School in California were charged with felony assault for attempting to anally penetrate another player with a javelin.[34]

To understand the gender symbolism involved in these sexually assaultive hazing practices, it is helpful to look at another context where men are raped. Rape by soldiers has been rampant in the Congo for many years, but more recently there has been a spike in the number of male victims. As with hazing by student athletes, the purpose is to humiliate in the most extreme manner possible. The men who are raped are sometimes referred to as "bush wives." One victim says, "I'm laughed at. . . . The people in my village say: 'You're no longer a man. Those men in the bush made you their wife.'"[35]

The term *wife* does not imply an ongoing relationship; it simply means that rape has been used to turn the man into a woman. The consequent humiliation has three elements. First, the victim has been penetrated, which is culturally understood to be something that is done only to women. Second, the victim has been subordinated by a dominant man, which does far more than lower the victim's status relative to that man: it feminizes the victim, because subordination is culturally programmed as feminine (and domination is culturally programmed as masculine).

That brings us to the third factor, which is rarely made explicit in discussions of male rape victims in contexts of hazing, prison, or war—namely, misogyny. To make a man into a woman by raping him does not merely flip him over to the other side of the gender binary; it does not merely make him something different. The gender binary is about more than differences, whether biological or culturally programmed. When a man is symbolically, forcibly transformed into a woman, he becomes a member of the other side in the "battle of the sexes."

The cultural militarism is crucial here, with its ubiquitous presumption that there are two "sides" who are enemies, and that every person must be on one side or the other, either friend or foe. When a man is made into a woman, he has been moved into the enemy group. As far as "real" men are concerned, he is their reviled enemy. In actual war the reviling of the enemy is crucial to fighting effectiveness. Thus, the enemy must be demonized and stigmatized. For men who view heterosexuality as inherently adversarial, which is typical in militaristic cultures, women are demonized as bitches and witches—they are the reviled gender. Such militaristic misogyny is a crucial factor in the humiliation of a boy who is raped by athletes as part of hazing, as well as in the humiliation of a man who is raped by soldiers in war. In both cases the humiliation relies on the rape symbolically making him a member of the reviled gender. Misogyny is also a factor in most prison rapes: the perpetrator turns the victim into "his bitch."

Thus, the misogyny of rape does not depend on the victim being female. When rape of a male is a way to make him symbolically female, and thus reviled, that dynamic works only if females are inherently reviled. The stigma inherent in femaleness becomes attached to the raped boy or man. While the cases of priests raping altar boys and scoutmasters raping boy scouts can be more complicated, it is important to note that the intensity of the humiliation reported by those victims is often related to the misogynistic factors we have considered.[36]

Misogyny has an additional function in cases of gang rape, regardless of whether the victim is male or female. The perpetrators of gang rape are bound together by their misogyny. This works in two ways. First, if one man shows any reluctance to join the attack, he may be taunted with any of the misogynistic slurs that are regularly used to control the behavior of men who display cowardice or who refuse to go along with the group, such as *wuss* or *pussy*. Second, the shared bond of the rapists is intensified by their shared misogyny. Such a shared hatred is often a source of broader social bonding in war-reliant societies, and particularly so among the warriors themselves.

That factor helps us see the synergy that occurs when misogyny and the capacity to suppress caring about suffering converge in the rapist. Misogyny, like any kind of hatred, powerfully enables the suppression of caring about the suffering of others. That's why haters can say such vile, hurtful, and mean-spirited things. Consider the total lack of empathy that is found among misogynistic Internet trolls, like the conservative commenters at breitbart.com writing about Lena Dunham, the writer and star of the television show *Girls* on HBO. *Girls* challenges misogyny on many levels. For instance, it calls into question beauty ideals that have been promulgated by the beauty-industrial complex. Perhaps even more threatening to conservatives, a recurring theme in *Girls* is women taking control of their sexual lives and even initiating sex. Here are some examples of what conservative commenters have said about Lena Dunham (with their spelling intact):

She's a skank so who gives a whip.

I wonder when this sleazy tramp will be showing genital warts on her face? Just HIV bait like most of her unHolywood contomporaries.

A conservative man would be repulsed by the flies buzzing around her lady parts, even after her whore bath. . . . no Republican man would date her, regardless of whether or not she was attracted to someone who opposed killing unborn babies or was opposed to rump ranger and twisted sister unions. Nice try at asserting your liberal ideals though. Now scamper along to your local Planned Parenthood Tattoo Piercing Parlor and have a spa day.

This from a girl who's willing to sleep with the whole 7th fleet.

Dating Lena Dunham is like dating a fish market.

This ugly hag gets lucky now she starts talking shiit . . . hope she saves her money

This is what happens when you put an ugly pear shaped chick in front of a camera. She's not a six packer—she's a 12-packer—and I am talking 12 high alcohol imports

This homely looking person is a hater, she should be tard and feathered and thrown in to the cesspool Chicago with the rest of the haters.

I wouldn't f*ck Lena Dunham with her own d*ck.

This little piggy can't even fasten the top hook of her dress . . .

You don't have to worry about dating any of us, Dunham. Bestiality ain't our bag.[37]

Internet trolls have a fascinating talent for confirming the problem of misogyny with hateful comments directed at anyone who calls attention to it. Anita Sarkeesian is a feminist blogger (feministfrequency.com) who makes videos for the Web on the subject "tropes vs. women in videogames." Here are some examples of the comments trolls have posted on Sarkeesian's YouTube videos:

Tits or GTFO

You're a bolshevik feminist Jewess

LESBIANS: THE GAME is all this bitch wants

Why do you put on make-up, if everything is sexism? . . . You are a hypocrite fucking slut.

Would be better if she filmed this in the kitchen.

I'll donate $50 if you make me a sandwich[38]

This selection is representative of a larger pattern of troll discourse that tends to blend misogyny, racism ("enlightened nigger" is another slur that has been hurled at Sarkeesian),[39] homophobia, and a latent longing for an imagined subordinate woman who cooks and offers unlimited but entirely passive sex. Violent fantasies are frequently added to the mix, like a flash game that encouraged players to beat an image of Sarkeesian's face until it appeared to be battered and bruised.[40] Sarkeesian reports that thousands of people came after her with "threats of rape, threats of death, threats of violence."[41] Such trolling reflects not only misogyny but also the suppressed empathy that is integral to a desire to hurt and defeat an enemy. Anyone who stands up against the hatred and subordination of women is an enemy, but the trolls and the entire misogynistic "manosphere" make it obvious that their larger enemy is women in general.[42]

That picture allows us to see, once again, a zero-sum game that undermines heterosexuality and synergistically harms both women as a group and men as a group. The men trolling Lena Dunham are doing their best to emotionally terrorize the overwhelming majority of women who do not fit the ideals of beauty that have been constructed and promulgated by the beauty-industrial complex. They are also trying to emotionally terrorize women who take control of their sexual lives. The men trolling Anita Sarkeesian are trying to emotionally terrorize women who point out the misogyny that is prevalent in video games. In both cases they are defending and reinforcing the misogyny that infects heterosexuality in militaristic cultures. They are inadvertently subverting the heterosexual eroticism they purport to embrace.

Thus, the attempts of misogynistic trolls to terrorize women don't just harm women, they also harm straight men. Indeed, what about the poor, pathetic, ostensibly straight trolls themselves? Is it possible even to imagine one of them having a mutually fulfilling relationship with a woman? They may imagine themselves to be players, but they are playing a zero-sum game in which they are doomed to be losers.[43] They are doomed to the hell of their inherently tragic desires for a phantom heterosexuality that exists only in their fantasies. They themselves are victims of misogynistic, militaristic cultural programming.

***

To the extent that misogyny is an essential component for the construction and maintenance of warrior masculinity, heterosexuality in militaristic cultures is inherently tragic. How can a man's disdain for women as a group not profoundly inflect his relationship with any particular woman?

But I'd like to close on a more optimistic note. Who knows what gender will look like, or whether it will exist at all, when men are finally free of sacrificial masculinity and its gendered harms aimed specifically at men? For now, there is at least one element of manliness that a man needs in order to engage in the project of gender liberation that has been launched by feminism (for both sexes)—and that is courage. Note that the cases of misogynistic terrorism we have considered involve women moving into traditionally male-only jobs. Those few cases are part of a larger pattern of some men responding to such women with sexual harassment, sexual assault, and discrimination. However, there has also been a pattern of some men allying with the women. If we look at the bigger picture, we can see that when those women and their male allies win, we all win. Those men who ally themselves with women against misogynistic terrorism—against discrimination and sexual harassment, against sexist jokes, against overblown claims of false rape accusations, against slut shaming, against all the other cultural mechanisms that are used to disempower women—those allies of women are the courageous men. They are also the smart men, who understand that feminism offers gains to both men and women.

Many men have been confused about the benefits feminism offers them, largely because they are confused about what feminism is. That is partly because of the plethora of myths about feminism that have achieved wide circulation, including, most notably, the myth that feminists are man haters (debunked in my article "Do Feminists Hate Men?").[44] Another significant factor in men's confusion is that there simply is no single, correct definition of feminism, as its proponents have espoused a wide range of definitions. Hence, there are many feminisms—or many versions of feminism. Nonetheless, I would propose a simple, minimal definition that accords with most versions of feminism: feminism is a preference that girls and women not be subjected (by society or individuals) to disadvantage just because they are girls or women. I consider feminism to be a preference, rather than an ideology or theory. People who share this preference might well strive to further it through political means, but the preference does not imply any *particular* political agenda. Likewise, people who share this preference will surely strive to implement it in their own lives, but the preference does not incorporate specific prescriptions for how to do that. It should also be noted that this definition of feminism does not in itself address any possible disadvantages that might be experienced solely as a result of biology, but rather only those that are imposed by society or individuals. There are least three further advantages of this definition over most others. First, it avoids any implicit ideological tests that could produce divisiveness among feminists. Second, it offers a way out of some of the less useful debates that have swirled around abstract notions like equality and rights. Third, it throws into relief the misogyny that is integral to opposition to feminism as I have described it: an antifeminist would be someone who rejects the preference that girls and women not be subjected to disadvantage solely on the basis of their being girls or women, thereby either endorsing such disadvantage or lacking concern about it, either of which allows an antipathy toward girls and women to come into full view.

This proposed minimalist definition of feminism offers a further benefit. In the context of the themes explored throughout this chapter, it helps us see that the misogynist preference for the gender-specific disadvantaging of women is interwoven with the gender-specific disadvantaging of men. The misogyny integral to antifeminism is also integral to the construction of warrior masculinity (as we have explored in this chapter and in chapter 3), which is the primary source of the gender-specific harms directed toward men (by themselves and other men more often than by women).

Now we can see how the embrace of feminism effectively serves the interest of men as a group. Without the use of misogyny to culturally program warrior masculinity, men are freed from the primary source of harm and disadvantage to which they are subjected as men.

We can also now see that misogyny is the linchpin of the gender binary. Without the use of misogyny to drive a wedge between men and women, and to police the boundaries of masculinity, the culturally programmed illusion of the gender binary dissipates. That dissipation of the gender binary is profoundly liberatory. Freed from the culturally programmed chains of gender, there are no longer two halves of the human race, defined by oppositionality and adversariality. But neither men nor women can be released from the cultural chains of gender unless both are. Men and women can escape from the zero-sum gender game only if they do it together.

7

THE DEGENDERING OF MILITARISM

WAR LOSES ITS SEX

Valor knows no gender.

—Barack Obama

War is gendered; it is something men do, and women suffer. That is not meant as a statement of fact; rather, it is a description of the cultural programming that has prevailed in almost all war-reliant societies. To engage in combat has been deemed masculine, and thus not feminine. This gendering of war has obscured the suffering of men in war and the ways that women have helped make war happen.

However, the nature and material conditions of war are changing, with profound cultural implications, including the gradual degendering of militarism and war itself. It is too early to say whether war will ever become entirely degendered. But there are several reasons why it makes sense to describe war as gradually becoming less gendered in the United States, and many other countries, and thus to speak of the degendering of war as a process that is underway—even if its approach to a complete and final separation of war and gender seems, for now, asymptotic.

Maybe the most obvious way of seeing the declining military importance of gender in the United States is the Obama administration's lifting of restrictions on women in combat roles in 2013. Moreover, the overall number of female troops continues to rise (now 15 percent), and there is a growing number of women ascending to high military rank (17 percent of officers are women).[1]

A window into some less obvious patterns of the degendering of war in American culture was provided by a uniquely qualified authority when former Secretary of Defense Robert M. Gates gave his last public speech on February 25, 2011, addressing the cadets at the United States Military Academy. Gates spent twenty-six years in the Central Intelligence Agency, becoming director in 1991. In 2006 he was appointed defense secretary by President George W. Bush and then was reappointed by President Barack Obama when he took office in 2009. Except for the president, who is commander-in-chief, Gates was the most powerful leader of the United States military. He is a lifelong conservative who served only in Republican administrations until being asked to continue as defense secretary by President Obama. He is highly respected within both the military establishment and the political establishment as an expert on the needs and capabilities of the military. He also had a strong reputation for being in touch with the lives of military personnel and their families. All these factors suggest that Gates's address to the West Point cadets may serve as a useful indicator of mainstream thinking about the military within both military culture and political culture.

The speech is clearly an attempt by an elder statesman to draw lessons from history and his own experience, and to assess the changing material conditions of national security, for the purpose of scouting the nation's future in relation to war and the military. I am going to pay particular attention to the ways in which the speech signals profound changes with regards to the cultural interplay of militarism and gender. Not surprisingly, Gates never uses the words *gender* or *sex*. He uses the word *men* four times and the word *women* twice. The latter term is found only conjoined with the former: he uses *men and women* to refer to the members of the current Army. The two instances where he uses the word *men* by itself are anecdotes about members of the Army in the 1930s. But, despite a paucity of explicit gender awareness, the speech offers some important signals about the degendering of war.

After some opening banter, the first substantive comment made by Gates is not about military strategy or leadership. And it is most definitely not meant to "pump up the troops." Rather, it is this: "No doubt the Army's challenges are daunting and diverse—supporting families, caring for wounded warriors, dealing with post-traumatic stress, doing right by soldiers, strengthening the NCO corps, training and equipping for the future, and finding a way to pay for it all."[2] This comment, especially considering its priority positioning in the speech, is noteworthy on two counts. First, none of the challenges Gates names here provide an incentive or rationale for going to war or for continuing any present war; instead, they are challenges to the very use of war as a way to achieve objectives or to solve problems. The challenges he names are, effectively, reasons not to engage in war: the harm to families, the disabling of troops by injury, the suffering of PTSD by troops, the need to provide health care and education and pensions for troops ("doing right by soldiers"), the insufficient number or quality of noncommissioned officers, the need for better training and equipment, and the huge financial cost of all of those things—not to mention (as Gates did not) the other even more huge financial costs of combat itself, including weapons, transport, food and housing for troops, training, recruitment, salaries, etc.

How does Gates's effectively cautionary stance about war relate to gender? Well, the warrior ideal of manliness has at its core the aforementioned "toughness," a concept that includes not only a readiness to engage in brutality but also a capacity to manage the capacity to care about the suffering of others and oneself and, more broadly, to suppress empathy. The Gates comment under consideration is utterly inconsistent with those demands of manly toughness.[3]

The first four of the challenges Gates identifies are about caring and compassion and not about fighting: caring for the families of soldiers, caring for physically disabled soldiers, caring for mentally ill soldiers, caring for soldiers and ex-soldiers by providing health care, education, and financial security in old age. To be sure, Gates is talking about caring that focuses on the military, rather than everybody else, but nonetheless his words reflect a profound change that has been taking place in American culture in recent decades—in the direction of becoming less "tough" in the ways veterans are treated. It's hard to say just when this cultural change began, but we can identify specific legislative acts that reflect it. After World War II, the "G.I. Bill" provided aid to veterans for education and housing. In 1974, there was the Vietnam Era Veterans' Readjustment Assistance Act, which brought Vietnam veterans the benefits of inclusion in affirmative action and equal opportunity laws. The "Post-9/11 Veterans Educational Assistance Act of 2008" provides tuition and housing assistance for veterans of the wars in Iraq and Afghanistan.[4]

This cultural change in the direction of becoming more compassionate toward veterans and their families has definitely ramped up during the wars in Iraq and Afghanistan. It did not happen right away. For example, President George W. Bush continued the policy started by his father, President George H. W. Bush, of not allowing news media to witness and photograph the flag-draped coffins coming home at Dover Air Force Base. But eventually President Bush began visiting wounded troops and having meetings with the families of dead soldiers. By 2008 his compassion for those families had reached a point where he said in an interview, "The president is commander in chief, but the president is often comforter in chief, as well." According to the interviewer, Bush's compassion for military families became so great that "the president often leaned on his wife, Laura, for emotional support. 'I lean on the Almighty and Laura. . . . She has been very reassuring, very calming."[5]

About that same time, there was also a swell of compassion for the casualties of war among the general public, bolstered by numerous emotionally gripping documentaries, such as *Hell and Back Again, Baghdad ER, Alive Day Memories, Body of War, The Soldier's Heart, Combat*

Hospital, and *War Against the V.A.* (a CNN documentary about veterans' struggles to get disability claims processed in a fair and timely manner by the Veterans Administration). The struggles of wounded soldiers to receive adequate care were widely covered in the mainstream news media, with many appalling reports about military hospital conditions and bureaucratic nightmares.

Eventually the phrase "support the troops" came to mean more than just "support the war." It gradually came to mean having empathy and compassion for the suffering of the troops and their families. In particular, awareness grew about PTSD and what came to be known as the signature wound of the wars in Iraq and Afghanistan, traumatic brain injury, or TBI. In 2010 there were two widely viewed, powerful films about war-related mental disorders: *The Wounded Platoon* (PBS) and *Wartorn: 1861–2010* (HBO); the latter in particular was warmly embraced by present and former members of the military.

This cultural shift toward caring about the suffering of soldiers and their families becomes more visible when it is contrasted with the lack of such caring after World War I, described by General Smedley D. Butler in a series of speeches given in 1933, later compiled as the powerful 1935 pamphlet *War Is a Racket*. I'm going to share an extended quote from Butler that foreshadows much of what Gates says in the passage quoted earlier.

> Who provides the [war] profits—these nice little profits of 20, 100, 300, 1,500 and 1,800 per cent? We all pay them—in taxation. . . .
>
> But the soldier pays the biggest part of the bill.
>
> If you don't believe this, visit the American cemeteries on the battlefields abroad. Or visit any of the veteran's hospitals in the United States. On a tour of the country, in the midst of which I am at the time of this writing, I have visited eighteen government hospitals for veterans. In them are a total of about 50,000 destroyed men—men who were the pick of the nation eighteen years ago. The very able chief surgeon at the government hospital at Milwaukee, where there

are 3,800 of the living dead, told me that mortality among veterans is three times as great as among those who stayed at home.

Boys with a normal viewpoint were taken out of the fields and offices and factories and classrooms and put into the ranks. There they were remolded; they were made over; they were made to "about face"; to regard murder as the order of the day. They were put shoulder to shoulder and, through mass psychology, they were entirely changed. We used them for a couple of years and trained them to think nothing at all of killing or of being killed.

Then, suddenly, we discharged them and told them to make another "about face"! This time they had to do their own readjustment, sans mass psychology, sans officers' aid and advice and sans nation-wide propaganda. We didn't need them anymore. So we scattered them about without any "three-minute" or "Liberty Loan" speeches or parades. Many, too many, of these fine young boys are eventually destroyed, mentally, because they could not make that final "about face" alone.

In the government hospital in Marion, Indiana, 1,800 of these boys are in pens! Five hundred of them in a barracks with steel bars and wires all around outside the buildings and on the porches. These already have been mentally destroyed. These boys don't even look like human beings. Oh, the looks on their faces! Physically, they are in good shape; mentally, they are gone.

There are thousands and thousands of these cases, and more and more are coming in all the time. The tremendous excitement of the war, the sudden cutting off of that excitement—the young boys couldn't stand it.

That's a part of the bill. So much for the dead—they have paid their part of the war profits. So much for the mentally and physically wounded—they are paying now their share of the war profits. But the others paid, too—they paid with heartbreaks when they tore themselves away from their firesides and their families to don the uniform of Uncle Sam—on which a profit had been made. They paid another part in the training camps where they were regimented and drilled while others took their jobs and their places in the lives of their communities. The paid for it in the trenches where they shot and were shot; where they were hungry for days at a time; where they slept in the mud and the cold and in the rain—with the moans and shrieks of the dying for a horrible lullaby.[6]

Perhaps it is obvious that, by the time he wrote this, General Butler had become an activist against war, unlike Gates. Both men wanted to draw attention to the plight of war veterans. But, in contrast to Butler, Gates did not go to West Point to tell the cadets that "war is a racket"—after all, he was there to address persons expected to have military careers.

Eighty years after Butler's indictment of America's treatment of its veterans, there continue to be incredible lapses in the health care afforded wounded troops (just as there are great lapses in the United States health care system generally).[7] Presently, there are almost 600,000 disability claims with the Department of Veterans Affairs that have been pending for over 125 days.[8] The department is still relying on paper to process claims. It was reported by the Associated Press in 2012 that "the piles of paperwork at a facility in North Carolina have grown so high that their weight had bowed the floor, prompting worries the building might collapse."[9]

In advocating for compassion for the suffering of the troops and their families, Butler and Gates diverge from cultural values that reflect the aforementioned emotional toughness required of the warrior: both leaders are amplifying, rather than suppressing, empathy for the suffering of soldiers and former soldiers, and they are failing to insist that wounded warriors repress caring about their own suffering.

The contextual difference between Gates and Butler is this: whereas Butler was a maverick, Gates's advocacy comes from the heart of the military establishment and reflects a widespread cultural shift in mainstream attitudes about war.

An incident that occurred in 1932 bespeaks the starkness of that difference. It happened in Washington, DC, where tens of thousands of World War I veterans, their families, and supporters were protesting against the continued deferment of "bonuses" the soldiers had been awarded in 1924 for their military service. General Butler visited with the marchers and then addressed them as a group; he told them they had the right to lobby Congress every bit as much as a corporation did. The next day, at the order of President Herbert Hoover, a force led by General Douglas MacArthur, including six battle tanks, infantry, and cavalry, drove the marchers, their wives, and children, from their campsite. The attack began with a cavalry charge, followed by infantry with fixed bayonets and using an arsenic-based gas that caused violent vomiting.[10]

So while the concerns of Butler and Gates have some similarity, the broader cultural context each faced is strikingly different, with Gates speaking at a time when compassion for the troops is both more widespread and more likely to be seen in political leaders. In contrast to 1932, American culture manifests a far less "tough" attitude toward the troops—that is to say, a less masculine attitude toward the troops. This itself is a powerful indicator of a cultural evolution toward degendering war.

The cultural shift signaled by the opening of Gates's speech to the West Point cadets also points to another, related, respect in which war is becoming degendered. In earlier chapters we have seen that war has always required that the lives and limbs and brains of men be sacrificed. To the extent that there is a greater reluctance to make that sacrifice of men—both in war and in violent sports like football—we are viewing men as less expendable. That means there is an attenuation of what I have suggested in earlier chapters may be the most substantial disadvantaging of men, their expendability. It is that particular disadvantaging of men that led to the earlier description of warrior masculinity as inherently sacrificial (in chapter 6). As the lives and well-being of soldiers, and men generally, are gradually coming to be deemed less expendable, a substantial element in masculinity is dissipating. A cultural ramification of increased compassion for the troops is that there is less masculine "toughness" in our attitudes toward men and that sacrificial, warrior masculinity is less demanded of men. In short, the degendering of war appears to be inseparable from the demilitarizing of gender.

* * *

The quote from Gates's speech that got the most press was a comment that some news outlets viewed as provocative ("Robert Gates' West Point Speech Sends Shockwaves" was the foxnews.com headline),[11] but that most military leaders probably saw as stating the obvious: "In my opinion, any future defense secretary who advises the president to again send a big American land army into Asia or into the Middle East or Africa should have his head examined."[12] Gates reiterates his point twice in the two ensuing paragraphs, first ascribing unlikelihood to "the prospects for another head-on clash of large mechanized land armies" and then describing as low "the odds of repeating another Afghanistan or Iraq." I think what made Gates's pronouncement seem so provocative and unexpected to many people (including some in the news media) is the continued prevalence in American culture of a simplistic, romanticized notion of war, largely built on images coming from popular representations of World War II. War, according to this widely circulating notion, has the following elements: large armies consisting entirely of men, the deaths of many of those men, and a heavy reliance on expensive technology, all for the purpose of attacking an evil enemy. In this notion of war there are always precisely two "sides"—one that will win and one that will lose—with victory determined by both control of territory and how many enemy combatants have been killed. Those are all ideas about war that call for a combination of brutal aggression against the enemy and the sacrifice of a lot of men in that effort. Culturally, therefore, it calls for a lot of boys and men to be imbued with the ideal of warrior masculinity. But, if Gates's assessment of the material conditions of national security now and in the foreseeable future is correct (and it seems to be shared by our military leaders), our culturally programmed faith in warrior masculinity may be unnecessary, and, if it is unnecessary, why would we want to conserve something we have seen in this book to be so detrimental to both men and women? But for an adequate assessment of whether our faith in violent masculine force is becoming less necessary we must look at the other kinds of threats, as well as the other uses of the military, that are examined in Gates's speech.

If, as Gates suggests, there will be no more major land wars for the United States, how will the military be used? Part of the answer must have been disconcerting to his audience of cadets planning careers in the Army. Gates says, "the Army also must confront the reality that the most plausible, high-end scenarios for the U.S. military are primarily naval and air engagements—whether in Asia, the Persian Gulf, or elsewhere." That blunt statement has substantial implications for the question of whether war is becoming degendered. While there are personnel in the Navy and Air Force who sometimes engage in the kind of combat that places a premium on warrior masculinity (e.g., Marines and SEALs, both in the Navy), their numbers are much smaller than is the case for the Army. Also, for the Navy and Air Force, direct combat confrontations comprise a far smaller portion of the overall mission, compared to the Army. Further, women may actually tend to be at an advantage relative to men for some jobs in the other two military branches. For example, a shorter distance from the heart to the brain is a physiological advantage for female pilots of fighter jets, which are used extensively by both the Air Force and the Navy.[13]

There are yet further developments in today's world that diminish the need for the military to be masculine and hence for men to be culturally programmed with the warrior ideal. Gates catalogues some of the present and future threats that may be faced by the cadets at West Point:

> We can't know with absolute certainty what the future of warfare will hold, but we do know it will be exceedingly complex, unpredictable, and—as they say in the staff colleges—"unstructured." Just think about the range of security challenges we face right now beyond Iraq and Afghanistan: terrorism and terrorists in search of weapons of mass destruction, Iran, North Korea, military modernization programs in Russia and China, failed and failing states, revolution in the Middle East, cyber [threats], piracy, [nuclear] proliferation, natural and man-made disasters, and more.[14]

Depending on how you count, there are approximately ten threats in that list. Keeping in mind that Gates has already ruled out a "traditional" land war, it is interesting to think about just how many of those threats call for responses that do not involve combat or at least not the kind of direct, violent combat that has led militaristic societies to gender war as a task for men.

Cyber threats call for a response with battalions of geeks, not hypermasculine warrior types. In the case of modern piracy, specifically off the coast of Somalia, there is no army to fight, but there are a lot of young men with military-style weapons and no hopes for nonpirate jobs. The roots of Somali piracy lie in the extreme poverty and inequality in Somalia, which can best be addressed with humanitarian aid, economic and educational development, and political reform.

When there are natural and manmade disasters, the need is for humanitarians of all sorts, including medical personnel and other rescue workers. In the particular case of "manmade" disasters, we may need more government safety regulations enforced by bureaucrats. (For example, the fertilizer plant in Texas that exploded in 2013, killing at least fifteen people, had not been inspected by the Occupational

Safety and Health Administration since 1985.)[15] To deal with nuclear proliferation we need highly skilled diplomats who can negotiate collaborative means of controlling and quarantining the materials used for making nuclear weapons, as well as scientists and engineers who can design safe means to disable already existing nuclear arsenals. The challenge of revolutions in the Middle East is incredibly complex, calling for an array of responses, among which would be still more geeks, to circumvent efforts of authoritarian governments to shut down Twitter, Facebook, and the Internet, as well as to provide political activists with Internet security against government surveillance.

None of those threats call for traditional, gendered military responses.

The threat of terrorism and terrorists is complex enough to call for an extended discussion. There is a wide array of potentially effective responses to terrorism. Most of them do not rely on hypermasculine warriors, but our militaristic cultural programming can make that hard to see. That was the case for many news commentators immediately after the attack on the World Trade Center, September 11, 2001, as Susan Faludi recounts in *The Terror Dream: Fear and Fantasy in Post-9/11 America*. She describes being interviewed by a *New York Times* reporter about "the return of the manly men."[16] In the resulting article, Patricia Leigh Brown notes that "war has traditionally brought out America's inner Schwarzenegger." Brown quotes the editor of *Esquire*, David Granger: "After a decade of prosperity that made us soft, metaphorically and physically, there's a longing for manliness. People want to regain what we had in World War II. They want to believe in big, strapping American boys."[17] Never mind that neither large physical stature nor "manliness" stopped any of the attacks on 9/11.[18]

It was not just hypermasculinity that commentators said we needed as a response to terrorism—it was also a return to hyperfemininity, which meant a rejection of feminism. Faludi received a call from a "*New York Observer* writer seeking comment on 'the trend' of women 'becoming more feminine after 9/11.' By which, as she made clear, she meant less feminist. Women were going to regret their 'independence,' she said, and devote themselves to 'baking cookies' and finding husbands 'to take care of them.'"[19] Faludi says the call left her "baffled," as well it should have.

The idea that traditional gender roles are an effective response to terrorism is absurd. But, as we have seen throughout this book, the cultural ideals of man as warrior and woman as breeder/nurturer have sometimes served as components of the cultural infrastructure of war. Hence, for societies that have relied on war as a way to solve problems in relation to other societies, the gender binary has often seemed necessary, not least because it has been culturally programmed with a facade of necessity that purports to be grounded in nature. But, as we saw in chapter 1, nature by no means determines or necessitates a gender binary. Rather, the gender binary is part of a larger package of cultural programming that culturally evolved to help war-reliant societies survive or triumph in conflict environments. Because terrorism involves violence and conflict, it seems similar to those past threats to which an effective response may have been war and a cultural infrastructure for war, including a gender binary that assigns the role of combatant primarily to men.

However, terrorism is not like those threats, partly because of its asymmetrical nature. This can be illustrated by the first suicide bombing in the modern Middle East. It was in 1980, during the Iran-Iraq war, in the battle of Kerbala. A thirteen-year-old boy, Hossein Famideh, strapped on explosives and threw himself in front of an Iraqi tank, utterly destroying it.[20] A boy destroying a tank presaged the incredible potential of suicide attacks in asymmetrical conflict, a potential most fully realized three decades later, on 9/11.

The Hossein Famideh suicide attack is instructive precisely because it occurred in the context of war. It serves to illustrate how traditional methods of waging war are often ineffective responses to the kind of threat emanating from terroristic techniques. Further, the asymmetry of suicide bombings and most other terrorist attacks make the gender of the attacker far less important; indeed, women or children have the advantage of being less subject to suspicion. The Kerbala suicide attack signaled what was to come in the United States wars in Iraq and Afghanistan, where traditional approaches to war have been largely impotent against terrorist tactics, including improvised explosive devices.

There is a particular aspect of the asymmetry of terrorism that is relevant for our present purposes. On the one hand, the terrorist must have what I have described throughout this book as an essential ability for a warrior: being able to manage the capacity to care about the suffering of others. Think of the case of the Boston Marathon bombers. They planted the backpacks containing their bombs at the very feet of the people they knew would be maimed or killed by the blast. Among their intended victims were eight-year-old Martin Richard, who was killed, and Martin's six-year-old sister, Jane, who lost a leg.[21] With the bombers in such close proximity to their victims, children and adults enjoying an athletic event, the ability to suppress empathy was as requisite for the attack as the bombs themselves. And, in the case of a suicide attack, one must also have the other essential quality of a warrior, the ability to manage the capacity to care about one's own suffering or death.

In a militaristic culture, responses to terrorism tend to be reactive, with the aim of killing as many terrorists as possible. In other words, the tendency is to approach terrorism in the same way militaristic cultures approach war: kill as many enemies as possible.

But the asymmetry of terrorism goes beyond the ability of one or two terrorists to bring a great city or nation to a standstill with bombs made out of pressure cookers and a few dollars worth of firecrackers and ball bearings. In the long term, killing as many suspected or potential terrorists as possible may not be the most efficacious way to protect a society from future terrorist attacks.

Consider that the majority of terrorist attacks in the modern era are carried out by men, often relatively young men. (Older men are often responsible for planning and organizing, but are less likely to carry out the attacks.) But only a fairly small percentage of men, in any society or in any religious group, become terrorists. It is not the possession of a Y chromosome that leads a person into terrorism, even though terrorists are more likely to be male than female.

Often the perpetrators of terrorist attacks, especially in the United States and Europe, are relatively young men who have been failures in a particular sense. They have been failures at becoming "real men," of living up to the culturally programmed ideals of masculinity. In militaristic cultures, masculinity is typically comprised largely of three factors. One of these is producing lots of offspring or at least seeming to have lots of the sort of sexual activity that might lead to procreation. But success at that first factor has generally required demonstrating potential or actual success at the second factor, which is fulfilling the role of provider—for example, by earning a salary, stealing cattle, accumulating quantities of grain, or having possession of a lot of land.

If a man seems unable to succeed as a provider, he is not viewed as an attractive heterosexual mate in a society that discriminates against female providers (as militaristic societies often do). Thus for a young man to establish his masculinity through those first two factors, as a procreator and provider, can be a substantial challenge. That is especially so in the context of a struggling economy with a shrinking middle class and with high unemployment rates. The situation is further complicated when women become more likely to take on the provider role, which has the cultural consequence of the provision of resources becoming a less specifically masculine role. And that, in turn, diminishes the power of masculinity to instill ambition in young men. But, if they lose their ambition, young men lose their potential for whatever residual masculinity they can attain as providers and, worse, begin to seem like potential dependents on either parents or a life partner. Either way, they are less likely to seem attractive as mates, especially if they are heterosexual and looking for a female partner.

The third way masculinity can be demonstrated in militaristic cultures is by taking on the warrior role or some semblance of it as defined by culturally programmed warrior masculinity. For most men, acting like a warrior can mean being emotionally reserved, being highly competitive (even to the extent of bullying other men), and, as we have seen in earlier chapters, demonstrating misogyny (proving your manliness by deprecating the "opposite" gender).

There is a relatively small number of young men for whom those ways of performing the warrior role seem insufficient or too difficult and who also have failed at being providers or procreators. Consequently they feel insecure about their masculinity. But attacking people is something every boy or young man can do. And, if he attacks for the sake of a larger cause, that enhances the sense that he is acting as a warrior. Thus the barriers to entry into a career as a terrorist are really quite low. Sometimes there is elaborate planning and organization, done primarily by other men, as with 9/11, and to a lesser extent with the "shoe bomber" and the "underwear bomber." But the Boston Marathon bombers had a less sophisticated approach; it was easy to buy the pressure cookers, fireworks for the gunpowder, and some ball bearings to maximize tissue damage. Assembling the bombs using Internet recipes was also easy. Finally, it was easy to take public transportation downtown, place the backpacks containing the bombs on the sidewalk near the marathon finish line, then nonchalantly stroll away.

Terrorism can be even easier than that, as we saw on a sunny day in the Woolwich area of London on May 22, 2013. Lee Rigby, twenty-five-year-old father and drummer in the British military, was walking down the sidewalk when he was set upon by two young men in their twenties. Using a meat cleaver and what looked like large kitchen knives, they hacked and stabbed him to death. The terrorist intent became clear when one of the suspects exclaimed to passersby, "We swear by the Almighty Allah we will never stop fighting you until you leave us alone. . . . We must fight them as they fight us. An eye for an eye and a tooth for a tooth. I apologise that women had to see this today but in our lands our women have to see the same. You people will never be safe. Remove your governments. They don't care about you."[22] The

Woolwich attacker's "eye for an eye and a tooth for a tooth" rationale is one of the classic justifications for war in militaristic cultures. So when a war-reliant society is attacked, the tendency is to attack back, typically using male warriors. But, as a means of dealing with the asymmetric threat of terrorism, the effectiveness of that reactive approach is questionable.

A different approach to shrinking the threat of terrorism would be to shrink the pool of young men who feel desperate enough to prove their masculinity that they will assume the mantle of the warrior by committing terrorist acts. One way to do that would be to promote economic and educational development in countries where there are millions of depressed and angry young men who have no hope for jobs, hence no hope for marriage, and who are sexually frustrated, for whom the remaining avenue to "proving their manhood" is to kill people, perhaps including themselves. Of course, the root of the problem is that these young men have been culturally programmed with antiquated ideas about masculinity, but does anyone really think that the military can fight those ideas out of them, using other young men who have the same antiquated ideas?

There is another gender-related factor regarding economic development as both a long-term response to terrorism and a way of abating most of the other threats named by Gates, including "failed and failing states." The fact that most economies are dominated by men can lead us to overlook one of the most important factors in enhancing the economic health of a society. According to a surprising source, the single most important factor contributing to economic development and stability is the expansion of economic and educational opportunities for women and girls. That is the conclusion reached in a recent report from the National Intelligence Council, an organization based in the office of the director of National Intelligence. The section of the report titled "Women as Agents of Geopolitical Change" is worth quoting at length:

> Economic and political empowerment of women could transform the global landscape over the next 20 years. This trend already is evident in the area of economics: The explosion in global economic productivity in recent years has been driven as much by fostering human resources—particularly through improvements in health, education, and employment opportunities for women and girls—as by technological advances. . . .
>
> • Demographic data indicate a significant correlation between a higher level of female literacy and more robust GDP growth within a region (e.g., the Americas, Europe, and East Asia). Conversely, those regions with the lowest female literacy rates (southern and western Asia; the Arab world; and Sub-Saharan Africa) are the poorest in the world.
>
> • Improved educational opportunities for girls and women also are a contributing factor to falling birth rates worldwide—and by extension better maternal health. The long-term implications of this trend likely include fewer orphans, less malnutrition, more children in school, and other contributions to societal stability.
>
> . . . Examples as disparate as Sweden and Rwanda indicate that countries with relatively large numbers of politically active women place greater importance on societal issues such as healthcare, the environment, and economic development. If this trend continues over the next 15–20 years, as is likely, an increasing number of countries could favor social programs over military ones. Better governance also could be a spinoff benefit, as a high number of women in parliament or senior government positions correlates with lower corruption.[23]

The bottom line here seems to be that the expansion of opportunities for girls and women—i.e., feminism—may be an effective way of dealing with many of the significant threats faced by the United States today. And to a considerable extent it appears that feminism may sometimes be a more effective response to those threats than the traditional militaristic and "manly" responses, relying on big guns, hypermasculine warriors, and combat of any kind.

This calls for a second look at the first sentence in the last quotation from Gates, right before he enumerates the threats: "We can't know with absolute certainty what the future of warfare will hold, but we do know it will be exceedingly complex, unpredictable, and—as they say in the staff colleges—'unstructured.'" Indeed, this "future of warfare" may be so "unstructured" that it may not be war in the traditional sense of ground combat at all. That kind of war is generally not the most effective way of dealing with the kinds of threats enumerated by Gates. Indeed, in some cases, like terrorism, war may actually exacerbate the threat. Further, the alternatives to traditional war lack its downsides, as mentioned by Gates early in his speech—including sacrifice of the lives, limbs, and mental health of military personnel who are overwhelmingly male.

Gates later says, "The need for heavy armor and firepower to survive, close with, and destroy the enemy will always be there." What he needs to add, though, is the following phrase, expressing what is already implicit in his speech: "even if that need continues to shrink." We should also note that "always" raises the burden of proof for a predictive assertion like this quite substantially, increasing the likelihood that it is based more on culturally programmed faith than on evidence. Indeed, Gates's assertion may be just one more example of the faith in masculine violent force that lies at the heart of cultural militarism.

✳ ✳ ✳

There are still more degendering factors in the evolving nature of war, and particularly with regard to the threats that traditional combat models may not be able to meet.

First, there is the "counterinsurgency doctrine," also known as "the Petraeus doctrine," which is articulated in *The U.S. Army/Marine*

Corps Counterinsurgency Field Manual,[24] first released in 2006. For our present purposes, the most interesting shift in the manual is a relatively greater emphasis on "winning hearts and minds" as a complement to the use of coercive violence. Toward that end, when the lead author, General David Petraeus, was commander of United States forces in Iraq, he emphasized the cultivation of empathy, listening skills, and responsiveness to the expressed needs, aspirations, and motivations not only of the civilian population but even of enemy combatants. For example, Petraeus ordered required attendance by United States troops in Iraq at showings of *Meeting Resistance,* a documentary film made by journalists to try to get into the minds of insurgents. His stated goal was to get soldiers to empathize with the insurgents. There are many other examples that could be given from counterinsurgency doctrine that also illustrate a greater emphasis on emotional skills, as well as on the demonstration of empathy through development projects like the building of schools, clinics, roads, and canals.

Of course, the goal of counterinsurgency doctrine is military success. But how that success is defined is itself undergoing evolution. Under Petraeus's leadership in both Iraq and Afghanistan, United States generals were scrupulously careful to avoid the traditional combat language of victory and defeat, winning and losing. And when General Ray Odierno, the last commander of United States forces in Iraq, presided over the end of formal military engagement in that country, he was quite clear about the limits of any continuing United States influence, including a lack of ability to limit the growing influence of Iran on the Iraqi government.

General Odierno's two deployments to Iraq provide revealing insight into how the military's faith in masculine violent force shifted throughout that war. During his first deployment in 2003, he had a reputation for the use of brutally aggressive, authoritarian tactics, including home invasions in which the male head of the family would be made to kneel and be humiliated in front of his family. Under Odierno's leadership,

American soldiers "kicked down doors, destroyed homes, killed civilians and arrested thousands—sometimes seemingly indiscriminately."[25] "Odierno, he hammered everyone," said a retired general working for Coalition Provisional Authority, which oversaw the U.S. occupation of Iraq. Sergeant Kayla Williams, an Army military intelligence specialist, described the soldiers under Odierno's command as typically "looking mean and ugly": "They stood on top of their trucks, their weapons pointed directly at civilians." Under Odierno, "every male from 16 to 60" was detained, leading to overcrowding at Abu Ghraib prison, overwhelming the staff there,[26] and ultimately resulting in publication of the notorious photographs that exposed the horrendous treatment of Abu Ghraib prisoners by American soldiers.

In that first deployment, General Odierno perfectly exemplified faith in hypermasculine, hyperviolent force. And the results of his aggressive tactics demonstrated that they were grounded only in faith and not in understanding. Hatred of Americans surged among Iraqis, as did their willingness to join the insurgency and kill Americans.

By the time General Odierno came to Iraq for his second deployment, everything had changed. General Petraeus had taken over command of United States forces in Iraq and introduced the counterinsurgency doctrine previously described. Odierno's return to Iraq was to replace Petraeus as commander of U.S. forces and to complete the implementation of Petraeus's plan for Iraq. Overcoming the skepticism of observers, based on his earlier performance in Iraq, Odierno embraced the new approach that was diametrically opposed to the one he had taken before. "Odierno began learning the religious and tribal breakdown of every district. He learned Arabic and walked around neighborhoods, as did the captains in charge of those districts."[27] They interviewed Iraqis about their concerns and aspirations, responding appropriately and with empathy. And it worked. While there were manifold intersecting factors involved, the level of violence plummeted, leading ultimately to U.S. troops exiting from Iraq not in "victory" but at least not ignominiously.

My overall point about counterinsurgency doctrine is just this: It represents a shift toward the use of skills and tactics that are decidedly less associated with masculinity than is coercive force. Indeed, some of those skills, like listening and empathy, have been culturally associated in militaristic societies with women, rather than men.

* * *

There are a number of interesting ways we can think about the shifts in military policies we have been considering. (1) To the extent that our military leaders are redefining the work of the military in those directions, it would seem that their militaristic faith in the efficacy and necessity of masculine force is diminishing, while their faith in the power of empathy and collaboration with others, including those who are potential or actual enemies, becomes a relatively more important element in the attainment of security. (2) To the extent that those shifts require human abilities and dispositions that rely on an enhanced capacity to care about the suffering of others, there is less reliance on people who have been socialized to be able to suppress the capacity to care, i.e., to have that emotional toughness that is the most crucial capability of a warrior. (3) Partly for that reason, it appears that our military leaders are moving us, however gradually, in the direction of degendered, or at least demasculinized, responses to threats. They are moving the military, and, with it, potentially the entire culture, in that direction precisely because it will be more effective than the traditional militaristic model, which relies so heavily on warrior masculinity, at assuring national and human security.

* * *

A quite profound way that combat itself is becoming degendered is the rapidly growing reliance by the military on combat technology that makes the gender of the operator irrelevant.

The most obvious case would be the drone fighter aircraft that are being used by the United States in Afghanistan, Pakistan, and Yemen. The activity of "piloting" a drone does not call on any of the qualities of a warrior that we have culturally presumed to be masculine. In particular, compared to a soldier involved in direct combat with enemy fighters, there is less need for the person engaged in drone attacks to be able to be "tough," to be able to manage the capacity to care about the suffering of himself and of others. That is a consequence of the physical remoteness of the operators: in the case of drones in Afghanistan and Pakistan, they are being operated out of bunkers and trailers in Colorado and Nevada by "pilots" who live in the suburbs and mow their lawns on Saturdays.[28]

One of the most radical technological trends toward degendering war lies in the field of robotics. The Pentagon's Defense Advanced Research Projects Agency (DARPA) has sponsored a plethora of projects and competitions that have resulted in robots with incredibly diverse combat capabilities. These robots are significant factors in the rapidly declining need to sacrifice men in war. A current DARPA Challenge (as the competitions are called) is described as follows: "By the end of next year, robots will walk into a disaster zone. They won't roll in on wheels or rumble in on treads. They will walk, striding across rubble, most of them balancing on two legs. Compared with human first responders, the machines will move slowly and halt frequently. But what they lack in speed, they make up for in resilience and disposability. Chemical fires can't sear a robot's lungs, and a lifespan cut short by gamma rays is a logistical snag rather than a tragedy."[29]

While DARPA is framing this project in terms of disaster rescue, this robot's usefulness in war is obvious, which makes it consistent with DARPA's military mission. What does not have to be specified by DARPA in the parameters of the competition is that the robot will not need to be culturally programmed with the ability that is crucial for human warriors and rescuers: managing the capacity to care about one's own suffering. Nor will it be necessary to culturally program a robot warrior to be able to manage the capacity to care about the suffering of others, which is another requisite of a human warrior. For now, the human operators of combat drones and robots do need some measure of that ability to suppress empathy, but the remoteness factor means that the operator needs it far less than does a soldier who is directly engaged in combat. As technology continues to evolve, robotic warriors and a plethora of other combat devices being developed by DARPA will become increasingly remote from the control of human operators, eventually becoming independent of that control. They will then have lethal autonomy, as it is called in the field of military robotics. At that point, lacking any direct connection with human gender, such devices may represent the ultimate degendering of war.

8

THE DEMILITARIZING OF GENDER

A TRUCE IN THE BATTLE OF THE SEXES?

> On the day when it will be possible for woman to love not in her
> weakness but in her strength, not to escape herself but to find
> herself, not to abase herself but to assert herself—on that day love
> will become for her, as for man, a source of life and not of mortal
> danger.
>
> —Simone de Beauvoir, *The Second Sex*

War-reliant cultures are masculine cultures, meaning that the values of
warrior masculinity are culturally pervasive. Thus war-reliant societies
view themselves as manly societies, even if a majority of the people are
not men and even if that majority of not-men are culturally deemed to
have unmasculine attributes. This cultural pervasiveness of masculinity
is partly because war-reliant societies are typically governed by men and
view men as generally dominant. Masculinity in militaristic societies is
inherently, culturally hegemonic. Hence, when such a society is ruled
or governed by a woman, there is generally an expectation that she will
display characteristics associated with warrior masculinity.

There are further ramifications of the overall masculinity of war-
reliant cultures, as they are suffused throughout with the core emotional qualities that are requisite for a warrior. The warrior must, above
all, be emotionally tough: that means he must be able to manage the

capacity to care about his own suffering and the suffering of others. That emotional toughness comprises the core of warrior masculinity, and so, in the case of a culture that is imbued with warrior masculinity, the suppression of empathy informs an array of social attitudes, not only regarding relations with potentially enemy societies, but regarding members of one's own group who are physically, educationally, economically, socially, or otherwise disadvantaged. Suppression of compassion and emotional hardening tends to be widespread in militaristic societies; however, there are culturally programmed expectations that boys and men will suppress compassion and display emotional hardness in noticeably greater measure than do girls and women.[1]

Thus the complex interplay of gender and militarism has sweeping ramifications, even beyond those assayed previously in this book regarding love and sexuality. As the material conditions that have given rise to cultural militarism change, including those considered in the previous chapter that affect whether and how war is conducted, the interrelatedness of war and gender will continue to evolve in profound ways, with broad implications for how people treat each other.

A ramification of the gradual degendering of war that was scouted in the previous chapter is the reciprocal demilitarizing of gender. To the extent a society becomes less likely to engage in the kind of war that relies on male warriors, there is a declining need to instill in males a gendered identity that conforms with the warrior ideal. The diminished social utility of warrior masculinity, along with a growing awareness of its detriments to both men and women, opens up a path for cultural evolution beyond the ideal of warrior masculinity. Likewise, when a society lessens its reliance on traditional forms of war, the reduction in loss of human life caused by war means less need for maximizing procreation, which opens up possibilities for freeing girls and women from the constrictive cultural programming associated with the maternal ideal, including the deprecation of abortion and contraception. Diminished procreative pressures can also lessen the homophobia that has characterized most modern militaristic societies.

As those traditional cultural patterns of gender differentiation and regimentation dissipate in response to changing historical conditions, the implications for the culturally programmed heterosexuality that has been described in this book could be immense. Specifically, if militaristic gendering recedes, the cultural expectation that heterosexuality must be premised on male domination and female subordination could also be expected to recede, along with the patterns of adversariality that flow from that model of heterosexuality. In sum, the degendering of war might lead to a truce in the "battle of the sexes" because of two factors: (1) a diminished need for male warriors who have been made emotionally tough through the use of misogynistic taunts and (2) diminished reproduction pressures that call for women to be culturally programmed as selfless procreators, nurturers, and providers of sexual services.

Such a truce in the battle of the sexes would have sweeping implications, and not just in the context of individual heterosexual relationships. In particular, misogyny and sexism are an ongoing, major source of social disharmony pervading every area of social, cultural, political, and economic life.

We see examples of this in a 2013 *New York Times* column by Frank Bruni titled "Sexism's Puzzling Stamina." Bruni takes note of "all the recent reminders of how often women are still victimized, how potently they're still resented and how tenaciously a musty male chauvinism endures. On this front even more than the others, I somehow thought we'd be further along by now."[2] As an example of that "musty male chauvinism" he cites a June 4, 2013 Senate hearing on sexual assault in the military. One month before, the Pentagon had released a report estimating twenty-six thousand sexual assaults in the military for fiscal year 2012, up dramatically from nineteen thousand in 2010.[3] A striking, widely published photograph of the Senate hearing showed a panel of experts consisting of eleven men and one woman. The Senate Armed Services Committee that was holding the hearing consisted of nineteen men and seven women (a record high number). Bruni notes that it had been twenty-two years since the Tailhook scandal, in which about one hundred Navy and Marine pilots were accused of sexually assaulting women at a convention. He also notes an additional measure of how little progress there has been since Tailhook, namely a statement by Republican Senator Saxby Chambliss, a member of the Senate committee: "Gee whiz, the hormone level created by nature sets in place the possibility for these types of things to occur."[4]

Expanding his focus regarding the persistence of sexism, Bruni proceeds to lament the small percentages of women in Congress and on corporate boards, the even smaller number of female heroes in movies and television shows, the lack of popular support for women's professional athletic teams, and the rarity of reviews for books by female authors. He also notes the panic by men on Fox News in response to the Pew Research Center study showing women to be the primary income earners in 40 percent of households with one or more children under eighteen. One of the Fox prophets of doom was Juan Williams, who said the rise in the number of female providers represents "something going terribly wrong in American society." Another Fox pundit was Erick Erickson, who said this: "When you look at biology, look at the natural world, the roles of a male and female in society, and the other animals, the male typically is the dominant role." Blending apocalypse with ignorance, he adds that the trend away from male dominance "is tearing us apart."[5]

Faced with these attitudes from the 1950s, and America's overall slowness in overcoming sexism, Bruni concludes his column with frustration and confusion:

> I'm mystified. Our racial bigotry has often been tied to the ignorance abetted by unfamiliarity, our homophobia to a failure to realize how many gay people we know and respect.
>
> Well, women are in the next cubicle, across the dinner table, on the other side of the bed. Almost every man has a mother he has known and probably cared about; most also have a wife, daughter, sister, aunt

or niece as well. Our stubborn sexism harms and holds back them, not strangers. Still it survives.[6]

It is easy to understand Bruni's frustration. However, the persistence of sexism can be explained. Let's begin that explanation with one important tip unwittingly provided by Erick Erickson. His comments about male dominance remind us of the discussion in the first two chapters of Friedrich Nietzsche's description of the traditional model of romantic love and sexuality.

Nietzsche says that at the heart of traditional heterosexual eroticism lie male domination and female subordination. A woman seeks love that results in utter devotion, and any "real man" seeks such devotion from a woman. This is a love, he says, in which a man takes a woman, and she gives herself to him. Such a love, premised on a man's dominance and a woman's subordination—with a woman being possessed by a man, as if she were a slave—leads inexorably to antagonism, Nietzsche observes. Regardless of what some women may have thought (or fantasized) about that kind of heterosexual love in the past, and regardless of how it continues to be glowingly portrayed in romantic fiction, we should note that few actual women today really want to be a man's slave, although there are examples of some semblance of that in the context of fundamentalist religion. A notably explicit example is a Yahoo group, "Masters and Slaves for Jesus," that advocates for "men being masters and head of their homes and women being slaves; just as the Bible teaches us to live."[7] That group is part of the Christian Domestic Discipline movement, which advocates for women to be spanked by their husbands.[8] The people in the CDD movement seem to take male domination and female subordination quite seriously— unlike secular BDSM folks, who view their practices as erotic play and for whom either sex can be dominant or submissive. A further example of the kind of heterosexuality described by Nietzsche is the continuing pattern of a large majority of women who take their husband's name when they marry, which is a cultural artifact of the idea that wives are the property of their husbands. But presumably most women now do not expect that archaic symbolism to imply actual legal possession or even to otherwise entail loss of respect for their personhood or professional status.

Nonetheless, as we saw in chapters 4 and 5, the idea that heterosexual love should be premised on male domination and female subordination continues to persist in fantasy and myth, often with the destructive effects in real heterosexual relationships that have been examined throughout this book. But the destructiveness goes beyond particular relationships.

The cultural inertia of this idea about erotic dominance by men and erotic subordination of women gives men a sense of entitlement to women that infects relations between men and women throughout society.

We see the consequences of these culturally programmed ideas about male entitlement in ways that are harmful to individual women, as well as extraordinarily costly to the economy: sexual assault justified by a belief that a woman was "asking for it," sexual harassment that men presume to be "invited," and sex discrimination resulting from a generalized belief that women are inferior and subordinate to men. All these social problems distract women from their work and obstruct their careers, impacting not just them as individuals, but women in general, with the further result of financial harm to their employers and the overall economy.[9]

Those damaging social problems continue, despite the fact that in real relationships actual behavior is moving away from traditional erotic myths and ideals. For example, there are growing numbers of men who are economically dependent upon women, or perform domestic and childcare tasks that were traditionally done by women, or have a diminished sense of male entitlement, or even all of the above. While the extent of such change is notable, its pace should not be exaggerated. In consonance with Frank Bruni's column, Lena Gunnarsson says that "while women have advanced their positions in the realm of sexuality and love—due above all to increased economic independence, the Pill, the possibility of divorce as well as a general loosening of the grip of marriage, and the dissemination of feminist consciousness—the most striking feature of contemporary heterosexual relations is perhaps that, despite all this, gender inequality continues its monotonous beat."[10]

Inadvertent help in understanding the persistence of gender inequality, as well as the sweeping patterns of misogyny and sexism that accompany it, comes from General David Morrison, the chief of army in Australia. He gave a brief but extraordinary speech following the announcement of an investigation into misogynistic e-mails that had circulated in the army during a period of three years. While details of the e-mails have not been released, they were said to be demeaning to female soldiers and contained both text and images that were "explicit, derogatory, demeaning and repugnant."[11]

Here are excerpts from General Morrison's fierce response, which was posted on YouTube (and which really needs to be viewed):

I have stated categorically many times that the Army has to be an inclusive organization, in which every soldier, man and woman, is able to reach their full potential and is encouraged to do so. . . .

Our service has been engaged in continuous operations since 1999, and in its longest war ever in Afghanistan. On all operations, female soldiers and officers have proven themselves worthy of the best traditions of the Australian Army. They are vital to us maintaining our capability, now and into the future.

If that does not suit you, then get out. You may find another employer where your attitude and behavior is acceptable, but I doubt it. The same goes for those who think that toughness is built on humiliating others. . . .

I will be ruthless in ridding the Army of people who cannot live up to its values and I need every one of you to support me in achieving this. . . .

If you're not up to it, find something else to do with your life. There is no place for you amongst this band of brothers and sisters.[12]

The general is surely on to something here, and it applies to the United States military every bit as much as the Australian military: Both women and men are now vital to maintaining the military's capability to carry out its missions. This growing military dependence upon large numbers of women is an extraordinarily important way in which war is becoming degendered. The growing numbers of women in the military have strengthened it, according to a consensus of military leaders. But the effectiveness of the military is diminished by adversariality between women and men. The military needs cohesion, regardless of gender. Hence General Morrison's vigorous demand that this "band of brothers and sisters" function cohesively is understandable.

The general says that anyone who is not on board with that goal should "get out"—an aggressively authoritarian approach. Then he adds this intriguing sentence: "The same goes for those who think that toughness is built on humiliating others." Now that is a radical idea, and it is where General Morrison's forceful approach to military cohesion may run into a daunting, maybe even insurmountable, problem.

Toughness. As we have seen in earlier chapters, toughness has generally been understood in militaristic cultures to be an essential element in masculinity, and misogyny has been crucial for inculcating masculine toughness in boys and men. The heart of toughness is being able to manage the capacity to care about the suffering of others and oneself. To instill that masculine toughness, and to police it, boys and men are subjected to humiliating taunts that are inherently misogynistic. Any sign of caring about suffering is seen as feminine, not masculine, and therefore met with taunts about being a pussy, little bitch, fag, wuss, etc. Sometimes it is crudely creative, for example, the suggestion that a man has "woman-like hormones" in the "Hurt Feelings Report" cited in chapter 3. The whole point is to humiliate a boy or man who is deemed not tough enough. In effect, he gets thrown over the fence separating the two adversarial groups, men and women, with the understanding that there is no greater insult, no worse fate, than to be deemed a woman, girl, or female.

But, if being deemed a woman is a horrible fate, that means the misogynistic humiliation of boys and men is simultaneously a vilification, and therefore humiliation, of girls and women. Militaristic cultural programming of masculinity relies crucially on this doubly misogynistic humiliation. So if General Morrison literally means it when he says "those who think that toughness is built on humiliating others" should "get out" of the army, either there would not be many people left or the military would be radically transformed. Considering that men coming into the military would have been misogynistically conditioned to be masculine as boys, General Morrison's imperative would have broad implications for all of Australian society.

Misogynist taunts have phenomenal power over boys and men. That's not to say that there is no other way of making soldiers, as well as peewee football players who might be future soldiers, emotionally tough. However, giving up misogynistic taunts as ways to culturally program the emotional toughness that is at the core of warrior masculinity would be a major shift, not just in the military, but in the entire cultural infrastructure of masculinity. It is culturally impossible to disentangle masculinity from the gender binary, and it is almost as hard to imagine how masculinity could be disentangled from the fear and loathing that boys and men have for the other side of the gender binary.

That is why misogyny persists so stubbornly, despite being dysfunctional in terms of military or social cohesion: misogynistic conditioning is integral to masculinity—or at least to major aspects of masculinity. We should note that it is not just the warrior dimension of masculinity that is premised on misogynistic cultural programming. In militaristic cultures, for a man to fail at the provider role is emasculating. And it is, more precisely, culturally feminizing for a man to be dependent on a female provider or to take on the domestic and childcare responsibilities that have been culturally defined as womanly.

In light of the degendering of war that was discussed in the previous chapter, are we gradually approaching the point when we will no longer need warrior masculinity? The growing reliance on technology for conducting war by remote control, along with the changes in the kinds of threats to national and human security that have been surveyed in the previous chapter, suggest a declining need to culturally program boys and men to be emotionally tough, and particularly to do that through misogyny, including taunts about wusses, pussies, and little bitches (as discussed in previous chapters). In the past, war-reliant societies have relied on men's anxiety about being deemed feminine to provide a supply of men masculine enough to brutally assault an enemy and to risk their own injury and death. But, to the extent that we rely on drones and robots to produce death and mayhem, we don't need to rely on making boys and men into warriors. And, to the extent there is no ongoing need to instill misogyny in boys and men to make them emotionally tough warriors, misogyny has surely become entirely dysfunctional—not just because of its corrosive effects on heterosexuality and women's lives generally but also because of its debilitating effects on men's emotional lives, as well as because of its sweeping social and economic detriment to society.

As we have seen in previous chapters, it is not possible to undermine half of human society with antipathy from the other half without undermining all of human society. Outside the context of militarism and warrior masculinity and traditional war, what social utility could possibly accrue from culturally programming one half of a species to hate the other half?

So just as war is becoming degendered, perhaps there is a need for gender to be demilitarized. Any past societal advantage that may have accrued from using misogyny to culturally program warrior masculinity seems to be dwindling and is becoming dwarfed by its societal disadvantages. In fact, there are signs that, as our military need for misogynistically conditioned tough guys diminishes, masculinity is shrinking, or at least culturally evolving. It is not evolving in a clear, linear direction, which is especially obvious when we take into account the popularity of rape jokes, popular music that glorifies violence toward women,[13] gonzo porn, violent and misogynist video games, and a trend among some men toward claiming they are victims of sexism or feminism or women.[14] Some men respond in fear to the ways masculinity is changing by clinging to the past with behavior that is reactive and hateful. Their stubborn misogyny can obscure any vision of the future of masculinity other than its gradual dissolution as its dysfunctionality becomes more glaringly obvious. But maybe it is more complicated than that: As Thomas Carlyle said about changing Victorian attitudes about masculinity in 1831, "The old ideal of Manhood has grown obsolete, and the new is still invisible to us."[15]

Nonetheless, there are some markers of the direction of change for masculinity. One indicator is the changing attitudes about women in combat. After the announcement by then Secretary of Defense Leon Panetta that the combat exclusion for women would be eliminated, a survey showed that 66 percent of Americans supported lifting the ban. Even more interesting, the numbers of women and men supporting women in combat were almost the same: 66 percent and 65 percent, respectively. Only 15 percent thought that having more women in combat would diminish the effectiveness of the military.[16]

This gradual embrace of women taking on the role of warrior signals a profound cultural shift regarding gender that is complementary to the diminution of the importance of warrior masculinity. Having women participating in combat roles in the military undermines the symbolic, gendered coherence of warrior masculinity and profoundly blurs the gender binary that has been integral to militaristic cultural programming. Similarly, the symbolic manliness of the provider role has been undermined by the rapidly growing number of women who are providers of financial resources for families. And the third symbolic pillar of masculinity, the procreator role, has been undermined by in vitro fertilization, the easy availability of contraception and abortion, and a general appreciation that an excess of people is burdening the environment. What happens to masculinity when women take on jobs and roles that were reserved for men, when it becomes obvious that many women can perform "masculine" toughness and aggression better than many men, and when major aspects of masculinity are seen as no longer having social utility?

What seems to be happening under those circumstances is that masculinity both expands and shrinks. As it expands to include a new female constituency, it shrinks in terms of its symbolic content. And some men and boys are clearly not handling that well. The same conservatives who panic over the effects of female providers on masculinity (as discussed previously) have also been panicking over the inclusion of contraception for women in health insurance policies under the Affordable Care Act—which becomes easier to understand when it is framed as diminishing the manly role of procreator. Greater access to contraception for women means smaller procreative power for men, thereby shrinking the symbolic content of masculinity. That may also help explain why conservative attempts to restrict abortion have been ratcheted up, with bizarre claims about masturbating fetuses, rape exceptions being unnecessary because rape kits are used so that a rape victim "can get cleaned out," and rape not causing pregnancy.[17] That kind of political flailing reflects the fact that conservative men cannot say openly, or even admit to themselves, that their opposition to women having control over their reproductive lives is because they are anxious about the cultural shrinking of masculinity. To say that would be unmanly.

That political flailing to preserve as much as possible men's control over procreation is one possible response to the shrinking symbolic content of masculinity. Another is the aforementioned advocacy of husbands spanking their wives as part of a larger effort to maintain, or at least simulate, men's dominance over women. More broadly, any opportunity to manifest misogyny offers an opportunity to cling to whatever residue is left of masculinity.

Violence toward women or other men can be a way to cling to the cultural residue of masculinity. Men's violence toward each other has been on the decline in recent decades with regard to criminal acts. A more complicated indicator of men's relationship to violence, and its role in the evolution of masculinity, comes from the sport of football. Football is surely one of the most militaristic and violent of team sports, calling upon players to act essentially like warriors. John Kass, a self-described lover of football, describes the violence of the sport: "It is about exploding into your opponent, refusing to break, while breaking others to your will and knocking them senseless." In a remarkable *Chicago Tribune* column recently, Kass proclaimed that "football is dead in America." He notes that four thousand former professional football players have filed a lawsuit against the National Football League for deliberately hiding the risks of brain damage in football. He also notes a rash of suicides by football players who shot themselves in the chest, specifically so that scientists could study the damage football had done to their brains. But it is not the cost of lawsuits that is going to shut down the NFL, according to Kass. Rather, it is the parents:

> What finishes football are the parents of future football players.
>
> The NFL desperately needs American parents. Not as fans, but as suppliers of young flesh.
>
> The NFL needs parents to send their little boys into the football feeder system. And without that supply of meat for the NFL grinder—first youth teams, then high school and college—there can be no professional football.
>
> And yet every day, more American parents decide they're finished with football. Why? Because parents can no longer avoid the fact that football scrambles the human brain.
>
> In cultural terms, parents who send their 10-year-olds to play football might as well hold up signs saying they'd like to give their children cigarettes and whiskey.[18]

Here is a broader cultural perspective: as our national and human security need for men to sacrifice themselves as warriors diminishes, our need to use football and similar sports to culturally program boys to have the qualities of the warrior diminishes. It's not just that it is beginning to make less sense to expose them to brain damage; it is also beginning to make less sense to motivate them to do that using misogynistic and homophobic taunts. And it is also beginning to make less sense to use those hateful taunts to prevent them from crying and from showing their fears and anxieties in ways that are essential to human psychological health.

As we have seen throughout this book, such changes in how we culturally program boys would have broadly sweeping implications. It means, in the long run, fewer men killing and beating and raping and harassing women and other men. It means less misogynistic harassment and discrimination that keep girls and women from reaching their full potential, which is debilitating both to them and to the entire economy. And, finally, it means less acrimony in heterosexual relationships. To say it in more positive terms: getting beyond the cultural programming of warrior masculinity opens whole new possibilities for men and women to love each other—as partners and spouses, as friends, as colleagues and coworkers, as neighbors. That is why this book was written.

NOTES

1. BATTLE OF THE SEXES

The Mike Tyson quotation of the epigraph is cited in the *Daily Telegraph*, February 1, 1989, from the *Columbia Dictionary of Quotations* (New York: Columbia University Press, 1993), p. 249.

1. Christie DZurilla, "Kim Kardashian Divorce Made Final the Day After Her Baby Shower," *Los Angeles Times*, June 4, 2013, www.latimes.com/entertainment/gossip/la-et-mg-kim-kardashian-divorce-final-kris-humphries-kanye-west-20130604,0,5019456.story (accessed July 8, 2013).

2. www.mylifetime.com/movies/obsessed (accessed February 4, 2011).

3. www.mylifetime.com/movies/friendship-die (accessed February 4, 2011).

4. www.mylifetime.com/movies/engaged-kill (accessed February 4, 2011).

5. Plato's cave allegory in *The Republic* can be helpful for explaining how cultural programming works. Plato asks the reader to imagine a society consisting of people sitting in a cave, chained so that they can only look at the wall of the cave in front of them. Behind them is a stone wall, beyond which is a fire. Between that wall and the fire there are people carrying puppets that cast shadows on the cave wall in front of the chained prisoners; the puppeteers also provide vocal dialogue that bounces off the wall of the cave so that it seems like the shadows are talking. Thus the prisoners' understanding of the world and their lives is derived entirely from what is provided by the shadows on the wall of the cave.

Plato's cave allegory was the inspiration for the 1999 film *The Matrix*. The "matrix" is a fabricated world of virtual experience produced by intelligent machines that is electrochemically fed into human brains, which then "have" those virtual experiences. Similarly (up to a point), our experience is largely fabricated by all the generators of culture in a wide variety of human and technological contexts, such as peer and family interactions, social media, religion, literature, and mass media (journalism, television, movies, sports, music, and so on). Borrowing the terminology of Plato's cave allegory, those kinds of culture generation are the sources of the shadows on the wall of our cave. They culturally program how we think, feel, desire, and choose.

Few cultures are static. Most evolve continually, as the material conditions faced by a society change. As we shall see in this book, cultural evolution generally benefits society as a whole, but does not necessarily serve the best interest of any particular member. Further, cultural evolution does not always keep pace with changing material conditions. Cultural inertia can result in the interests of most or all members of a society being poorly served. Thus cultural programming presents challenges for the flourishing of any given individual person.

Although my notion of cultural programming is both broader and narrower than the notion of "cultural belief systems" in anthropology, its similarity to that notion can be seen when Marilyn Grunkemeyer usefully notes that "[cultural] belief systems tend for the most part to reside at the level of assumptions and presuppositions," rather than evidence and reason. See Marilyn Grunkemeyer, "Belief Systems," in D. Levinson and M. Ember, eds., *Encyclopedia of Cultural Anthropology* 1:125–30 (New York: Holt, 1996), pp. 126, 125.

6. Lizette Alvarez and Deborah Sontag, "When Strains on Military Families Turn Deadly," *New York Times*, February 15, 2008, www.nytimes.com/2008/02/15/us/15vets.html (accessed July 1, 2013).

7. Wendy Wang and Kim Parker, "Women See Value and Benefits of College; Men Lag on Both Fronts, Survey Finds," *Pew Research Social and Demographic Trends*, August 17, 2011, www.pewsocialtrends.org/2011/08/17/women-see-value-and-benefits-of-college-men-lag-on-both-fronts-survey-finds/ (accessed June 9, 2013).

8. In the absence of nonobvious countervailing factors.

9. Justin Kaplan, ed., *With Malice Toward Women* (New York: Dodd, Mead, 1952); the quotes are from pp. 1 and 4.

10. Camille Paglia, *Sex, Art, and American Culture* (New York: Vintage, 1992), pp. 68, 74.

11. Robert Louis Stevenson, *Virginibus Puerisque and Other Works* (New York: Scribner's, 1896), pp. 39–40.

12. For a plethora of examples of such variation, see David D. Gilmore, *Manhood in the Making: Cultural Concepts of Masculinity* (New Haven: Yale University Press, 1990). On the Semai, see Robert Knox Dentan, *Overwhelming Terror: Love, Fear, Peace, and Violence Among Semai of Malaysia* (Lanham, MD:

Rowman and Littlefield, 2008). On the Tahitians, see Robert I. Levy, *Tahitians: Mind and Experience in the Society Islands* (Chicago: University of Chicago Press, 1975). On the Mosuo, see Judith Stacey, "Unhitching the Horse from the Carriage: Love and Marriage Among the Mosuo," *Utah Law Review* 2 (2009), http://epubs .utah.edu/index.php/ulr/article/view/170/143 (accessed July 2, 2013). Also on the Mosuo, see Cai Hua, *A Society Without Fathers or Husbands: The Na of China* (Cambridge: MIT Press, 2008).

13. While the term *militaristic* may technically imply the existence of military institutions, I shall use *militaristic* in a broader sense, as an approximate synonym for *war-reliant*, except when I am writing about cultural militarism, which refers to broad cultural patterns, including faith in force, suppressed empathy as a virtue, etc.

14. David Buss, *Evolutionary Psychology: The New Science of the Mind,* 3d ed. (Boston: Allyn and Bacon, 2008), p. 327.

15. Edward O. Wilson, *On Human Nature* (Cambridge: Harvard University Press, 1978), p. 99.

16. Douglas P. Fry, *Beyond War: The Human Potential for Peace* (New York: Oxford University Press, 2007), p. 219.

17. Ibid., pp. 237–238; the list is also in Douglas P. Fry, *The Human Potential for Peace: An Anthropological Challenge to Assumptions About War and Violence* (New York: Oxford University Press, 2007), pp. 92–93. There is also considerable information about societies that are not war reliant at the Web site nonkilling.org.

18. Fry, *Beyond War*, p. 26.

19. Ibid., p. 31.

20. Dentan, *Overwhelming Terror,* pp. 192–97. Also see his *The Semai: A Nonviolent People of Malaya* (New York: Holt, Rinehart, and Winston, 1968). And the Semai are discussed extensively throughout Fry, *Beyond War.*

21. Fry, *Beyond War,* pp. 17–18.

22. Joshua S. Goldstein, *War and Gender* (New York: Cambridge University Press, 2001), chap. 1; also available at www.warandgender. com/wgch1.htm (accessed July 1, 2013); Maria Lepowsky, *Fruit of the Motherland: Gender in an Egalitarian Society* (New York: Columbia University Press, 1994); Gilmore, *Manhood in the Making,* chap. 9.

23. Henry Adams, *Letters of Henry Adams, 1858–1891,* ed. Worthington C. Ford (Boston: Houghton Mifflin, 1930), p. 484.

24. Gilmore, *Manhood in the Making,* p. 203.

25. Lu Yuan and Sam Mitchell, "Land of the Walking Marriage (Mosuo People of China)," *Natural History* 109, no. 9 (2000): 58–60; Heide Gottner-Abendroth,

"The Structure of Matriarchal Societies," *ReVision* 21, no. 3 (1999): 1–6. For another example of matriarchy, see Peggy Reeves Sanday, *Woman at the Center: Life in a Modern Matriarchy* (Ithaca: Cornell University Press, 2002).

26. Amanda Alpert, Final Exam for PHIL 180: Existentialism, December 17, 2002 (quoted with permission of the author).

27. Steve Keating, "Girl Power Carries U.S. Back to Top of Medal Table," www .sbs.com.au/news/olympics/articles/UK-OLY-USA-REVIEW-2012-BRE87B0JE .html (accessed August 12, 2012).

28. "Serena Williams in Burberry—Wimbledon Championships 2012 Winners' Ball," www.redcarpet-fashionawards.com/category/blog/blog-celebrities/serena -williams/ (accessed August 12, 2012).

29. For extensive evidence of the illusoriness of the gender binary, with hundreds of examples from throughout nature, see Joan Roughgarden, *Evolution's Rainbow: Diversity, Gender, and Sexuality in Nature and People* (Berkeley: University of California Press, 2004).

30. The most notable exception would be the "amazon soldiers" in Dahomey; see Stanley B. Alpern, *Amazons of Black Sparta: The Women Warriors of Dahomey* (London: Hurst, 1998).

31. Associated Press, "Baby Killed After Interrupting Mom's Facebook Time," October 28, 2010, www.foxnews.com/us/2010/10/28/baby-killed-interrupting-moms-facebook-time/ (accessed July 1, 2013).

32. Victoria Taylor, "Colorado Woman Left Estranged Husband a Note Before Shooting Their 9-Year-Old Son: Police," *New York Daily News*, June 1, 2013, www .nydailynews.com/news/crime/mom-left-note-shooting-son-9-cops-article -1.1360604?print (accessed June 2, 2013).

33. Dave Grossman, *On Killing: The Psychological Cost of Learning to Kill in War and Society,* rev. ed. (Back Bay, 2009).

34. Eric T. Dean Jr., *Shook Over Hell: Post-Traumatic Stress, Vietnam, and the Civil War* (Cambridge: Harvard University Press, 1997), p. 54; quoted in Joshua S. Goldstein, *War and Gender* (Cambridge University Press, 2001), p. 254.

35. Stephen E. Ambrose, *Citizen Soldiers: The U.S. Army from the Normandy Beaches to the Bulge to the Surrender of Germany June 7, 1944–May 7, 1945* (New York: Simon and Schuster, 1997); quoted in Goldstein, *War and Gender*, p. 255.

36. Gwynne Dyer, *War: The Lethal Custom* (New York: Basic Books, 2006), p. 59.

37. Ibid., p. 59.

38. Gilmore, *Manhood in the Making*, p. 210.

39. Genesis 38:9–10.

40. Paul Cartledge, *The Spartans* (New York: Vintage, 2004); P. J. Rhodes, *History of the Classical Greek World, 478–323 BC*, 2d ed. (Hoboken, NJ: Wiley-Blackwell, 2009), pp. 240–256; Simon Hornblower, *The Greek World, 479–323 BC* (London: Routledge, 2011), pp. 250–251; Robert K. Fleck and F. Andrew Hanssen, "'Rulers Ruled by Women': An Economic Analysis of the Rise and Fall of Women's Rights in Ancient Sparta," www.law.virginia.edu/pdf/olin/0708/hanssen.pdf (accessed July 2, 2013).

41. See Josef Meisinger, "Combating Abortion and Homosexuality as a Political Task," in Günter Grau, ed., *Hidden Holocaust? Gay and Lesbian Persecution in Germany, 1933–45* (New York: Routledge, 1995), pp. 113–15. Meisinger was appointed as the first director of the Reich Central Office for Combating Homosexuality and Abortion.

42. See, for example, Sunshine Hillygus and Todd Shields, "Moral Issues and Voter Decision Making in the 2004 Presidential Election," *PS: Political Science & Politics*, April 2005, www.apsanet.org/imgtest/PSApro5HillygusShields.pdf (accessed July 1, 2013).

43. Patrick Healy, "The Clinton Conundrum: What's Behind the Laugh?" *New York Times*, September 30, 2007, www.nytimes.com/2007/09/30/us /politics/30clinton.html?_r=0 (accessed July 3, 2013); after Healy's repeated use of the expression "Clinton Cackle," I recall hearing television commentators use it frequently.

44. James Campbell, "Gillard's Rivals Should Ditch the Witch Attack," *Sunday Herald Sun*, March 27, 2011, www.heraldsun.com.au/news/opinion/gillards-rivals -should-ditch-the-witch-attack/story-e6frfifo-1226028789433; Van Badham, "Julia Gillard Ousted: Achievement Does Not Equal Respect If You're a Woman," *Telegraph*, June 27, 2013, www.telegraph.co.uk/women/womens-politics/10143834 /Julia-Gillard-ousted-by-sexism-Achievement-does-not-equal-respect-if-youre-a-woman.html; Kathy Marks, "What Sank Julia Gillard? The Truth About Sexism in Australia," *Independent*, June 28, 2013, www.independent.co.uk/news/world /australasia/what-sank-julia-gillard-the-truth-about-sexism-in-australia-8679285 .html?printService=print (all accessed July 3, 2013).

45. In modern industrialized societies, men who are economically privileged are less likely to go to war than less privileged men, but nonetheless they are socialized with the qualities of the warrior and encouraged to display those qualities in business and professional contexts.

46. *FHM*, November 2008, cover at www.fhmus.com/site/incoming/Default. aspx?categoryid=2142&cpr=1, article at http://fhmonline.com/site/content /article.aspx?ID=36842 (both accessed October 3, 2008).

47. Elizabeth Cady Stanton, *Elizabeth Cady Stanton as Revealed in Her Letters, Diary and Reminiscences* (New York: Harper, 1922), 2:82.

48. Stephanie Coontz, *Marriage, a History: How Love Conquered Marriage* (New York: Viking Penguin, 2005), pp. 149–150.

49. T. S. Arthur, *Advice to Young Ladies on Their Duties and Conduct in Life* (Boston: Phillips, Sampson, 1849), pp. 148–49, 156.

50. Friedrich Nietzsche, *The Gay Science,* trans. Walter Kaufmann (New York: Random House, 1974), p. 319.

51. Ibid.

52. Ibid.

53. "The War Within," CNN, aired June 17, 2007, 2:00 pm EDT, transcript at http://transcripts.cnn.com/TRANSCRIPTS/0706/17/siu.01.html (accessed February 10, 2013).

54. Ibid.

55. Nietzsche, *The Gay Science,* p. 319.

56. www.cnn.com/US/OJ/suspect/note/ (accessed March 24, 2011).

57. www.endabuse.org/content/action_center/detail/754 (accessed March 24, 2011).

2. LET'S MAKE A DEAL

The epigraph is from "Unhappily Married," lyrics by Pistol Annies (Angaleena Presley, Ashley Monroe, Miranda Lambert), from the album *Annie Up* (Nashville: RCA Records, 2013). Credit/permission: Ashley Monroe (BMI), Reynsong Publishing Corporation/Ayden Publishing (BMI).

1. By "heterosexual homicide" I mean a killing in the context of a present, former, or sought-for heterosexual relationship.

2. Nelly said in an October 2010 interview that he was thinking of turning the *Tip Drill* video into a movie, www.sohh.com/2010/10/nelly_hints_at_tip_drill_movie_everybody.html (accessed March 22, 2011).

3. Susan Faludi, *Backlash: The Undeclared War Against American Women* (New York: Crown, 1991).

4. http://radioboston.wbur.org/2011/03/21/feminist-response-haslander (accessed March 22, 2011).

5. Tim Murphy, "If You Thought Michele Bachmann Was Out There . . . ," *Mother Jones,* May 14, 2012 (accessed August 16, 2012).

6. Eric W. Dolan, "Fox Contributor: Liberals Who Reject That Men Should Dominate Women Are Anti-science," www.rawstory.com/rs/2013/05/29/fox -contributor-liberals-who-reject-that-men-should-dominate-women-are-anti -science/ (accessed May 30, 2013)

7. www.focusonthefamily.com/marriage/gods_design_for_marriage/marriage _gods_idea/covenant_the_heart_of_the_marriage_mystery.aspx (accessed March 22, 2011).

8. "God designed men, not women, to be the breadwinners," May 29, 2013 http://www.youtube.com/watch?v=c_Dc_loZfMQ (accessed May 30, 2013).

9. "Police: Dad Says He Killed Girl for Texting Boy," Associated Press, February 16, 2008, www.msnbc.msn.com/id/23203367/ns/us_new-crime_and_courts/ (accessed March 23, 2011).

10. Friedrich Nietzsche, *The Gay Science*, trans. Walter Kaufmann (New York: Random House, 1974), p. 319.

11. Even the *Urban Dictionary* has only this definition of "penis whipped," submitted as a synonym for *enraptured* by a visitor to the Web site named Barry Flomar: "When a female is so enraptured by a certain man's penis size and power to pleasure her that she goes through a state of emotional chaos. This mental mind warping can last hours, days, weeks, or even months before it is shaken. It is harder to shake if the penis whipping act is repeated while she is still in the original phase of the mind state. This mind-fuck status festers from fearing she will lose the best fuck she has ever had. *I was so penis whipped after he tagged me the first time that I feared I wouldn't be able to think straight for months*," www.urbandictionary.com/ define.php?term=enraptured (accessed June 23, 2011).

12. http://bauerfamilylaw.blogspot.com/2008/02/groom-taking-brides-last-name.html (accessed March 23, 2011).

13. Richard Fry and D'Vera Cohn, "New Economics of Marriage: The Rise of Wives," http://pewresearch.org/pubs/1466/economics-marriage-rise-of-wives (accessed March 23, 2011).

14. Wendy Wang and Kim Parker, "Women See Value and Benefits of College; Men Lag on Both Fronts, Survey Finds," *Pew Research Social & Demographic Trends*, August 17, 2011, www.pewsocialtrends.org/2011/08/17/women-see-value-and-benefits-of-college-men-lag-on-both-fronts-survey-finds/ (accessed June 9, 2013).

15. Randy Dotinga, "For Depressed Young Women, Girlfriends Are Better Bet Than Boyfriends," http://story.news.yahoo.com/news?tmpl=story&cid=97&97 &e=3&u=/hsn/20020404/hl_hsn/for_depressed_young_women__girlfriends

_are_better_bet_than_boyfriends (retrieved April 5, 2002), also available at http://tech.groups.yahoo.com/group/psychiatry-research/message/3251; the study itself is Shannon E. Daley," *Journal of Consulting and Clinical Psychology* 70, no. 1 (February 2002), pp. 129–141.

16. *ABC World News* broadcast, March 13, 2008, recorded by the author.

17. "20/20: Prostitution in America: Working Girls Speak," ABC broadcast, March 20, 2008, recorded by the author.

18. Kate Linthicum, "Erotic Massage Parlors Proliferate in L.A. Communities," *Los Angeles Times*, March 23, 2011, www.latimes.com/news/la-me-massage-parlors -20110323,0,1398011.story (accessed March 23, 2011).

19. Gail Dines, *Pornland: How Porn Has Hijacked Our Sexuality* (Boston: Beacon, 2010); also see the resources at stoppornculture.org.

20. The term *gonzo porn* is also used in another sense, for pornography that strives to give the viewer a sense of being part of the scene. That meaning was presumably borrowed from the term *gonzo journalism,* made famous by Hunter Thompson. Gail Dines's use of the term reflects the pre–Hunter Thompson definition of gonzo as extremely bizarre. I suspect that this earlier definition was initially why the term *gonzo* was applied to Thompson's work, and then his proclivity for inserting himself in bizarre ways into the political action he narrated led to a lexical evolution that produced the notion of gonzo porn as making the viewer feel present in the action. In any case, I use the term *gonzo porn* to mean pornography that misogynistically, and often brutally, degrades the women it features, as illustrated by the examples I give in chapter 3.

21. Amanda Walker-Rodriguez and Rodney Hill, "Human Sex Trafficking," *FBI Law Enforcement Bulletin*, March 2011, www.fbi.gov/stats-services/publications /law-enforcement-bulletin/march_2011/human_sex_trafficking (accessed July 20, 2013).

22. www.realdoll.com/cgi-bin/snav.rd (retrieved March 22, 2011).

23. Interviewed in the documentary film, *The Price of Pleasure* (Media Education Foundation, 2008).

24. Nietzsche, *The Gay Science,* pp. 319–20.

25. Sandra Bartky, *Femininity and Domination: Studies in the Phenomenology of Oppression* (New York: Routledge, 1990), p. 102.

26. Ibid., p. 104.

27. Ibid., p. 102–3.

28. Ibid., p. 103.

29. Wang and Parker, "Women See Value and Benefits of College."

30. ABC News broadcast, February 6, 2006.

31. Robert L. Jamieson Jr., "Why Won't the Coach's Wife Be at the Super Bowl?" www.seattlepi.com/jamieson/257978_roberto2.html (accessed March 22, 2011).

32. Pepper Schwartz, *Love Between Equals* (New York: Free Press, 1994).

33. Shulamith Firestone, *The Dialectic of Sex* (New York: William Morrow, 1970), p. 123.

34. ABC News *Nightline* broadcast, February 14, 2008; also see John Berman and Shani Meewella, "Partners in Crime, and Life," http://abcnews.go.com /Nightline/story?id=4291491&page=1; also see Julia Hoppock, "The Two Cop Couple" http://abcnews.go.com/blogs/headlines/2008/02/the-two-cop-cou/ (both accessed July 1, 2013).

35. Richard Wasserstrom, "Preferential Treatment, Color-Blindness, and the Evils of Racism and Racial Discrimination," *Proceedings and Addresses of the American Philosophical Association* 61, no. 1, supplement (Sep., 1987), pp. 27–42.

3. HOW TO MAKE A WARRIOR

Andrej Pejić models both men's and women's clothing, and describes herself as living in between genders. The chapter epigraph comes from Alex Morris, "The Prettiest Boy in the World," *New York*, August 14, 2011, http://nymag.com /fashion/11/fall/andrej-pejic/index2.html (accessed June 21 2013).

1. Homer, *The Iliad*, trans. Robert Fagles (New York: Penguin, 1991), pp. 423–24.

2. See Terrence Real, *I Don't Want to Talk About It: Overcoming the Secret Legacy of Male Depression* (New York: Fireside, 1997); William Pollack, *Real Boys* (New York: Random House, 1998).

3. Alissa J. Rubin and Sangar Rahimi, "Nine Afghan Boys Collecting Firewood Killed by NATO Helicopters," *New York Times*, March 2, 2011, www.nytimes .com/2011/03/03/world/asia/03afghan.html (accessed March 3, 2011).

4. See Michael B. Poliakoff, *Combat Sports in the Ancient World* (New Haven: Yale University Press, 1987); and David D. Gilmore, *Manhood in the Making* (New Haven: Yale University Press, 1991).

5. A host of examples from many different societies is provided in Gilmore, *Manhood in the Making.*

6. *Raising Cain* (2006) is a documentary narrated by Michael Thompson, based on his book *Raising Cain: Protecting the Emotional Lives of Boys* (New York: Ballantine, 2000). The film is viewable at www.pbs.org/opb/raisingcain/ (accessed March 18, 2011).

7. "Battles with Taliban Take Heavy Toll," www.msnbc.msn.com/id/5424809 /ns/nightly_news-about_us/t/richard-engel/ (accessed May 14, 2011). There is a follow-up report transcript here: https://a248.e.akamai.net/7/1635/50139/1d /origin.nbclearn.com/files/nbcarchives/site/pdf/51460.pdf (accessed May 14, 2011).

8. "Back Home, Soldier Wrestles with Wounds of War," *NBC Nightly News*, November 21, 2010, www.nbcnews.com/video/nightly-news/40301979#40301979 (accessed December 5, 2013).

9. Bill Chappell, "U.S. Military's Suicide Rate Surpassed Combat Deaths in 2012," *NPR*, January 14, 2013, www.npr.org/blogs/thetwo-way/2013/01/14/169364733 /u-s-militarys-suicide-rate-surpassed-combat-deaths-in-2012 (accessed June 26, 2013).

10. For the soldier even to be concerned about his psychological health can be a problem; see Andrew Goldstein, "Even Soldiers Hurt," *Time*, October 7, 2001, www .time.com/time/magazine/article/0,9171,1000997,00.html (accessed July 1, 2013).

11. For a contrary view on the privilege differential between men and women, see the blog entry "Why Gender Privilege Does Not Exist," February 27, 2011, 12:09 A.M., http://clarissasblog.com/2011/02/27/why-gender-privilege-does-not-exist / (accessed July 1, 2013).

12. Mark McCormack and Eric Anderson, "'It's Just Not Acceptable Any More: The Erosion of Homophobia and the Softening of Masculinity at an English Sixth Form," *Sociology* 44, no. 5 (October 2010): 843–59.

13. Karen Snyder, "Offensive Survey Leads to Buffalo Head Coach Resignation," *K2 Radio*, November 9, 2011, http://k2radio.com/offensive-survey-leads-to -buffalo-head-coach-resignation/ (accessed July 21, 2013)

14. David Gilmore, *Manhood in the Making* (New Haven: Yale University Press, 1990), pp. 158–159.

15. Anonymous, final paper for Introduction to Philosophy, Springfield College, fall 2009.

16. A paraphrase of a comment by Michael Herzfeld about Glendiot manhood in *The Poetics of Manhood: Contest and Identity in a Cretan Mountain Village* (Princeton: Princeton University Press, 1988), p. 16.

17. Those particular examples are from Gail Dines, *Pornland: How Porn Has Hijacked Our Sexuality* (Boston: Beacon, 2010), p. 64.

18. Ibid., pp. 68–69.

19. www.foundrymusic.com/bands/displayinterview.cfm/id/130 (accessed May 17, 2011).

20. NPR Staff, "'Badass' Guys: Giving History a Kick (and a Punch)," www .npr.org/2011/05/14/136205194/badass-guys-giving-history-a-kick-and-a-punch (accessed May 17, 2011).

21. Ben Thompson, *Badass: The Birth of a Legend* (New York: Harper, 2011). The quote is from a book excerpt at www.npr.org/2011/05/14/136205194/badass -guys-giving-history-a-kick-and-a-punch (accessed July 21, 2013).

22. So a primary criterion of the highest military honor in the United States, the Medal of Honor, is that the recipient's combat effectiveness be "at the risk of his own life." http://edocket.access.gpo.gov/cfr_2002/julqtr/32cfr578.4.htm (accessed March 18, 2011).

23. Bill Chappell, "U.S. Military's Suicide Rate Surpassed Combat Deaths in 2012," *NPR*, January 14, 2013, www.npr.org/blogs/thetwo-way/2013/01/14/169364733 /u-s-militarys-suicide-rate-surpassed-combat-deaths-in-2012 (accessed June 26, 2013).

24. Daniel Somers, "'I Am Sorry That It Has Come to This': A Soldier's Last Words," *Gawker*, June 22, 2013, http://gawker.com/i-am-sorry-that-it-has-come-to-this-a-soldiers-last-534538357 (accessed June 25, 2013).

25. Hamilton Nolan, "Bushmaster Firearms, Your Man Card Is Revoked," *Gawker*, December 17, 2012, http://gawker.com/5969150/bushmaster-firearms -your-man-card-is-revoked (accessed June 26, 2013).

26. Robert Siegel, "A Turning Point for Talking About Suicide and Guns in Wyoming," *NPR*, March 19, 2013, www.npr.org/templates/transcript/transcript .php?storyId=174761612 (accessed June 26, 2013).

27. Ibid.

28. Kevin Powell, "Manhood, Football, and Suicide," *CNN*, December 3, 2012, www.cnn.com/2012/12/03/opinion/powell-football-manhood-suicide/index .html (accessed December 3, 2012).

4. KEEPING THE BATTLE OF THE SEXES ALIVE

The epigraph is from "Unhappily Married," lyrics by Pistol Annies (Angaleena Presley, Ashley Monroe, Miranda Lambert), from the album *Annie Up* (Nashville: RCA Records, 2013). Credit/permission: Ashley Monroe (BMI), Reynsong Publishing Corporation/Ayden Publishing (BMI).

1. The notion of some men's rights activists and other antifeminists that this policy indicates an anti-male attitude coming from women generally, or feminists

specifically, is absurd, not least because it is primarily men who decide this policy. See the discussion of antifeminist Warren Farrell in chapter 6.

2. See the discussion of Sparta in chapter 1.

3. Friedrich Nietzsche, *The Gay Science*, trans. Walter Kaufmann (New York: Random House, 1974), p. 319.

4. David Ellis and Barbara L. Goldberg, "Hedda's Hellish Tale," *Time*, December 12, 1988, www.time.com/time/magazine/article/0,9171,956490,00.html; "Interview with Hedda Nussbaum," *Larry King Live*, CNN, June 16, 2003, www.rickross.com/reference/abusive/abusive1.html; Kathy A. Gambrel, "Hedda Nussbaum: Still Reclaiming Her Life," www.upi.com/Top_News/2003/01/23/Hedda-Nussbaum-Still-reclaiming-her-life/UPI-32721043352467/ (all accessed March 25, 2011).

5. Judson W. Van DeVenter, "I Surrender All" (1896), http://library.timelesstruths.org/music/I_Surrender_All/ (accessed May 30, 2011).

6. Nietzsche, *The Gay Science,* p. 319.

7. Ibid.

8. "A Take-Charge Kind of Guy" aired January 29, 2009, www.tv.com/web/romance-buy-the-book/a-take-charge-kind-of-guy-2754318/ (accessed June 5, 2013).

9. www.amazon.com/Taken-Prince-Christina-Dodd/dp/0451413040 (accessed March 30, 2011).

10. George Michael, "Faith"; lyrics at www.metrolyrics.com/faith-lyrics-george-michael.html (accessed July 22, 2013).

11. Terri Orbuch, "Are Men More Romantic Than Women?" *Huffington Post*, January 6, 2011, www.huffingtonpost.com/dr-terri-orbuch/are-men-more-romantic-tha_b_796099.html; Piper Weiss, "Why Men Are More Romantic Than Women," January 12, 2011, http://shine.yahoo.com/channel/sex/why-men-are-more-romantic-than-women-2439559; "It's Official: Men Are More Romantic Than Women," February 2007, http://findarticles.com/p/articles/mi_pwwi/is_200702/ai_n17220307/ (all accessed April 6, 2011).

12. Orbuch, "Are Men More Romantic Than Women?"

13. Ibid.

14. Lisa Wade, "The Banal, Mundane Lives of College Students," *Sociological Images*, June 25, 2013, http://thesocietypages.org/socimages/2013/06/25/the-banal-mundane-sex-lives-of-college-students/ (accessed July 25, 2013).

15. *African Americans' Lives Today*, June 2013; study conducted by Harvard School of Public Health, Robert Wood Johnson Foundation, and NPR, www.rwjf

.org/content/dam/farm/reports/surveys_and_polls/2013/rwjf406076 (accessed June 5, 2013); also available at www.hsph.harvard.edu/news/files/2013/06/AfrAmer _report_final_with_topline.pdf (accessed June 5, 2013).

16. Michelle Buonofiglio, "AuthorView: Christina Dodd," November 10, 2005, www.click2houston.com/entertainment/5298876/detail.html (accessed March 30, 2011).

17. Orbuch, "Are Men More Romantic Than Women?"

18. Anna Breslaw, "Casting Call: Bit-Player, Male," *New York Times*, March 10, 2011, www.nytimes.com/2011/03/13/fashion/13ModernLove.html (accessed June 12, 2011).

19. Ibid.

5. CAN MEN RESCUE HETEROSEXUAL LOVE?

1. Wendy Wang and Kim Parker, "Women See Value and Benefits of College; Men Lag on Both Fronts, Survey Finds," *Pew Research Social & Demographic Trends*, August 17, 2011, www.pewsocialtrends.org/2011/08/17/women-see-value-and-benefits-of-college-men-lag-on-both-fronts-survey-finds/ (accessed June 9, 2013).

2. Gene Demby, "So Single Black Men Want Commitment. Really?" *Code Switch: Frontiers of Race, Culture, and Ethnicity*, June 8, 2013, www.npr.org/blogs /codeswitch/2013/06/08/189581139/so-single-black-men-want-commitment-really (accessed June 9, 2013).

3. Wang and Parker, "Women See Value and Benefits of College."

4. Clyde W. Franklin II, "Black Male-Black Female Conflict: Individually Caused and Culturally Nurtured," *Journal of Black Studies* 15, no. 2 (December 1984), pp. 139–54, www.jstor.org/stable/2784005 (accessed June 28, 2013).

5. David M. Buss, "Sex Differences in Human Mate Preferences: Evolutionary Hypotheses Tested in 37 Cultures," *Behavioral and Brain Sciences* 12 (1989): 1–49; there is a briefer discussion of the study in David M. Buss, "Sexual Conflict: Evolutionary Insights Into Feminism and the 'Battle of the Sexes,'" in David M. Buss and Neil M. Malamuth, eds., *Sex, Power, Conflict: Evolutionary and Feminist Perspectives* (New York: Oxford University Press, 1996), pp. 296–315.

6. That was the premise of the MTV show *Exposed,* www.mtv.com/shows /mtv_exposed/series.jhtml (accessed July 1, 2013).

7. Dan Savage, Savage Love Podcast, episode 237, May 3, 2011, www.thestranger. com/SavageLovePodcast/archives/2011/05/03/savage-love-episode-237 (accessed June 13, 2011).

8. Season 3 (2010), episode 2, at about 18:30; see www.tvfanatic.com/shows /friday-night-lights/episodes/season-3/tami-knows-best/ (accessed Juy 1 2013).

9. See chapter 4.

10. *BBC World Service Documentaries*, "Family Matters: Episode 2—Mexico," broadcast March 21, 2011, www.bbc.co.uk/programmes/p00fc7vd (accessed July 23, 2013).

11. Friedrich Nietzsche, *The Gay Science*, trans. Walter Kaufmann (New York: Random House, 1974), p. 319; Friedrich Nietzsche, *The Gay Science,* ed. Bernard Williams, trans. Josefine Nauckhoff (Cambridge: Cambridge University Press, 2001), pp. 227–28.

12. Simone de Beauvoir, *The Second Sex* (New York: Vintage, 1989), p. 642.

13. The most notable exception being the Spartan women, who owned property and experienced fitness training comparable to the Spartan men, including wrestling and foot races. See Sarah B. Pomeroy, *Spartan Women* (New York: Oxford University Press, 2002); and Robert K. Fleck and F. Andrew Hanssen, "'Rulers Ruled By Women': An Economic Analysis of the Rise and Fall of Women's Rights in Ancient Sparta," www.law.virginia.edu/pdf/olin/0708/hanssen.pdf (accessed July 2, 2013).

14. Beauvoir, *The Second Sex*, p. 643.

15. Ibid., p. 653.

16. Ibid., p. 653.

17. Ibid., p. 644.

18. David D. Gilmore, *Manhood in the Making: Cultural Concepts of Masculinity* (New Haven: Yale University Press, 1990), p. 15.

19. *BBC World Service Documentaries*, "Family Matters: Episode 2—Mexico."

20. See www.npr.org/blogs/health/2014/02/18/279035110/ivf-baby-boom -births-from-fertility-procedure-hit-new-high.

21. Richard Whitmire and Susan McGee Bailey, "Gender Gap," *Education Next* 10, no. 2 (Spring 2010), http://educationnext.org/gender-gap/ (retrieved April 13, 2011); "Left Behind in America: The Nation's Dropout Crisis," Center for Labor Market Studies, Northeastern University, May 5, 2009, www.clms.neu.edu /publication/documents/CLMS_2009_Dropout_Report.pdf (retrieved April 13, 2011); James Vaznis, "Hub Grads Come Up Short in College," *Boston Globe*, November 17, 2008, www.youthworkersalliance.org/news/hub-grads-come-up -short-in-college (retrieved April 13, 2011); Wang and Parker, "Women See Value and Benefits of College."

22. www.npr.org/blogs/money/2010/07/07/128359804/unemployment-rate -men-vs-women (accessed June 18, 2011).

23. http://economix.blogs.nytimes.com/2011/04/08/men-unemployment-and
-disability/ (retrieved June 18, 2011).

24. David Brooks, "The Missing Fifth," *New York Times*, May 9, 2011, www
.nytimes.com/2011/05/10/opinion/10brooks.html (accessed June 18, 2011).

25. Ibid.

26. Ibid.

27. Gail Dines, *Pornland: How Porn Has Hijacked Our Sexuality* (Boston: Beacon, 2010), p. 62.

28. Matthew B. Ezzell, "Pornography, Lad Mags, Video Games, and Boys: Reviving the Canary in the Cultural Coal Mine," in S. Olfman, ed., *The Sexualization of Childhood* (Westport, CT: Praeger, 2009), pp. 7–32, quoted in Dines, *Pornland*, p. 62.

29. Michael Kimmel, *Guyland: The Perilous World Where Boys Become Men* (New York: HarperCollins, 2008), pp. 183–85.

30. Elizabeth A. Armstrong, Laura Hamilton, Brian Sweeney, "Sexual Assault on Campus: A Multilevel, Integrative Approach to Party Rape," *Social Problems* 53, no. 4 (2006): 483–99.

31. On women choosing to remain single, see Kate Bolick, "All the Single Ladies," *Atlantic*, November 2011, www.theatlantic.com/magazine/archive/2011/11/all-the
-single-ladies/308654/ (accessed July 27, 2013); Bella DePaulo, *Singled Out: How Singles Are Stereotyped, Stigmatized, and Ignored, and Still Live Happily Ever After* (New York: St. Martin's, 2006); Eric Klinenberg, *Going Solo: The Extraordinary Rise and Surprising Appeal of Living Alone* (New York: Penguin, 2012). On women choosing to be in relationships with other women, see Kira Cochrane, "Why It's Never Too Late to Be a Lesbian," *Guardian*, July 22, 2010, www.guardian.co.uk
/lifeandstyle/2010/jul/22/late-blooming-lesbians-women-sexuality/print (accessed July 27, 2013); Vicki Iovine, "Switching Sides Later in Life," *Huffington Post*, May 15, 2009, www.huffingtonpost.com/vicki-iovine/is-lesbianism-the-latest_b_203837.html (accessed July 27, 2013); Lindsay Miller, "Queer by Choice, Not by Chance," *Atlantic*, September 12, 2011, www.theatlantic.com/health
/archive/2011/09/queer-by-choice-not-by-chance-against-being-born-this
-way/244898/ (accessed July 27, 2013). Of course, the evidence is strong that in the vast majority of cases a lesbian orientation is not the result of choice.

6. GENDER TERRORISM, GENDER SACRIFICE

The epigraph to this chapter is quoted by Michael Kimmel, *Manhood in America* (New York: Oxford University Press, 1995), p. 178.

1. This cultural programming of women to be breeders takes place in manifold ways. For example, stereotypes about only children have been used to guilt-trip mothers into having more than one child, despite all the myths about only children being thoroughly debunked and despite all the emotional and economic disadvantages that accrue with each additional child. See Lauren Sandler, *One and Only: The Freedom of Having an Only Child, and the Joy of Being One* (New York: Simon and Schuster, 2013); Susan Newman, *The Case for the Only Child: Your Essential Guide* (Deerfield Beach, FL: HCI, 2011); Bill McKibben, *Maybe One: The Case for Smaller Families* (New York: Plume, 1999).

2. Warren Farrell and James P. Sterba, *Does Feminism Discriminate Against Men? A Debate* (New York: Oxford University Press, 2008), p. 70.

3. "Sex, Race, and Granite: One More Lesson from the Vietnam War," *Injustice Studies* 1 (Summer 1997), http://wolf.its.ilstu.edu/injustice/ (online-only journal, link inactive May 27, 2004); reprinted in *Henniker Review* 27 (1997).

4. Farrell and Sterba, *Does Feminism Discriminate Against Men?* p. 38.

5. Ibid., p. 108.

6. Ibid., p. 19.

7. "When It Comes To Brain Injury, Authors Say NFL Is in a 'League of Denial,'" NPR, *Morning Edition*, October 7, 2013; transcript at www.npr.org/templates /transcript/transcript.php?storyId=229181970 (accessed October 7, 2013); "League of Denial: The NFL's Concussion Crisis," PBS *Frontline* broadcast, October 10, 2013, transcript at www.pbs.org/wgbh/pages/frontline/sports/league-of-denial /transcript-50/ (accessed October 11, 2013).

8. Allen Schwarz, "Dementia Risk Seen in Players in N.F.L. Study," *New York Times*, September 29, 2009, www.nytimes.com/2009/09/30/sports/football /30dementia.html (retrieved July 4, 2011).

9. Ken McLeod, *We Are the Champions: The Politics of Sports and Popular Music* (Burlington, VT: Ashgate, 2011), p. 219.

10. www.factcheck.org/2008/07/mccains-veteran-voting-record/ (accessed July 8, 2012) and www.newsreview.com/reno/newsview/blogs/post?oid=855494 (accessed July 8, 2012).

11. See Terrence Real, *I Don't Want to Talk About It: Overcoming the Secret Legacy of Male Depression* (New York: Fireside, 1997); also William Pollack, *Real Boys* (New York: Random House, 1998).

12. Farrell and Sterba, *Does Feminism Discriminate Against Men?* p. 4.

13. Mariah Burton Nelson, *The Stronger Women Get, the More Men Love Football: Sexism and the American Culture of Sports* (New York: Harcourt Brace, 1994).

14. Pierre Bourdieu, *Masculine Domination* (Palo Alto: Stanford University Press, 2002), p. 23.

15. Helen Benedict, "The Private War of Women Soldiers," *Salon*, March 7, 2007, www.salon.com/news/feature/2007/03/07/women_in_military/print .html (accessed July 2, 2013).

16. Molly O'Toole, "Military Sexual Assault Epidemic Continues to Claim Victims as Defense Department Fails Females," *Huffington Post*, October 6, 2012 (updated October 9, 2012), www.huffingtonpost.com/2012/10/06/military -sexual-assault-defense-department_n_1834196.html (accessed January 19, 2013).

17. Ibid.

18. Tim Beneke, "Men on Rape," in Michael S. Kimmel and Michael A. Messner, eds., *Men's Lives*, 5th ed. (Needham Heights, MA: Allyn and Bacon, 2001), pp. 384–89.

19. Tom Digby, "Male Trouble: Are Men Victims of Sexism?" *Social Theory and Practice* 29, no. 2 (April 2003): 263.

20. Joan Walsh, "Men Who Hate Women on the Web," www.salon.com /2007/03/31/sierra/ (accessed July 16, 2012).

21. Ibid.

22. Hyde Park Johnny, "Murder of Derrion Albert Was a Turnaround School," www.dailykos.com/story/2012/01/20/1054298/-Murder-of-Derrion-Albert-was -a-Turnaround-School (accessed July 19, 2012).

23. Quoted in the film *No Safe Place* (1996), transcript available at www.pbs .org/kued/nosafeplace/script/script.html (accessed July 5, 2011).

24. Ibid.

25. See, for example, the explanations given by rapists of how they were able to commit their horrific acts in the documentary, *Rape: Face to Face,* http://filmakers .com/index.php?a=filmDetail&filmID=74 (accessed July 17, 2012).

26. Robert Prentky, "Rape: Behavioral Aspects." *Encyclopedia of Crime and Justice, 2002,* www.encyclopedia.com/doc/1G2–3403000218.html (accessed July 05, 2011).

27. Ibid.

28. Jennifer Schuessler, "The Dark Side of Liberation," *New York Times*, May 20, 2013, www.nytimes.com/2013/05/21/books/rape-by-american-soldiers-in-world -war-ii-france.html?smid=fb-share&_r=1&&pagewanted=print (accessed June 6, 2013); see also Mary Louise Roberts, *What Soldiers Do: Sex and the American GI in World War II France* (Chicago: University of Chicago Press, 2013); and J. Robert Lilly, *Taken by Force: Rape and American GIs in Europe During WWII* (New York: Palgrave Macmillan, 2007).

29. "Heroes, Villains, and the Invisible," *New York Times*, June 14, 2012, http://movies.nytimes.com/2012/06/15/movies/human-rights-watch-film -festival-at-lincoln-center.html (accessed July 18, 2012).

30. Bronwyn Ladd, "How Suicide Rates in the Military Compare to Civilian Populations," www.examiner.com/article/how-suicide-rates-the-military-compare -to-civilian-populations (accessed July 18, 2012).

31. "Military Suicides Hit Record High in 2012," NPR, *All Things Considered*, January 14, 2013 (accessed January 15, 2013). See also David Zucchino, "Military Suicides Spike—Nearly 1 per Day, Pentagon Reports," *Los Angeles Times*, June 8, 2012, http://articles.latimes.com/2012/jun/08/nation/la-na-nn-military -suicides-20120608 (accessed July 18, 2012).

32. Bureau of Justice Statistics, http://bjs.ojp.usdoj.gov/index.cfm?ty =tp&tid=31 (accessed July 15, 2013).

33. Jon Seidel and Becky Schlikerman, "Police Report: Maine West Coach Witnessed Sexual Hazing, Congratulated Victim," *Chicago Sun-Times*, November 28, 2012, www.suntimes.com/news/metro/16675179-418/police -report-maine-west-coach-witnessed-sexual-hazing-congratulated-victim.html, (accessed January 15, 2013).

34. Sid Garcia and Christina Salvo, "Lawyer Details Alleged Hazing at La Puente High," KABC-TV, September 24, 2012, http://abclocal.go.com/kabc /story?section=news/local/los_angeles&id=8822343 (accessed January 15, 2013).

35. Jeffrey Gettleman, "Symbol of Unhealed Congo: Male Rape Victims," *New York Times*, August 5, 2009, www.nytimes.com/2009/08/05/world /africa/05congo.html (accessed January 15, 2013).

36. Wikipedia has a comprehensive survey of scouting rape, with an extensive bibliography: http://en.wikipedia.org/wiki/Scouting_sex_abuse_cases (accessed January 20, 2013).

37. Charles Johnson, "Breitbart.com Incites Another Deluge of Misogynist Hate Speech Against Lena Dunham," http://littlegreenfootballs.com/article41463 __Breitbart.com_Incites_Another_Deluge_of_Misogynist_Hate_Speech _Against_Lena_Dunham (accessed March 9, 2013).

38. Helen Lewis, "Dear The Internet, This Is Why You Can't Have Anything Nice," *New Statesman*, June 12, 2012, www.newstatesman.com/blogs/internet/2012/06 /dear-internet-why-you-cant-have-anything-nice (accessed March 10, 2013).

39. Ibid.

40. Alyssa Pry and Alexa Valente, "Women Battle Online Anti-Women Hate from the 'Manosphere,'" ABC News *20/20*, October 16, 2013 (accessed October 17, 2013); Sarah Rybek, "Women in Gaming: Anita Sarkeesian and Internet Criticism,"

Uloop, March 11, 2013, http://umich.uloop.com/news/view.php/75712/women-in-gaming-anita-sarkeesian-and-internet-criticism (accessed July 28, 2013).

41. Pry and Valente, "Women Battle Online Anti-Women Hate."

42. Ibid.

43. They are also losing in another way: Anita Sarkeesian's campaign for funding of her work on Kickstarter had a goal of $6,000, but it surpassed that goal by $152,922: www.kickstarter.com/projects/566429325/tropes-vs-women-in-video-games/ (accessed March 10, 2013).

44. Tom Digby, "Do Feminists Hate Men? Feminism, Antifeminism, and Gender Oppositionality," *Journal of Social Philosophy* 29, no. 2 (September 1998): 15–31, available online at http://onlinelibrary.wiley.com/doi/10.1111/j.1467-9833.1998.tb00105.x/abstract.

7. THE DEGENDERING OF MILITARISM

The epigraph to this chapter is from the "Statement by the President on the Opening of Combat Units to Women," www.whitehouse.gov/the-press-office/2013/01/24/statement-president-opening-combat-units-women (accessed May 27, 2013).

1. "By the Numbers: Women in the U.S. Military," January 24, 2013 (the data is from 2011), www.cnn.com/2013/01/24/us/military-women-glance (accessed June 7, 2013). Of mainly symbolic importance for the degendering of war was when a former Navy SEAL came out as transgender: Kristin Beck was formerly Chris Beck; see Kristin Beck, *Warrior Princess: A U.S. Navy SEAL's Journey to Coming Out Transgender* (New York: Advances, 2013).

1. www.defense.gov/speeches/speech.aspx?speechid=1539 (accessed May 20, 2013).

2. It should be noted, however, that Gates's comments on this matter are not entirely without historical precedent. For example, Luna Najera has pointed out that in the early modern Spanish military manuals she has researched and written about there are sentiments that are similar, if not nearly as pronounced and particular as they are in Gates's speech. Strategy, she tells me, was sometimes focused on not killing others and, of course, not having your own men killed. A good war was sometimes one where strategy enabled defeat of the enemy without combat.

3. "President Bush Signs H.R. 2642, the Supplemental Appropriations Act, 2008," http://georgewbush-whitehouse.archives.gov/news/releases/2008/06/20080630.html (accessed June 7, 2013).

4. John Solomon, "EXCLUSIVE: Bush, Cheney Comforted Troops Privately," *Washington Times*, www.washingtontimes.com/news/2008/dec/22/bush-cheney -comforted-troops-privately/?page=all (accessed May 20, 2013).

5. Smedley Butler, "War Is a Racket," originally published in 1935, based on speeches he gave in 1933; the text of the pamphlet is available at www.ratical.org /ratville/CAH/warisaracket.html (accessed May 20, 2013).

6. As in the failure to provide funding for what may be the most effective kind of therapy for many brain injury cases; see www.npr.org/2010/12/20/132145959 /pentagon-health-plan-wont-cover-brain-damage-therapy-for-troops.

7. James Dao, "Criticism of Veterans Affairs Secretary Mounts Over Backlog in Claims," *New York Times*, www.nytimes.com/2013/05/19/us/shinseki-faces -mounting-criticism-over-backlog-of-benefit-claims.html?pagewanted=all&_r=0 (accessed May 20, 2013).

8. "VA Paperwork Could Buckle N.C. Office Building," *Associated Press*, August 30, 2012, www.armytimes.com/article/20120830/NEWS/208300324 /VA-paperwork-could-buckle-N-C-office-building (accessed June 7, 2013).

9. http://en.wikipedia.org/wiki/Smedley_Butler and http://en.wikipedia.org /wiki/Bonus_Army.

10. http://nation.foxnews.com/robert-gates/2011/03/02/robert-gates-west -point-speech-sends-shockwaves (accessed May 20, 2013)

11. www.defense.gov/speeches/speech.aspx?speechid=1539 (retrieved February 26, 2011).

12. James P. Sterba, *Does Feminism Discriminate Against Men?* (New York: Oxford University Press, 2007).

13. www.defense.gov/speeches/speech.aspx?speechid=1539, retrieved May 20, 2013, 11:52 am EDT.

14. Theodoric Meyer, "What Went Wrong in West, Texas—and Where Were the Regulators?" *ProPublica*, April 25, 2013, www.propublica.org/article/what -went-wrong-in-west-texas-and-where-were-the-regulators (accessed June 10, 2014).

15. Susan Faludi, *The Terror Dream: Fear and Fantasy in Post-9/11 America* (New York: Holt, 2007), p. 20.

16. Patricia Leigh Brown, "Ideas & Trends; Heavy Lifting Required: The Return of Manly Men," *New York Times*, October 28, 2001 (accessed May 22, 2013).

17. It's not clear exactly what happened on Flight 93 before it went down in Shanksville, Pennsylvania. From phone calls it appears four large men may have charged the hijacker in the front of the plane, but also that a petite female flight attendant was preparing hot water to pour on the hijacker. Whether either factor made any difference is unclear. See Andrew Alderson and Susan Bisset,

"The Extraordinary Last Calls of Flight UA93," *Telegraph*, October 21, 2013, www.telegraph.co.uk/news/worldnews/northamerica/usa/1360088/The -extraordinary-last-calls-of-Flight-UA93.html (accessed June 12, 2013); Dennis B. Roddy, Cindi Lash, Steve Levin, and Jonathan D. Silver, "Flight 93: Forty Lives, One Destiny," *Pittsburgh Post-Gazetter*, October 28, 2001, http://old.post-gazette. com/headlines/20011028flt93mainstoryp7.asp (accessed June 12, 2013).

18. Faludi, *The Terror Dream*, p. 20.

19. *The Cult of the Suicide Bomber,* written and directed by Robert Baer (an ex-CIA agent), 2006.

20. Ashley Fantz, "Boy Killed in Boston Blast Wrote, 'No More Hurting People,'" www.cnn.com/2013/04/16/us/boston-boy-killed (accessed May 25, 2013, 1:59 pm EDT)

21. Alexandra Topping, Paul Owen, and Martin Williams, "London Attack: Police Make Two Further Arrests After Woolwich Killing," www.guardian. co.uk/uk/2013/may/23/woolwich-latest-developments-live (accessed May 26, 2013).

22. From pp. 16–17 of "Global Trends 2025: A Transformed World," released in November 2008 by the National Intelligence Council, and available at www .dni.gov/files/documents/Newsroom/Reports%20and%20Pubs/2025_Global _Trends_Final_Report.pdf (accessed June 12, 2013). See also Thomas P. M. Barnett, *The Pentagon's New Map* (New York: Putnam, 2004); and Nicholas Kristof, "Divorced Before Puberty," *New York Times*, March 4, 2010.

23. Available here: www.fas.org/irp/doddir/army/fm3–24.pdf (accessed May 26, 2013).

24. Nancy A. Youssef, "Odierno: Former Door-kicker Now Reflects Iraq Progress," *McClatchy Newspapers*, September 16, 2008, www.mcclatchydc.com /2008/09/16/52636/odierno-former-door-kicker-now.html#.UbtnBBaPJzV (accessed June 14, 2013).

25. Thomas E. Ricks, "'It Looked Weird and Felt Wrong,'" *Washington Post*, July 24, 2006, www.washingtonpost.com/wp-dyn/content/article/2006/07/23 /AR2006072300495_pf.html (accessed June 14, 2013).

26. Youssef, "Odierno."

27. It should be noted that the remoteness factor is also relevant to Gates's comment about greater reliance on naval and air warfare.

28. Erik Sofge, "How to Build a Hero," www.popsci.com/technology/article /2013–01/how-build-hero (accessed May 5, 2013); also see the DARPA Challenge official announcement: www.darpa.mil/NewsEvents/Releases/2012/10/24.aspx (accessed May 5, 2013).

8. THE DEMILITARIZING OF GENDER

1. It has not always been the case that militaristic societies have placed cultural expectations on girls and women that exclude altogether those warrior qualities; consider, for example, the Spartan women, who were expected to be physically fit and in some limited respects capable of fighting. Sarah Pomeroy, *Spartan Women* (New York: Oxford University Press, 2002).

2. Frank Bruni, "Sexism's Puzzling Stamina," *New York Times*, June 10, 2013, www .nytimes.com/2013/06/11/opinion/bruni-sexisms-puzzling-stamina.html?emc =eta1&_r=2&&pagewanted=print (accessed June 12, 2013).

3. *Department of Defense Annual Report on Sexual Assault in the Military, Fiscal Year 2012,* www.sapr.mil/index.php/annual-reports (accessed June 16, 2013).

4. "Saxby Chambliss on Sexual Assault and 'Hormone' Levels in the Military," *Atlanta Journal-Constitution,* June 4, 2013, www.ajc.com/weblogs/political -insider/2013/jun/04/saxby-chambliss-sexual-assault-and-hormone-levels-/ (accessed June 16, 2013).

5. Emily Arrowood, "Fox Figures: Rise in Female Breadwinners Is a Sign of Society's Downfall," May 29, 2013, http://mediamatters.org/print /blog/2013/05/29/fox-figures-rise-in-female-breadwinners-is-a-si/194263 (accessed June 16, 2013).

6. Bruni, "Sexism's Puzzling Stamina."

7. www.christiandomesticdiscipline.net/assets/dd-in-a-christian-marriage-by -ned-and-maria.pdf (accessed June 21, 2013).

8. www.christiandomesticdiscipline.net (accessed June 21, 2013).

9. There is extensive information about this in the National Intimate Partner and Sexual Violence Survey (NISVS), www.cdc.gov/violenceprevention/nisvs/ (accessed June 21, 2013).

10. Lena Gunnarsson, *On the Ontology of Love, Sexuality and Power: Towards a Feminist-Realist Approach* (Örebro, Sweden: Örebro University, 2013), p. 23.

11. "Australian Military Investigates 'Explicit Emails,'" *BBC News Asia,* June 13, 2013, www.bbc.co.uk/news/world-asia-22885465 (accessed June 16, 2013).

12. David Morrison, "Chief of Army, Lieutenant General David Morrison— Unacceptable Behaviour," http://lybio.net/chief-of-army-lieutenant-general- david-morrison-unacceptable-behaviour/people/ (accessed June 15, 2013).

13. For a few examples see Roxane Gay, "What Men Want, America Delivers," *Salon,* July 5, 2013, www.salon.com/2013/07/05/what_men_want_america _delivers/ (accessed July 7, 2013). Of course, the range of available examples is monstrously large.

14. I have addressed the matter of whether men are victims of sexism and feminism in two articles: Tom Digby, "Male Trouble: Are Men Victims of Sexism?" *Social Theory and Practice* 29 (April 2003): 247–73, and "Do Feminists Hate Men? Feminism, Antifeminism, and Gender Oppositionality," *Journal of Social Philosophy* 29 (Fall 1998): 15–31. On whether men are victims of feminism, see also Warren Farrell and James P. Sterba, *Does Feminism Discriminate Against Men? A Debate* (New York: Oxford University Press, 2008).

15. James Eli Adams, *Dandies and Desert Saints: Styles of Victorian Masculinity* (Ithaca: Cornell University Press, 1995), p. 1.

16. "Broad Support for Combat Roles for Women," January 29, 2013, www .people-press.org/2013/01/29/broad-support-for-combat-roles-for-women/ (accessed May 28, 2013).

17. Dana Milbank seems to get this connection between masculinity and Republican efforts to further constrict women's access to abortion in his article "Trent Franks's Abortion Claim and the Manly Republican Party," *Washington Post*, June 12, 2013, http://articles.washingtonpost.com/2013–06–12 /opinions/39921015_1_men-todd-akin-20-weeks (accessed June 20, 2013). That article also reports on the various Republican claims that pregnancy cannot result from rape. The masturbating fetuses idea comes from Texas congressman Michael Burgess: Adam Edelman, "Texas Republican Rep. Michael Burgess Suggests Fetuses Can Masturbate," *New York Daily News*, June 19, 2013, www.nydailynews .com/news/politics/texas-republican-rep-michael-burgess-suggests-fetuses -masturbate-article-1.1376894 (accessed June 20, 2013). On the rape kit claim, see Alexander Abad-Santos, "Sponsor of New Texas Anti-Abortion Bill Thinks Rape Kits Are Contraceptives," *Atlantic Wire*, June 24, 2013, www.theatlanticwire.com /politics/2013/06/new-texas-anti-abortion-bill-rape-kits/66531/ (accessed July 7, 2013).

18. John Kass, "American Football Industry Is on Its Deathbed" *Chicago Tribune*, April 24, 2013, http://articles.chicagotribune.com/2013–04–24/news /ct-met-kass-0424–20130424_1_future-football-players-nfl-draft-the-nfl (accessed May 29, 2013).

INDEX